HOUSE DESIGN

Alfredo DeVido, FAIA

HOUSE DESIGN

Art and Practice

JOHN WILEY AND SONS, INC.
New York • Chichester • Brisbane • Toronto • Singapore

Designed by Monika Keano
Typeset by Laura Lindgren

Library of Congress Cataloging-in-Publication Data:
De Vido, Alfredo, 1932–
        House design : art and practice / Alfredo De Vido.
            p.   cm.
        ISBN 0-471-52980-X (cloth : acid-free paper)
        1. Architecture, Domestic—United States—Planning.   I. Title.
    NA7205.D365 1996
    728—dc20   95-42940

Printed in the United States of America

10   9   8   7   6   5   4   3   2   1

CONTENTS

FOREWORD

The author of this book, Alfredo De Vido, designed the only house my wife and I have ever built, and now—15 years later—he is working with us on an addition that will serve us for the next 15 years.

In some ways, I am an unusual client. Although I have built only one new house, I have spent my lifetime as a design journalist, first as the editor of a group of magazines about building and remodeling, then as the editor-in-chief of *House & Garden* and then *Elle Decor*, and now as the editor-in-chief of *House Beautiful*—all magazines devoted to reporting on the design and building of houses.

From the initial design process to determining the budget to the actual building, a house project is fraught with potential pitfalls. A careful reading of this book is one way to help keep pitfalls to a minimum.

De Vido has spent the major part of his practice on residential architecture and has frequently worked as a designer–builder, assuming both the conceptual and practical aspects of bringing a design to fruition. He is a man who likes to design but who also likes to help buildings get built. He knows that the conversation(s) between client and architect are crucial and that it is, ultimately, the client's house. He also knows that the architect is there to guide the client in the high art of design.

Architects are often the best at the grand gesture; clients, on the other hand, care about the livable moments. De Vido, and his book, try to help make both of these things happen.

A house has a relationship, not only with its inhabitants, but also with the land on which it is built and the community within which it resides. De Vido, who stands in the tradition of Alvar Aalto and Marcel Breuer, designs buildings that work with both the natural and the built environment, as the chapters that deal with these issues reveal.

Most important, De Vido likes creating buildings. His own house and studio, situated a few miles east of our house on Long Island, is always a work in progress. And it is the process of design and building that this book is all about.

Nothing is more crucial to that process than the communication between the designer and the client who will ultimately live in and be enriched by the building that results from their dialogue. This book, *House Design: Art and Practice*, was written to facilitate that communication.

Louis Oliver Gropp
Editor-in-Chief, *House Beautiful*

INTRODUCTION

The main purpose of this book is to propose that house design is a matter of care—care on the part of the clients who generate the need for houses and greater care on the part of the people with expertise, the architects and builders of houses. People who care about their houses will spend time looking at them and thinking about what they like in what they see. They'll review their houses' colors and textures in the same way they review those features in their clothing. Some will go further, looking at a space and the way it is defined, the types of historical styles, regional characteristics, and the polemics of design. Others will start to assemble clipping books and information on the designers and architects who speak most directly to them, stylistically, visually, and sometimes philosophically.

Innovation does not mean bizarre ways of assembling materials in cacophonous juxtaposition. Most such attempts will merely be jarring to the senses. Innovation can be highly successful in the hands of an artist. In fact, innovation comes rather easily by tailoring the design to its occupants and the site. It is the means of putting the information together in concert with the client that is important.

The aim of working with your client is, therefore, to discover what is unique about the client, the location, and the site characteristics. With this knowledge, the designer can proceed with a responsive design that will meet most of the aims of the client. In some cases, the design will transcend sound, appropriate well-constructed planning. It will become a unique work of art. Witness the villages and towns in countries such as Italy, Spain, and Greece.

Mainstream design is difficult to define in a pluralistic world. Better to analyze the givens, namely, client, site, and budget, and tailor your efforts accordingly. Many houses that are built today reveal a slipshod and careless approach. In the past, houses were built better, owing to various factors, including a less diverse society that had fewer choices, a lower rate of mobility that gave people the stability and time to plan carefully, and the presence of models and patterns to be copied. It is not a bad thing to use a pattern or a good example. Too often architects are determined to reinvent form. This is really impossible, since a study of form will reveal that there isn't anything new under the sun. What is new is the right assemblage of materials fitting the program, site, and local conditions.

1 |
HOUSES, HOMES, AND HOUSING

As we enter the twenty-first century, we have to ask what a house should be. Houses have a practical aim—to give protection from the elements. They also reassure their occupants. The space that a house delimits is a step toward ordering the universe. Though most of the world's building budget goes into the production of houses and housing, houses are rarely discussed in a meaningful way, and new and unlikely stylistic attempts are produced in which the original idea of a house is totally missing.

In a traditional vein, houses are built with imitation shutters and applied entrance features. The image is skin deep and suffers from excessive repetition. Contemporary-looking work is often subject to shifts in style, sometimes based on philosophical ideas that do not relate to visual art. Hardly do these stylistic and polemic ideas correspond to the practical needs of builders or to the needs of the occupants of houses.

BASIC NEEDS

There are many different types of houses and housing. All are intended to satisfy their occupants' real and perceived needs, which are functional, constructional, social, and symbolic. There may be other labels, but these four provide the basis for an introductory discussion about houses.

FUNCTIONAL

Most important, functional needs include keeping the effects of weather extremes out of the house. This is broadly called protection from the environment, which means no leaky roofs or basements and no baking heat caused by large expanses of unprotected glass. A few parts of the world, such as Hawaii, don't require much protection against climatological stress, but most places do. Protection from the environment can most easily be accomplished by employing the basic principles of physics. Too often we forget those principles in our high-tech culture, where any interior climate can be established through electronically controlled heating and air conditioning.

Functional

People need shelter from the cold and wet, hot and dry, or hot and humid climates. Where the climate is cold and wet, thick walls keep out the cold and store heat generated from within the house and gained from the sun's rays. Larger windows provide more light in the interior. Pitched roofs shed rain and snow. Simple devices that are integral parts of a house can help, such as shutters to protect openings from wind, rain, and snow, and overhangs designed to block the sun during the summer and admit it during the winter when its rays are welcome.

In hot, dry climates, thick walls keep out the heat by day, and if these walls are painted in light colors, they reflect the sun's rays. Small windows also limit the amount of sunlight entering the house. At night, the thick walls radiate the heat gained during the day to mitigate interior temperatures.

When the climate is hot and humid, walls made of porous screens let air pass through and cool the house. Overhangs and porches provide shade from the hot sun and serve as outdoor rooms. They also shed rain. Sometimes houses are built on raised platforms to keep them above periodic flooding and above the insect and reptile zone found close to the ground in tropical climates.

CONSTRUCTIONAL

Early constructional ideas were based on the use of locally available materials (timber from forests, stones from mountains, mud in delta areas, ice in the Arctic) and on accessible transportation systems that made it possible to use materials not immediately available. Technology created lightweight, strong materials that enabled greater distances to be spanned, greater heights to be scaled, and unusual shapes to be constructed. Larger living spaces could be treated with more flexibility. Transparent materials permitted new kinds of thinking about sheltered space. Machinery that tempered interior environments allowed almost limitless possibilities for designing an environment in relation to the surrounding physical climate. However, despite new constructional freedoms, the cost and inefficiency of some combinations of enclosure and services are prohibitive. Increasingly, important constructional considerations are cost-effectiveness and the correct use of ecologically sound, nonpolluting materials.

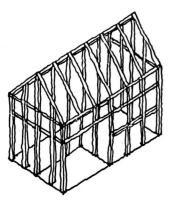

Constructional

Social

SOCIAL

Because people mostly live together in towns or cities, we have devised social arrangements for working and living together in physical proximity. This proximity suggests and often mandates how our houses will work, look, and be protected. A person's social status is often a motivating factor in the physical appearance of his or her house. For instance, a prominent citizen in a community may want his house to look grander than a neighbor's whose position is more modest or less successful. Houses thus become expressions of sociological differences between people. "Keeping up with the Joneses," or the Ramirezes or the Yangs, is a very real phenomenon that must be taken into visual account.

People also like to live with others with whom they have common beliefs and ideals. Such arrangements can be accomplished physically in groupings of individual dwellings with common areas, or in houses where there are two master bedroom setups for people who want to share a dwelling, yet maintain some individual privacy. There are groupings of extended families in a single house, whereby parents take in their children and the children's families, or vice versa. Many of these groupings are due to economic necessities in a world of high building and financing costs.

SYMBOLIC

Through the ages, people have communicated with each other about life's functional and physical aspects and its sometimes illogical, magical aspects such as religion, philosophy, and the esoteric aspects of art and ritual. Architects, primitive and otherwise, have spent time studying art and rituals that invest buildings with symbols corresponding to these rituals. It is easier to suggest older societies; their symbols were simple and few. Today we have many historical options to choose from, and, as a result of nomadic life patterns, geographical ones as well. Architects sometimes select historical precedents as a substitute for symbolic meaning, as, for example, in adorning houses with classical colonnades. They believe these symbolize domesticity and the daily life cycle within the house. However, the contemporary house can make gestures to symbolic beliefs as well as keeping out the rigors of the local climate. A pitched

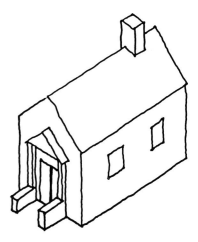

Symbolic

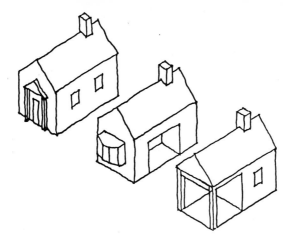

roof in a temperate climate, for instance, is not only symbolic, but also answers practical demands to shed water and snow.

THE BUILDERS OF HOUSES

There are different categories of people who build houses and housing: house builder/developers, governmental agencies and autonomous groups, and architects/custom builders all produce houses, but their backgrounds and the uses of their products are diverse. They operate differently, with different financial goals. Studies reveal that the various social and economic groups engage different kinds of builders. The results are sometimes surprising. For example, people with a lot of money to spend may not necessarily turn to architects/custom builders. They may decide that it is too difficult to determine what their own needs are, so they seek shelter in an existing house or multifamily dwelling. Toward the other end of the economic scale, people with small budgets may have a strong desire to build their own houses, and will do so despite the additional costs of building.

HOUSE BUILDERS/DEVELOPERS

In general, house builders and developers build homes for a broad market, including single-family detached homes, still the most popular if they can be afforded, and the multifamily type, ever more common because of increases in land and site development costs. These are the larger builders of suburban or exurban housing in larger developments. Their houses are designed in a conservative manner, sometimes with architects, but usually without them. The development team tries to deliver the right product for the market. For example, in the houses they build, they will attempt to include the right number and kinds of bedrooms for the life-styles of the market and to provide "curb appeal," the salability of the look. Their market usually dislikes experimentation and prefers conventional ways of living. However, buyers may also be interested in new ideas that have been marketed in the media. For example, a popular

Architects and custom builders

concept in this country includes big bedrooms, equipped with spacious bathrooms, whirlpool baths, and multijet showers. House builders/developers note these trends and cater to them. To ignore popular concepts in housing is to incur the penalty of failure to sell the product.

Houses may be provided with consumer features such as bay windows, assemblages of building materials facing the street, a variety of window shapes, and a grand front entrance. The house is a consumable, with design features to "sell" the house. Unfortunately, these features are often visual gimmicks, poorly coordinated. Architects often denigrate them. It should be possible to design salable houses that will satisfy high aesthetic criteria. To this end, it may take a closer union of the architectural profession with the people who build houses. Meshing the financial and administrative ability of builders and developers with the conceptual organizational ability of the architectural profession may be of advantage to both groups.

GOVERNMENTAL/AUTONOMOUS GROUPS

Multifamily housing, high-rise or low-rise, is frequently built by governmental or autonomous community groups as well as developers. As the population ages, there are increasing numbers of senior citizen housing complexes, as well as nursing homes. There are also many types of housing for various income groups and units for groups with special problems, such as people with AIDS and those who are homeless. Because of the inherent structure of funding for housing of this type and the conservatism of program administrators, such housing units are mostly stripped to bare essentials. Builders are often closely regulated, and the range of amenities available to users is limited as a result of the regulations. In these complexes, there is an emphasis on such aspects as collective recreational and common areas. Increasingly, greater priority is given to security and the ability to provide a crime-free living environment. Architects are employed in these projects, but they are not generally encouraged to do an architecturally distinguished job. Their fees are low, and bureaucratic paper shuffling discourages creativity.

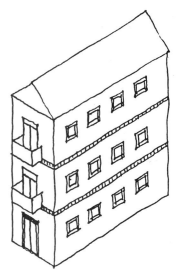

Governmental and autonomous groups

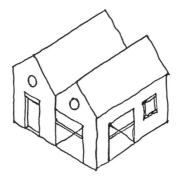

Two- to four-family detached, attached

ARCHITECTS/CUSTOM BUILDERS

The third and smallest group of people who build houses are architects and builders who have architects working for them. The users of the houses they build, usually well educated and sophisticated, are from various social and economic groups. They may previously have built or renovated houses or apartments and have frequently given some thought to the mechanics and comforts of living.

TYPES OF HOUSES

Houses are designed as detached buildings or arranged in different groupings. The grouped varieties are as numerous as their underlying economic and social reasons. Economics are dictated mostly by the high cost of land and utility/infrastructure. Houses are also grouped for ease of maintenance, because a grouped dwelling requires less care than a single-family house with surrounding property. Another reason for grouping houses is that taxes are generally lower per unit than for a detached house.

SINGLE FAMILY/DETACHED

The most common housing type in the United States is the single-family detached house on its own piece of land. It is significantly less common in older cultures, including most of Europe, where traditions include collective living at all levels of society. In contrast, the history of the single-family house is long and continuous in this country. It has occasionally been architecturally distinguished in the sense of a grand monument such as Monticello or Falling Water. For the most part, however, the single-family dwelling has been distinguished by finely scaled domesticity, with historical periods mined for precedents.

TWO- TO FOUR-FAMILY DETACHED/ATTACHED

In urban areas, houses are grouped for reasons of land scarcity and the need to maximize the use of utilities and roads. Rows of two-family houses, narrowly

HOUSES, HOMES, AND HOUSING

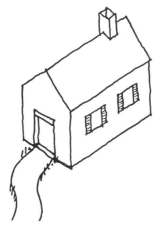

Single-family, detached

detached or sharing a common wall, are common. They often form attractive townscapes and are widely extolled by many groups as a good housing type for urbanized areas. Such paired houses offer many advantages. In addition to maximizing the use of infrastructure, they simply take less land, which is crucial in a densely built area. This housing type has also been cited as a safer kind of urban housing; it provides good street visibility from the interior, thereby allowing occupants to be aware of activities (possibly criminal) in the street.

The salient features of two- to four-family buildings, either detached or sharing common walls, is that they are relatively low-rise and have land around them, usually in the form of front and rear yards. Increasingly, variations provide ingenious side yards that are also private. The buildings' relative low height makes them desirable for reasons of livability, safety, and economics. For instance, if the dwelling units are low, egress to the street or backyard is easy, without necessitating an elevator. This kind of development has long existed in Europe, where communities have three-dimensional zoning regulation by which town planners create site plans that legislate where windows and access points can be located. The use of planned sites is increasing rapidly in this country. Some of the more common variations are discussed in the following paragraphs.

LOW-RISE WITH MULTIPLE ACCESS

Low-rise, multiple-access units, sometimes called garden apartments, generally do not exceed two stories and are serviced by the off-the-shelf, relatively inexpensive elevators. Some units were formerly built without elevators as well, but that design is mostly a thing of the past since access for disabled persons has been mandated. Stair and elevated access is called "multiple" because more than one family has access to the individual units. The entire complex is set on landscaped land held jointly by the owner of the apartments and by the co-op or condominium organization. Qualitatively, the units are quite livable, economical to build, and acceptable to most communities because they look domestic. Rents or purchase prices are low, making them good starter dwellings for first-time users of housing and affordable housing for seniors.

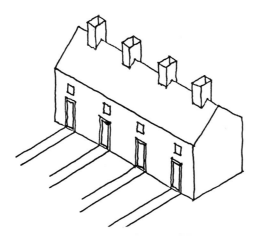

Low-rise with private access

LOW-RISE WITH PRIVATE ACCESS

Low-rise, private-access units are up-down buildings grouped in a row or cluster. Variations are numerous. They can have split levels, two-story spaces, basements used as living areas, and garages. These buildings are not generally provided with elevators, although current legislation must be observed for use by disabled persons.

The name of this dwelling type varies widely. The dwellings have been called row houses, town houses, and planned units. They are popular and attractive, have a good residential scale, and are acceptable in most communities, because they look like, and actually are, single-family dwellings. Many communities recognize that these units use less land and minimize the demand on infrastructure.

ZERO LOT LINE

With the increasing use of planned subdivisions that have three-dimensional planning restrictions, architects can now design many imaginative combinations of dwelling units. For example, if zoning ordinances permit, dwellings can have one wall on one lot line, with a mandated minimum on the adjacent lot line and no windows on the lot line wall. This then permits the use of the resulting side yard as a private outdoor living space. The side yard can also be used for vehicular access to the rear of the lot. The provision of garages on the street for densely built low-rise housing usually results in an unattractive streetscape.

Other combinations of houses are possible. A notable concept that has not been used widely in this country, but has been accepted in Scandinavia, is the court house, in which each dwelling has a private court that abuts blank walls of the adjacent buildings. This arrangement ensures a private outdoor area for each housing unit. In general, zero lot line solutions are for private-access buildings, although it is possible to build them for multiple-access units as well.

DENSE URBAN GROUPINGS

In an urban world, high-rise solutions (more than two stories) are increasingly called for by builders and clients who need higher density to achieve an economic return on investment where infrastructure and land are expensive.

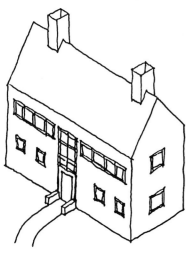

Low-rise with multiple access

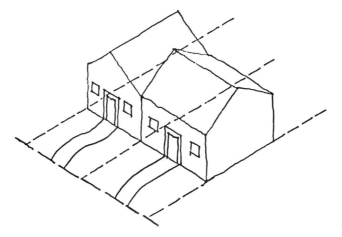

Zero lot line

High-rise buildings, of the type found in large cities, are beyond the scope of this discussion, which concerns the design of houses or groups of houses by architects or architect builders for specific sites and clients.

However, the combinations of houses in denser agglomerations are increasingly designed as diverse entities in which specific clients and groups of clients are part of the design process. Ralph Erskine, A British-Swedish architect, designed a large multiple-family housing complex called Byker, in England, in which he involved the users of these apartment and town house units in site and unit-specific decisions.

HIGH-RISE MULTIPLE FAMILY/MULTIPLE ACCESS

Taller multiple-access buildings are usually built with elevators, because access to buildings of more then two stories via staircase is difficult or prohibited by local codes or disability requirements. Various configurations of these buildings are possible, ranging from those with two to four units stacked around the stairs and elevator, to corridor types. The stacking of units around a single staircase and elevator is generally not permitted in North America because of the requirements of fire codes to provide more than one means of egress in case of fire. Some of the numerous possibilities are discussed in the following paragraphs.

TOWERS/POINT BLOCKS

Towers and point blocks generally have small per floor areas to which semi-private access is provided to each unit via a staircase and an elevator. The number of units surrounding this kind of compact access is generally restricted to four. The number of units can be increased, but short corridors will then become necessary and, with them, additional fire stairs and elevators. Because towers limit the number of units per access point, costs are higher, due to the large amount of vertical circulation required to gain access to a limited number of apartments per floor. Views and exposures can be maximized, thus enhancing the appeal of the individual apartments. The absence of long public corridors improves security, because surveillance of a corridor is then possible from apartment doors.

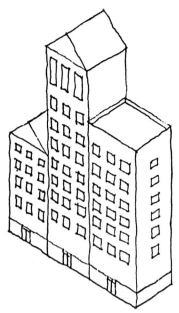

High-rise multiple-family, multiple access

Variations are possible within the concept of point blocks, such as the connection of several towers to form streets in the air. In appropriate climates, these aerial streets can be open, also a security plus.

CORRIDOR BUILDINGS

Although corridor groupings of dwelling units are not limited to high-rise buildings, they are quite commonly used for high-rises, because they can maximize the ratio of usable living space to circulation space, both vertical and horizontal. These buildings are of two basic types, with variations.

Single-Loaded Corridor Buildings

A plan with corridors on one side of a slab building is usually referred to as a single-loaded corridor building. The idea is to provide all dwelling units with a single orientation toward a view or desirable climatic exposure. Buildings can be designed to have a corridor on every floor or to have a corridor on every other floor or every third floor. Configurations with corridors on every other floor or every third floor require interior stairs. Although these can be spatially interesting within the dwellings, they entail the accompanying cost and inconvenience of providing the staircases. However, the amount of public corridor is lessened and the intermediate floors without public corridors can then have more than one orientation.

Double-Loaded Corridor Buildings

Double-loaded designs provide units on both sides of a central corridor and are more common than single-loaded types, because they lessen the amount of corridor needed per dwelling. As in single-loaded corridor buildings, it is possible to skip floors, providing internal stairs, to alternate the position of the corridor from one side of the building to the other, to provide corridors every third floor, or to provide split levels. The combinations are also limitless, governed only by the restrictions of site and budget.

PROJECT: FOLLY FARM, *Sulhampstead, England*

Architect: Edwin Lutyens

- Two additions to a basic farm cottage.

- Around the wings of the house, the site has been arranged into landscaped courts, terraces, and water features.

- Multipaned bay windows combine with pitched and hipped overhanging roofs.

- Vernacular building materials—brick, slate, and stone—have been utilized.

- Interiors are classically ornamented.

Rear garden foliage and bay windows combine to accentuate the relationship of the house and its natural surroundings.

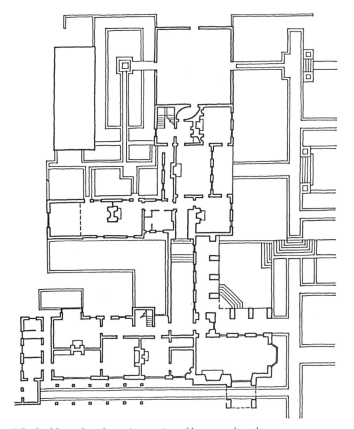

The building plan shows integration of house and garden.

The great hall has an overlook from the second floor.

PROJECT: GROUPED HOUSES, *Asunto Oy Liinasaarenkuja 3–5, Westend, Espoo, Finland*

Architects: Gullichsen, Kairamo, Vormala Architects
Erkki Kairamo, Juhan Maunula, Aulikki Jylhä

- Two-story paired houses are lined up on pedestrian paths.

- Privacy fences are included.

- Detailing of garden trellis, roof access ladder, necessary railings and circular stairs, and site paving provide visual interest and decoration to an otherwise simple building mass.

- Windows and doors are carefully composed.

- Private gardens soften the geometry of the site.

Entrances from a pedestrian way.

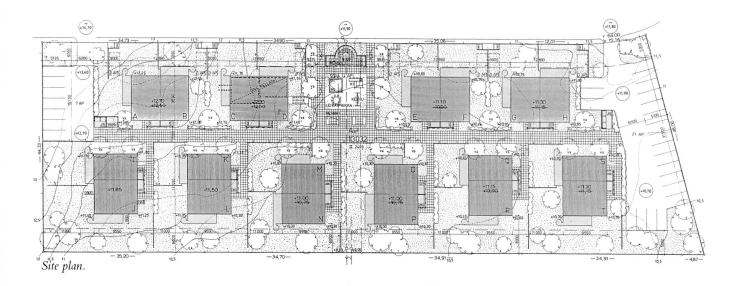

Site plan.

Gardens rendered private by fences and planting.

Pedestrian path.

Delicate steelwork provides detailing to solid building cube.

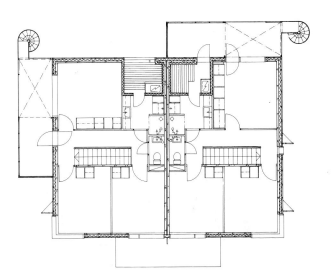

Second floor plan.

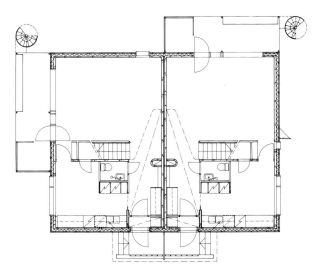

First floor plan.

PROJECT: WERTHEIMER HOUSE, *Bethany Beach, Delaware*

Architect: Alfredo De Vido, FAIA

- The octagonal form of this house recalls nautical buildings.
- The seaside landscape is left untouched. Because of tidal conditions, the house is raised on piers, concealed behind cedar boards.
- Within, the living spaces are organized around a heightened living area.
- Low-maintenance wood finishes in the interior are lightly whitewashed.

The house and its site.

Interior beam structure is exposed as a decorative feature.

Sketch.

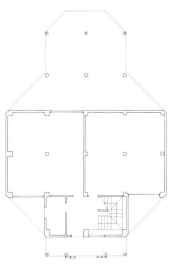

Ground floor plan.

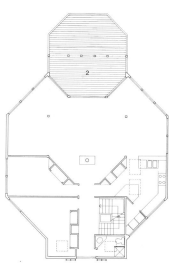

First floor plan.

Screened porch invites open-air dining.

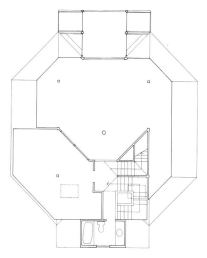

Second floor plan.

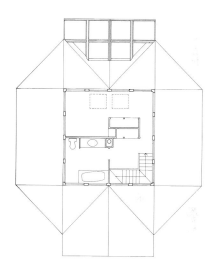

Third floor plan.

Light fills the lofty living area.

Lighting fixtures are designed into the beams.

PROJECT: APARTMENT, *Rittenhouse Square, Philadelphia, Pennsylvania*

Architects: Wesley Wei Architects

- Converted from two former apartments, this living space totals 3,000 square feet.

- An existing column grid was visually reinforced by additional cabinets to create a T-shaped circulation pattern.

- The cabinets have symbolic and poetic meanings to both architect and client.

Living area looking toward the kitchen.

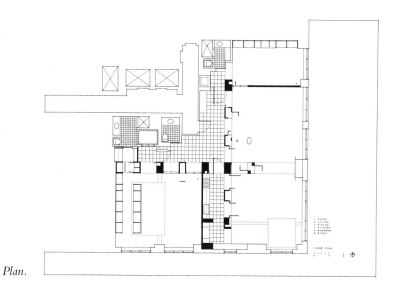

Plan.

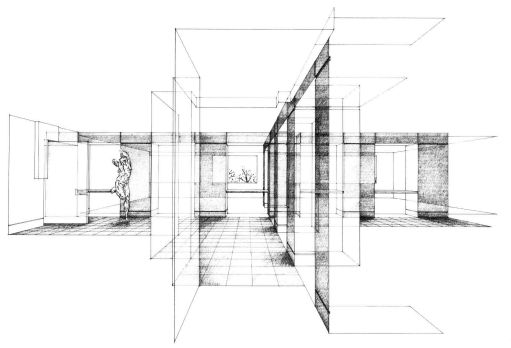

Planar drawing.

Detailing of space.

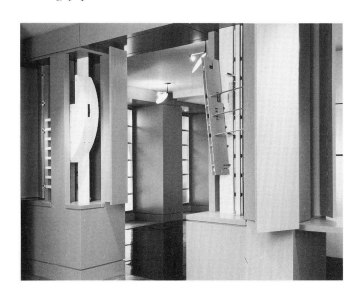

Architectural sculpture.

View of a corridor flanked by column/storage elements and architectural sculpture.

PROJECT: SAMETZ HOUSE, *Garrison, New York*

Architect: Alfredo De Vido, FAIA

- The house features a cube form that is economical to build and easy to heat and cool, because it exposes little surface area to the elements.
- The 30-foot height of the house enables key rooms to capture splendid views of the Hudson River Valley.
- The strong geometric form is reinforced by simple detailing and window alignment.

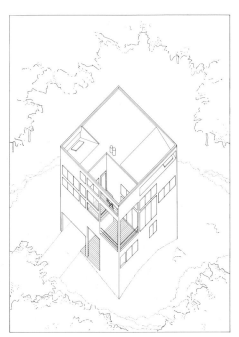

Axonometric view.

View toward entry showing two outdoor porches.

River view facade of house.

Prospect from the upper porch.

Dining area and fireplace.

Window pattern framing verdant landscape.

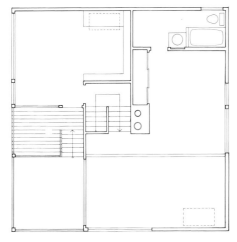

Entry level plan.

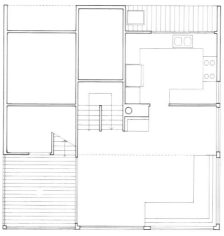

Living/kitchen level plan.

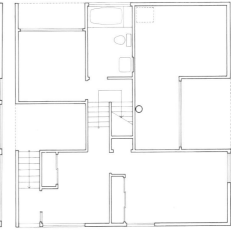

Master bedroom level plan.

PROJECT: RURAL HOUSE, *Alabama*

Architects: Samuel Mockbee and Auburn University Students

- This low-cost rural housing utilizes stuccoed hay bales for substructure and a corrugated acrylic shed roof.
- The 850-square-foot interior contains a living room, master bedroom, and three sleeping niches expressed on the exterior as rounded huts attached to the main structure.

Entrance facade shows translucent roof over hay bale structure.

Rear facade shows sleeping niches.

Interior.

PROJECT: PIERRAKOS HOUSE, *Oxylithos, Euboea, Greece*

Architects: Suzana and Dimitris Antonakakis
Atelier D'Architecture

- Siting this house on the crest of a hill allows it to command extraordinary views.

- The grouping of units protects against strong northeastern winds.

- Within a protected courtyard, open and closed spaces look out toward different views.

- Atelier, living room/kitchen/dining area, and bedrooms are housed in separate buildings connected with trellises.

- Open spaces between buildings are landscaped on descending terraces.

- Vernacular construction techniques were used for this house.

Spaces between buildings are connected by beams and overhangs.   *Thick, textured masonry forms are outlined as shadows are cast.*

Openings and windows are recessed and shaded against the hot Mediterranean sun.

The house sited in the natural landscape.

Interior court is terraced and defined by walks and trellis.

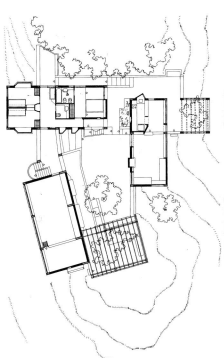

Plan.

Sketch elevation.

Diagram showing site and building organization.

PROJECT: GARRATY HOUSE, *Sag Harbor, New York*

Architect: Alfredo De Vido, FAIA

- Modular design allocates space for a variety of uses.
- The concrete block and weathered wood construction emphasizes the modular aspect of the design.
- Recesses and projecting walls give protection against the sun and the sometimes strong winds.

Elevation overlooking Peconic Bay.

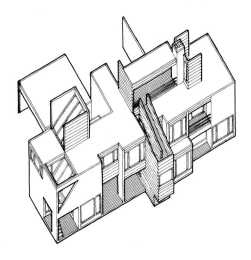

Axonometric view.

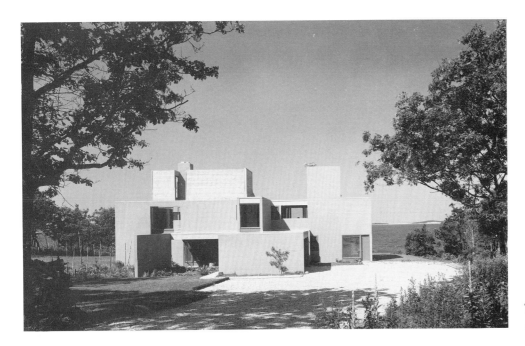

The approach to the house shows a relatively closed facade.

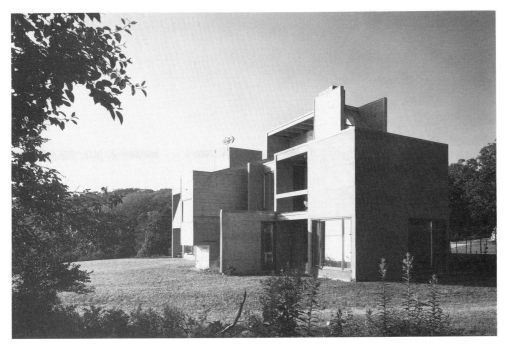

Angled view demonstrating sunshades.

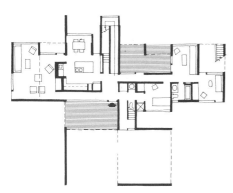

First floor plan.

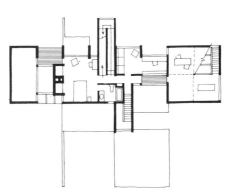

Second floor plan.

PROJECT: NORNEY, *Shackleford, Surrey, England*

Architect: C.F. A. Voysey

- The roofline draws attention with its steep pitch, numerous chimneys, and picturesque massing.

- Strong modeling of the exterior blends bow windows with square gables.

- The entrance is grand, with its striking roof, circular window, and patterned door.

- There is a sense of order, with several emphases: the heavy gable overhanging the bay windows, the prominent porch, and the layout of the interiors.

An exterior view shows paned bay windows and overhanging gables.

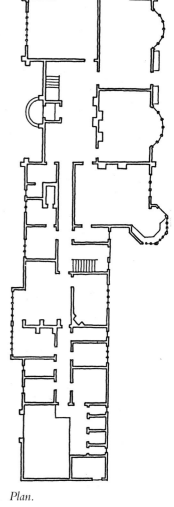

Plan.

Main entrance with embellished door and round window.

2|
THE CLIENT

In custom building a house, the client is all-important. Not only does the client generate the project and provide the financing, but also he or she determines the intangible content of the project, in the sense of stylistic direction. It is best to make your client a collaborator in the design process. The client will then feel part of it and will be faced with no surprises later.

WHY DO PEOPLE WANT HOUSES?

People want houses to meet their needs for shelter and to express their desires about living space. Besides a habitable space in which to live their lives comfortably, people want to establish a territory that is uniquely theirs. Ideally, a house should be at one with its natural or man-made surroundings. People want their houses to be economically constructed, of sound materials, well put together, and able to withstand the elements, without requiring excessive maintenance and high utility bills. In addition, they want their houses to accommodate their activities, the day's rhythms, and their dreams. A house is a small part of the big world, but to the people living in it, a house can be their entire world. It contains their clothing, machines, workspaces, collections, artworks, and places of repose and relaxation.

Each house is located within a context of some sort, be it a parcel of land in a woods or a prairie, a town or city, or an allocated area within an existing building. Within the new or allocated space or structure, inhabitants want to claim the place with their own furniture, color, light, and reshaped spaces.

AFFORDING THE NECESSITIES AND DREAMS

The cost of houses preoccupies every home builder. Chapter 5 suggests a series of questions and leads the architect to a meaningful assessment of what the budget might be. Beyond that, budget determination is a juggling act requiring careful probes into the client's financial position, such as how much money is really available or can be borrowed, to reach a considered judgment of how the client really wants to spend his or her money. People who build houses choose architects mostly on the basis of their perceived ability to put together those intangibles that people always try to introduce wherever a house is established. These intangibles include nooks and crannies, unexpected views, grandness (where that is wanted), and the "feel" of the space. If clients could do this themselves, they probably would. Fortunately for architects and builders, the act of building requires a knowledge of construction techniques and the ability to fit together spaces and the walls and apertures defining them. Within a house, the occupant is the master, escaping external constraints other than those imposed by co-occupants or the restrictions required by the community. Perhaps the greatest restriction lies in fitting the dreams to the costs.

INNOVATIONS, DESIRES, CHOICES

Among architects, builders, and marketers of houses innovation is of strong interest. Inevitably, though, tradition plays an important part in house design and actually enables us to offer a wider group of choices than would be possible were we restricted to the latest fads or designer items. To some extent, house design is a matter of style. Recently, a number of books have been written defining various regional or national "styles." These are handsome books, usually codifying what the authors believe to be the salient characteristics of the groupings. A book on Santa Fe style, for instance, depicts bright colors, ethnic and craft collections, methods of building with adobe that make sense in the hot, dry climate, and other features that the author feels are characteristic of the region and its strong architectural and decorating styles. Another book, on Turkish style, illustrates the richness of the decorative motifs found in carpeting and textiles, as well as the careful woodworking of older houses set in what used to be forested areas.

The designers of houses devote considerable time to the arrangement of walls defining space, their apertures, and the innovative decoration of these elements. Ezra Pound succinctly suggested that it was good to "make it new." Although he didn't elaborate, most people think his intent was to advocate the exploration of new ways of assembling words. Throughout literary, art, and architectural history, the practitioners of those crafts have often tried to do the same within their fields. Some have appointed themselves experts on matters of taste and style. A larger group, including many house makers, dispute the elitist claims of taste and style trendsetters, and just do it.

PROFILE OF A CLIENT

One of the client's early decisions was the selection of an architect. Find out how this was done. If you have been referred by a third party, consider the person who made the recommendation and whether this person might have qualified his or her opinion in any way. Knowing the client's attitude toward your abilities will help you to approach the project. For example, someone may have cautioned that you create a well-built, beautiful house but regularly exceed your budget—a common caveat. If you find that the client is apprehensive in this regard, emphasize your concern for budget and how you propose to deal with it during subsequent discussions to allay fears. If you do exceed your budgets, it may be better to remain silent, leaving the client to draw his or her own conclusions. Or you may want to point out that most budgets are routinely exceeded because of the architect's desire to accommodate as many of the client's requests as possible. To compensate, you might suggest a lower original budget target to give the job a cushion.

Find out whether the client has worked previously with an architect, either on this project or another one. If so, it is likely that you will know the other architect's reputation. Nevertheless, it will give you needed background to ask the client how the job was performed and whether there were any problems. A discontinued relationship may seem to indicate problems, so it would be wise to find out what, if any, they were. If another architect has worked on the same project for which you are being interviewed, and if that architect has been terminated, make sure that his or her services have been terminated properly. If the client reveals that the other architect is still on the job, inquire about the reason. If you are doing sketches because the client is unsure about staying with the original architect, it's probably better to back off. Either ask the client to dispense with the other architect, or try to work out a clear arrangement that leaves you in an unambiguous situation. The client and the other architect will respect your professional integrity if you are frank and open in dealing with them.

CLIENTS COME WITH DIFFERENT QUALITIES

Architects have different levels of ability. Some are experienced and have a high degree of personal integrity and sincerity. Others have the same good qualities, but lack the artistic talent to put together a meaningful design that will work for a client.

Just as some house builders have different qualifications and interests in building houses, clients also vary as to their characteristics. Despite the architect's best efforts to do a job properly, a client may be difficult to work with. However, architects should be able to handle difficult clients. The best policy is to remain professional. Ask questions courteously and explain things carefully.

Clients for the three groups of people who build houses can be divided into two broad categories: (1) private individuals/families or groupings functioning as family units and (2) public groups or governmental agencies. The latter, public groups serving as clients for the builders of multifamily housing, may not be logically included here, because the governmental agencies or autonomous groups that shape this type of housing depend on sociological data or market consultants to determine the design of the houses and how they fit together. Individuals are involved in the design process, but they do not project their own preferences for living patterns into the design.

PRIVATE CLIENTS

Clients in the first category can be organized into fairly distinguishable groups:

Group A. People in this group usually turn to house builders/developers. They tend to be leery of the design process, because they have heard the usual stories about exceeded budgets, and they are unsure of their own capability to visualize things from a paper rendering. Some, however, will have exhausted the possibilities of existing houses in the area where they would like to live, so they approach the architect/custom builder. These people make good clients if the architect is patient while sorting out their goals and matching them with appropriate budgets. They do not make such good clients if they are very indecisive. The best policy for the architect with indecisive clients is to adopt a strongly positive attitude and suggest only one or two options.

Group B. Most in this group are people of high creativity. Their life goals stress personal satisfaction and individuality. If they have inspected the architect's work and have sold themselves on it, or have been sold on it by one of the architect's former clients, they will be good clients. They will get along with the architect and be decisive. However, the architect should be aware that not all in this group are ideal clients. Among the things to be prepared for are the following:

THE CLIENT

1.　The inability to find one job among those in the architect's portfolio that the client can identify with strongly. This creates a lack of certainty that his or her ideas will be properly realized. The architect can counter this fear with careful note taking or by suggesting that the client collect pictures of any architect's work and indicate what he or she likes or does not like in the pictures.

2.　An opposite problem is strong identification with one particular project. Sometimes the architect will be requested to make a few changes in an existing house to achieve a satisfactory design. Because different sites, programs, and budgets usually make that approach difficult, the architect can point this out and suggest that other ideas should be reviewed. On the other hand, the client may be quite right; one of the architect's designs may be basically appropriate for that client, site, and budget. The architect can then modify it as necessary, negotiate an appropriately lower fee, which the client will expect, and proceed.

A good analysis of these two broad groups was documented in a study of two Chicago architects, Mark van Doren and Frank Lloyd Wright. The study revealed that van Doren's clients tended to be conservative, had inherited money or businesses, and were creative within limits. Wright's clients were mostly self-made people who had built their own businesses and were receptive to new ways of thinking and innovative design.

The most important ownership goal of both sets of clients is psychological in nature. Simply put, it's the satisfaction of living in one's own home.

PUBLIC AND PRIVATE GROUPS/AGENCIES

Public and private groups and agencies commission houses and house groupings. These clients also come in two distinguishable groups.

Group A. With the growing desire of people to live with others of similar interests and backgrounds, and with the high cost of land and the infrastructure needed to service the buildings on that land, an increasing number of groups commission house groups or subdivisions. Sometimes these people share common areas or buildings for social purposes or for day-care services. Ecological reasons, such as preservation of a scenic site, may be the group's focus. Or a trade union may decide to build houses for its members. Groups of this sort usually form associations. The people the architect deals with are members of the association's building committee. These groups can be difficult to work with, because the members may not agree with one another and the architect must mediate between individual members. There's no easy recommendation. Above all, try to get a clear program from the committee, and prepare your proposals from that. You can do this by addressing the group's questions, as many as possible, about the proposed housing.

Group B. Public agencies of a municipality, county, or state government commission houses. Such dwellings are frequently connected in rows or groups or can be stacked as low- , medium- , or high-rises. The houses are wholly or partially subsidized with public money. Architects work with sociological data or market consultants to determine the design of the houses and how they fit together. The clients are involved, but they do not have the opportunity to project their own living patterns on the design.

Cost considerations are paramount. Regulations are numerous. The architect must bring patience and a mind for detail to negotiations with this type of client.

WORKING WITH FAMILIES (OR OTHER GROUPS)

In traditional times, family units were composed of parents and children, bound together by common needs and goals. Adults entered family life through marriage and, frequently, having children. This elemental and ancient relationship has changed—sometimes radically, sometimes not—throughout the world. Although statistics change often, the modern house is inhabited by any number of groupings, same sex or opposite, single or married, with children or without. Depending on the closeness of the relationship, the inhabitants will want to do certain things within the house either individually or together.

TRAFFIC FLOW

Classifying the kinds of activities that the people within a house will probably engage in is a helpful practice, rather than trying to choreograph family activities according to some abstract ideal. For instance, any grouping will include adults, perhaps children, and invited guests who will occupy the house for varying periods, as well as pets and service people such as repair persons and nannies.

An easy way to approach the analysis is by patterning a day's activities for the typical inhabitant. Short of psychoanalyzing them or living with them for a while, the architect can perform the analysis using a series of questions such as those suggested by the listed program in Chapter 5. The answers generally provide a framework for the relationship of rooms and the activities within them. This sort of classification offers clues to the flow of people and material, and where the machinery of living will be accommodated. It's a start.

Another way to approach the analysis relates to the grouping of people within the house: determine their preferred flow of activity. For instance, one adult may like to get up earlier than the other and exercise in private, then shower and dress. The other person may like to sleep later, eat something, then dress. Children may arise sleepily and shamble off to school or to their morning activity without any routine, generally leaving it to a responsible adult to get them moving in the right direction more or less on time. In this instance, an arrangement suggests itself whereby a room is placed adjacent to the sleeping chamber in which the early riser can exercise and wash in private without disturbing the other person. At some point, he or she may mobilize the child, which suggests a different chamber for the child, not too far distant but sufficiently removed so that noise from the early riser's activities will not disturb the sleeping child. To find out what the daily flow for house members will be, list a typical day's sequence for each inhabitant, limiting that sequence to one double-spaced sheet of paper. This will not provide all the answers, but with the other information gathered, it will at least give a clearer understanding of who lives in the house and what they do there.

AVOIDING STEREOTYPES

Above all, avoid stereotyping the individual members of a household. Not only does it annoy the clients, who regard themselves as individual enough to have come to an architect in the first place, but it is also intrinsically wrong to force the inhabitants into a predetermined traffic flow within the house. For example, there are certain accepted rules of planning in kitchen design, such as having counters on each side of the sink and range and on the latch side of the refrigerator. Although it is important to point out these customs as a practical matter, it is wrong to insist on them if the user of the kitchen wants to have the sink immediately next to the cooktop for reasons unique to him- or herself, such as ease of emptying a pot directly into a waiting colander in the sink.

ASPECTS OF LIVABILITY

The livability of a house concerns comfort. Comfort is physical, emotional, and intellectual—the best state of being, in a truly livable house. To most people comfort means a good place to sit or lie down, with good natural light or a convenient lamp, some cushions for the back, and a place to put a well-filled cup or glass. Comfort also means ease of use and privacy from others who are occupying the house. It means good ventilation and the ability to regulate temperature and control drafts.

ACTIVITIES

Living patterns affect the design of houses, and vice versa. When a client communicates the program to the architect and the architect determines all aspects of the site, the house as designed and built should represent the best efforts of both architect and the client to provide a three-dimensional diagram of the living functions and patterns that will take place in the house. Because compromises are always a part of the design process, owing to budget, site constraints, or adjustments in living patterns to accommodate more than one person, the completed house will also exert its own influence on the occupants. The architect will inevitably influence the living patterns as well, although it is a mistake for an architect to impose his or her own life patterns and habits on a client.

HOUSE AREAS

The areas of a house that make up the whole can be usefully divided into private, semiprivate, and social. Concepts of privacy have changed over the centuries. In ancient times, the owners of a house lived in the same room as their family, help, and livestock. In Renaissance villas, circulation routinely passed through spaces now considered private. In our present age, privacy is relatively more important.

Classifying the various activities that take place in a house is useful. Try lumping them together according to the presently perceived need for varying degrees of privacy.

Private activities generally include those that take place in the bedroom and bathroom, though some individuals may wish to bathe together. Some people, who find it acceptable to wash together, ask the architect to provide adjacent sinks. Contemplative activities are usually done in private when, for instance, undistracted attention must be paid to the pages of a book, the creation of a painting or drawing, the study of some skill or educational matter, or the pursuit of a money-making activity. Increasingly, smoking is an activity of enforced isolation. Sleeping is a solitary activity for which people prefer quiet.

Those activities that people can do with or without other people include such manual activities as cooking, housekeeping, listening to or making music, sewing, and fixing things that break. Looking at art or doing nothing can be either a private or a social activity.

Social activities include conversing with others, entertaining, dancing, and playing of all sorts using games or one's wits. Most people particularly like to eat with others.

In addition to the activities that take place at specific points within the house, there are others of a more general nature. It is necessary to store things and to get to and between the various points. Access to these points is generally on foot, but attention must be paid to those who are disabled whose locomotion is mostly mechanized. The relationship of all activities relates to the site. Vehicular access should be considered, inasmuch as some people want to see, from certain points in house, who's coming in the drive or up the walk.

Changing family patterns are another important consideration. For instance, as children grow up they need their own spaces in which to work or study, or guests may be present for brief or extended periods. The architect and client are asked to perform a difficult juggling act, inasmuch as the ideal space allocation for any given situation may be at odds with that for another situation.

DESIGNING FOR PRIVACY AND FLEXIBILITY

Once the architect has determined which activities the client wants to keep private and what relationships should be between the spaces used for different purposes, he or she can employ various means to achieve levels of privacy and flexibility. A bubble diagram is a useful tool to determine the proximity and interrelation of spaces. It may even be desirable to show such a diagram to your client if it appears that he or she is indecisive about relationships between rooms. Arrows can be added to the diagrams to show the effects of exterior site factors.

Long or Spread-Out House

The site and external factors permitting a long or spread-out house can be useful in zoning the house. However, travel distances should be reviewed with the client, because there may be mitigating considerations. A two-zone house in which

Long or spread-out house (Hammer house, Sagaponack, NY)

children are allocated their own space or spaces, detached or semidetached from the rest of the house, may produce good sound isolation for the adults. But many parents may have reservations about leaving children without supervision.

The Weather

The effects of the weather or the sun on the various activities within a house should be measured and provided for. For example, people usually gravitate to the sun and like to live in sunny spaces. A person who wants to have a greenhouse should be asked which orientation he or she prefers. South is not necessarily the only option, because some plant species need relatively shady or sun-sheltered space. Unpleasant winds usually come from a specific direction, and thick walls with few openings can be designed to guard against them. Precipitation, another factor, must be channeled away from exterior surfaces.

Materials

The materials chosen for the inside of a house will have an effect on the privacy of the occupants. Dense materials such as masonry will block the passage of sound. Ordinary Sheetrock can be doubled up to provide additional sound-blocking mass. Sound absorbent material such as cork or carpet on the floor will quiet footsteps. Even color can have a soothing effect. The presence of dark natural wood, subdued colors, or a book-lined wall contributes to a feeling of privacy.

Size

The size of specific rooms must be considered. Psychological studies have explored the degree of physical proximity with which various people are comfortable. This "hidden dimension" varies from one person to another. For instance, two people in the same room may be quite comfortable in separate chairs, but not so on the same sofa. Although few budgets are sufficiently ample to provide large rooms throughout a house, the effects of large rooms should be considered, especially for their drawbacks. Some people prefer intimate spaces and nooks for certain, usually private, activities.

Cozy work area (Whitton/Dailey house, Southampton, NY)

Windows provide light and air.
(Morton house, Middletown, NJ)

Sound Insulation

Sound insulation between rooms is almost always a good idea. Few people think of it, but insulation is relatively cheap and can be used to reduce sound transmission between various rooms to good effect. The services of an acoustician are not required to design sound insulation, because the necessary information is commonly available in standard reference books. However, it is a good idea to consult an acoustician for such activities as watching TV or making or listening to music. Strategic placement of reflective and absorptive material within the room is important to the enjoyment of sound-producing activities.

In houses of more than one story, or within apartments that are part of a multifamily complex, sound insulation is of primary importance; it must be discussed with your client and provided for. Even in apartments with concrete slabs between units, it's possible to line the ceilings and walls with layers of absorbent material that will do the job.

Movable Sound Isolation Walls

Movable sound isolation walls and panels are almost always a poor investment. To function properly, the gasket commonly provided for these walls needs maintenance, and people generally tend not to move large objects within a house. It's best to avoid flexible arrangements of walls or furniture that require great physical effort.

Doors

Doors are commonly undercut at the bottom to provide easy clearance over the floor finish. This gap can be a passageway for unwanted sound. Gaskets and strip-

Maximize space and convenience in the kitchen. (Tarnopol house, Bridgehampton, NY)

ping of all sorts are available to cut off noise. Where soundproof rooms are required, sound-isolating doors are available, although they tend to be expensive.

Windows

Windows and the views they provide are frequently desirable, but not for all activities. Although windows are a good source of light and ventilation, they can also be distracting. Sometimes the urge to look out of windows and noise coming in through them can be detrimental to the pursuit of certain activities, such as intense study or a close following of the Super Bowl on TV.

Bathrooms

Bathrooms can be handily placed next to bedrooms or between them. This works particularly well if the bathroom will be used by the occupants of both bedrooms. Although some people may request doors directly to this bathroom from the bedrooms, it's not the best idea, because one door may be left locked by a departing occupant.

Labor-Intensive Spaces

In labor-intensive spaces, such as kitchens, the requisite activities necessitate optimum distances and clearances. For instance, the "work triangle" between refrigerator, sink, and cooktop should provide convenient counter space, yet not be so distant that the preparation of a large meal will exhaust the cook. There are also many good rules of proper kitchen planning that the architect should study and provide for, if only to avoid the intrusion of "kitchen planners," who tend not to have the overall traffic flow of the house in mind.

Some of the more important rules of good kitchen planning include the following: counter space on each side of the sink, range, and refrigerator; shelving that is not so high that reaching heavy dishes is difficult or hard on the back; pantry closets that permit stored goods to be readily viewed and reached; and surfaces that are properly sized and easy to keep clean.

THE CLIENT

Odors

Odors from kitchens and bathrooms should be exhausted using mechanical devices such as hoods and fans. Bathroom fans are frequently required by code if there's no window. Windows are very desirable in kitchens and bathrooms both for exhausting odors and for light, as well as to compensate for the inevitable failure of the fan at some point in its life cycle.

Buffers

Buffers such as closet and storage spaces provide sound insulation. It is good planning to incorporate them between bedrooms. Machinery areas are also good buffers, but care should be taken with venting and handling the noise they may emit.

Mechanical Equipment

Mechanical equipment—and the noise and odor it may produce—can be bothersome. For instance, it is wise to be careful in locating a noisy air handler next to or under a bedroom. Oil burners can leak oil and are best placed as far as possible from all human activity. Kitchen and bath fans can be obtrusive. Quiet models are usually more expensive than noisy ones, but they may be worth the expense if the client is sensitive to noise.

Pets

Pets and their travels can be important not only in regard to the health of their owners—for instance, asthmatic sufferers who are allergic to cats—but also in regard to mitigating odors and protecting rugs and furniture. The comings and goings of a pet must be taken into account. Some dog species, for instance, cannot bark and require special egress to go outdoors whenever they want.

THERMAL COMFORT

The temperature, purity, and circulation of the air within a house can all be tempered. Pollutants contained within building materials and generated by the occupants have been studied in recent years. Asbestos is a well-publicized danger to human health, as is cigarette smoke. Most pollutants in materials have been identified and eliminated, including most toxins in paints. Still present are the pollutants generated by machine exhaust and produced through nature's cycles, such as pollen.

Air temperature, its humidity content, and its movement and freshening quality are of importance to the comfort of the occupants. The following paragraphs present some useful considerations.

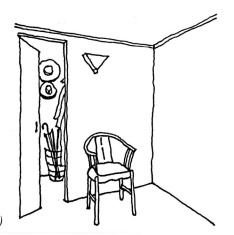

Closets are good sound buffers.
(De Vido house, East Hampton, NY)

Heating and Cooling

The desired type of heating and cooling system should be discussed at an early stage with the client, inasmuch as the routing of pipes and ducts throughout the house takes space and must be thoroughly planned. Air is heated at some central point and conveyed to the various spaces with fans pushing it through a system of ducts. It is possible to heat space with electric coils and panels, sometimes with fans, sometimes without. Cooling is conveyed in much the same way as heating. Most commonly, an air handler passes air over cold pipes filled with refrigerant and the resulting cool air is distributed throughout the house.

Various energy sources are available for heating and cooling interior spaces, ranging from oil, gas, and electricity to the sun itself, by using its power through passive or active means. In applying solar principles, it is important to know some rules of physics, such as a cold surface nearby pulls heat from the human body, and air moving over a surface, also known as a "cooling breeze," has an evaporative effect.

The selection of heating and cooling systems entails the consideration of many aspects, such as the cost of the various types of energy, the space required and the location of the equipment, and the quality of the air after it has been tempered. Among the items the architect should review with the client are the following:

• What allergies, if any, should be considered in filtering the air? Consider airborne contaminants, such as pollution and pollen, as well as allergies to pets and, in rural areas, agricultural sprays.

• What are the cost considerations of the various available kinds of energy? For instance, electric resistance heating can have a low initial installation cost, but can cost more to operate, canceling out any savings in a short time. The perennial public relations battle between the oil and gas industries, each touting its own product, is confusing at best. It is also subject to the changing winds of international disputes affecting the price of oil.

• Solar heating and cooling is generally desirable in passive modes that employ the path of the sun and its absorption on, or blocking by, the surfaces of the house. The costs and operating procedures of active modes, such as rooftop solar collectors, must be considered.

• How sensitive are the clients to the noises generated by the equipment, such as the movement of air through ducts and grilles, the sound of the burners in the furnace, or even the "ping" of lightweight convection systems when they heat up or cool down?

Humidity Content

In addition to the thermal aspects of a space, the humidity content is important. At one end of the scale is an excessively dry environment caused by hot, dry air. Steam and hot water in pipes can produce this type of environment. At the other end, summer heat near a large body of water such as the ocean or a lake can be much more oppressive than the same air temperature in a drier climate. For example, a temperature of 100° F in the desert is much more tolerable than the same temperature in a moist, closed-in environment, assuming there are no other mitigating factors such as breezes or strong, direct radiation from the sun. Humidity can be varied through the use of humidifiers, which provide moisture in the air, or dehumidifiers, which remove it.

The type of heating or cooling selected also affects the quality of moisture in the air. For instance, warm air heating tends to be dry without the provision of a humidifier. Air conditioners normally have dehumidifiers built in. Natural means are also available to regulate moisture content, ranging from boiling water in an iron kettle on top of a wood stove to the evaporative effects of moving air. It should be noted that air moves best within a space when it can actually move through it. For example, opening windows on two sides of a room, rather than just one, significantly reduces humidity.

Conditioned Air

It is important to conserve expensively conditioned air. There are devices, for instance, that provide for the replacement of stale indoor air with fresh air. The stale air is exhausted through a system of baffles in such a way that it gives its heat to the incoming air while being exhausted. These devices were popular during the energy crunch in the 1970s. They are still available, although difficult to find, since most of the manufacturers are foreign. It is also possible to design and build such air-to-air heat exchangers. The installation of a ceiling fan that moves the air in a room is a very simple way to provide a cooling effect.

Airborne Pollutants

Airborne pollutants within a house constitute another concern. The pollutants in building materials have been mentioned briefly; the list seems to grow as scientists identify additional injurious substances. It is a good idea to follow the news stories about newly discovered polluting substances and to respond according to a logical assessment of the given facts. Airborne asbestos particles and certain lead particles, when ingested into the human system in large quantities, have been proven to be a serious health threat. Remedial measures for eliminating life-threatening pollutants require expert care, so seek help.

For some varieties of pollutants, devices such as precipitators can work. These devices collect pollutants and destroy them by electronic means. Make it clear to your clients that certain pollutants, when taken into their systems, can be treated only by medication.

Pests

Other considerable pollutants to the well-tempered house environment are pests of all sorts, ranging from ants, termites, roaches, and flies to mice, rats, raccoons, and bats. Some people do not seem to be bothered by a certain level of pest inhabitation, although some are carriers of disease and should be kept out of a house for safety's sake.

To control the intrusion of these outsiders, the best protection is a tightly built house. Careful caulking under foundation sills and tight closure of the points of entry of pipes help to close these routes of intrusion during construction. Soil treatments are available to limit the infestation of termites, but they can have harmful ecological side effects. If they are used when the house is under construction, it is mandatory to engage a certified pesticide applicator, because some of the chemicals are toxic to humans.

Bats are a special problem, inasmuch as they are most comfortable in tight spaces. These creatures are actually beneficial, because they eat a great number of insects every night. However, most people do not like them searching for food within the house. To exclude them, the architect can make sure that all openings to the cavities of the structure, such as the voids above the insulation within the roof and wall structure, are carefully screened. "Carefully" is the operative word; one small hole can accommodate the entry of hundreds of bats.

SAFETY

Household accidents are the single greatest cause of injury to people. The safety precautions discussed in the following paragraphs therefore merit the architect's attention.

Code Regulations

Code regulations, particularly in regard to the operation of electrical outlets and appliances, should be strictly adhered to. Use only licensed plumbers, heating and cooling installers, and electricians. Go beyond the minimum in following safety rules and regulations.

Level Changes

Avoid single- or even double-riser changes in levels. These are notoriously dangerous, owing to people's difficulties with depth perception. Yet they are surprisingly common in houses, because people like subtle changes in level between rooms or between areas within a room. Although the permanent occupants of the house may get accustomed to such changes, it should be pointed out that visitors may not see them, so they should be routinely avoided. Level changes of three or more risers are safer, if properly provided with handrails.

Three or more risers make level changes safer. (Rothschild house, Greenwich, CT)

Slippery Floors

Avoid the installation of slippery floor surfaces wherever possible. Polished stone or tile can look elegant if properly maintained. Yet the polished surface is dangerous in spaces where people come and go with wet feet, as in an entry or bathroom. The architect should be very careful about specifying finishes that people can slip on, even at a client's request, because that does not relieve the architect of responsibility should there be an accident. For instance, some clients may want glazed tile on bathroom floors because it is attractive. However, it is also dangerous, and for that reason manufacturers don't recommend it. It also has poor wearing qualities underfoot. Floors within tubs and showers, particularly dangerous, should be provided with no-slip surfaces.

Door Swings

Check the direction of all door swings. It is generally agreed that the doors to a room should open into that room, rather than into the corridor or access point. Give thought to where the doors will rest when open within the room. Doors work better resting against a wall or closet instead of standing in the line of traffic or in a

Door swings away *from living room (Ferguson house, Pound Ridge, NY)*

position where they are maddeningly in the way wherever the occupant wants to cir-culate. Never open doors above a void, such as to a basement if there is no landing at the top of the stairs.

Heavy Materials Overhead

Do not install potentially dangerous, heavy materials overhead where a change in temperature or lack of maintenance can work them loose.

Avoid sticking large pieces of stone on a wall or ceiling with mastic. Better to use noncorrodable fasteners. It is common practice to put tile on the ceiling of a high-humidity area such as a shower stall. Just make sure the tile setter knows how to do it, because even a short fall of a large piece of tile can cause injury. Better still, avoid the installation completely and use vaporproof paint on Sheetrock or plaster. Think defensively. With the general lack of maintenance that building materials get, the potential for calamities in the future looms large.

Designing for Disabled People

People with disabilities deserve special attention. Not only is this mandatory by law, but necessary in any long-range plan for a house. The client will inevitably age, so some thought should be given to the location of the master bedroom in a two-story house. A second floor location may be desirable at present for a number of reasons, but perhaps not desirable in the future. Without offending your client, ask if there are any health problems you should plan for.

Handrails and Grab Bars

Provide grab bars and handrails where required and desirable. Most codes mandate handrails for stairs. Grab bars in bathrooms are a good idea, particularly for older people, and are mandatory for disabled persons.

Awkward Protrusions

Avoid protrusions that may not be easily seen, such as doors that swing out from cabinets at eye height. Many people lack depth perception, or simply aren't careful about where they're going, and may bump into such protrusions.

LIGHTING: 24-HOUR ARCHITECTURE

Many houses are used most intensively when there is little daylight. It is therefore important for the architect to design the house for use during periods of little or low-level natural lighting. The services of a competent lighting designer are desirable, but they involve an extra fee that your client may be reluctant or unable to pay. If a lighting designer is not to be consulted, the following guidelines can be helpful.

Discussion with Client

Discuss the concept of lighting in general with your client, in order to avoid pitfalls. Some people simply do not like overhead lighting and will never be convinced of its merit in some locations. Irrational, perhaps, but this is a real factor in the design of the system.

Safe Levels of Lighting

Safe, appropriate levels of lighting should be provided at all changes in floor level. Consider, for example, how to set up the switching of lights on stairs, since stairs

Triangular wall sconces and hanging overhead lights provide overall illumination. (Frocht house, East Hampton, NY)

are generally used to go from one level to another. Placing a switch at the foot of the stairs without placing one at the head means that the user has to go back down the stairs to turn the light off.

Conveniently Located Switches

Give some thought in general to the mechanics of switching lights on and off. Go over the plan with your client before construction, because light switching habits are highly individual. Consider the desirability of lighting particular locations, such as the area in front of a closet to illuminate its contents.

Locate a switch at the entrance to a room or space so as to provide convenient illumination. Place a switch at the customary height to control overhead lights or outlets that floor or table lamps are plugged into. Give some thought to the type of switching for a bedside lamp that has to be turned off when a person retires. It is possible to split the outlets within a duplex outlet so that one remains permanently active, while the other is switchable. This is especially convenient at a bedside where a clock radio requires a steady supply of electricity.

Switching Devices

Investigate different kinds of switching devices and the use of dimmers. For example, programmed scenarios control fixtures within a room to create different levels of lighting for various kinds of activity. These devices, controlled by mini-circuit boards and low-voltage wiring, are expensive at present. They are not appropriate for use in small spaces with simple lighting schemes. However, for large living spaces, it is possible to program different lighting level arrangements, say, for a party, during which lower levels of lighting are desirable, versus a family evening when light levels should be higher. Exercise caution in using these sophisticated devices if your client is not mechanically oriented, because their cost and installation will be wasted if they are not used.

On a simpler level, dimmers are commonly used to good effect and can save energy as well as provide a broad range of lighting options. Check with your client to see that these devices will be understood and used properly. Some good spots for dimmers are areas that will accommodate a change in activities, such as living rooms used both for quiet, low-level conversation and for reading and game playing, for which visibility is important.

Some types of light switches, for instance, the heat-sensing variety, have pre-programmed light levels that must be used in certain ways. Many would-be users

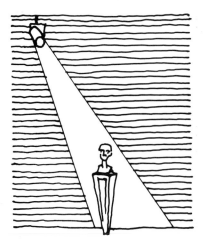

Directional lighting can illuminate a special object.

don't understand that it is necessary to keep a hand on a heat-sensitive switch in order to get the illumination to an adequate level. Another kind of problem may be caused by slide switches. Ask your client whether this type of high-tech device is necessary or desirable. Many visitors to high-tech houses have washed in the dark or gloom because they did not understand how to use the light switch and were too embarrassed to ask.

Energy-Efficient Lighting

Energy-efficient lighting of all kinds is important. There are many color-corrected lighting fixtures that save on energy costs. There is also a great deal of unwarranted prejudice against this type of lighting because older fluorescent fixtures remain notorious for their poor light color and a subliminal flicker that is tiring to the eyes. A new world of lighting, which arrived with the era of expensive energy, merits the attention of architects and their clients. If costs are a problem, however, use these fixtures judiciously.

Task Lighting

Task lighting is important at kitchen counters and in bathroom areas. Kitchen lighting is best located directly above the counter or work surface rather than behind the person engaged in a task, in order to avoid shadows.

If fluorescent lighting is used in kitchens, it's better to specify color-corrected lamps so that food will look good. The same rule applies in the bathroom, because people like to look good when they look in the mirror.

Directional Lights

Directional lights that illuminate a wall, book, or work of art are easily specified. Their location is important in terms of determining the proper distance from the wall and their spacing from each other so as to avoid "scalloping" of light patterns on the surface to be lit.

Security Lighting

Consider security lighting. It is possible to provide low-voltage circuiting to allow switching at several locations that will illuminate the fixtures within a house and on the exterior. This feature can be comforting if the presence of a prowler is sensed at night. The sudden, bright illumination of the house will probably frighten away any potential intruder. The actual location of these fixtures, such as at bedside, should be considered, and their possible tie-in with a burglar alarm system investigated.

THE EFFECTS OF WEATHER

The sound of rain on a roof can be quite soothing. It can also be objectionably noisy if the roof is of metal placed directly on top of thin planking. Also of concern is how rain passes from the roof to the ground. If it is allowed to fall off the roof directly onto the top of an open casement window on a hot, humid night, the window will have to be closed. This is where an overhang is useful. However, some architects do not like overhangs for aesthetic reasons, and they are truly ugly when applied in a certain insensitive way (when the roof beams are simply carried out a foot or so and cut square, with a large facia board at the ends). Good-looking overhangs usually have their bottom sides shaped or modeled in some fashion to give them a graceful appearance from below. It's possible to protect windows from falling precipitation in other ways, of course, such as recessing them in some sort of niche. The important thing to remember is that windows need protection during inclement weather. Other effects of weather that concern both architect and client are discussed in the following paragraphs.

Wind

Thought must be given to wind and its effects in various climates—at the seashore, for instance. Some kinds of windows, such as casements or awnings, will be damaged if left open in high winds, because the open window serves as a sail that catches the wind. Hinges on many such windows cannot take the wind load.

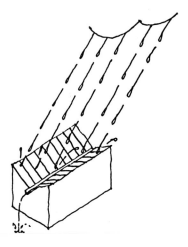

Always consider how rain moves from the roof to the ground.

Sun

Sun, in large, unmodulated quantities, can raise the interior temperature of a house to unacceptable levels and cause fading of fabrics and darkening of natural woods. Many artworks, particularly textiles and those on paper, suffer from direct exposure to the sun.

Heavy Snow

In areas of heavy snow, steps must be taken to protect a house from snow and ice slides that may injure the inhabitants, and from snow dams that cause leaks. In cold climates, the overhangs and lower ends of pitched roofs are commonly provided with a band of metal roofing to prevent the penetration of water into the house. As it melts on a roof, a buildup of water is created beneath the standing snow. When the sun goes down and the temperature on the roof drops, this standing water moves sideways and pushes under shingles. It is then reheated by normal heat loss from the house and causes what may seem to be a leak within the house. The solution is a "cold roof" in which a layer of cold air is permitted to flow between the insulation and the roof covering via eaves and ridge vents.

Steps should also be taken to cope with big pileups of snow around the house. This necessitates higher than normal windows on the ground floor and impervious surfacing at entrances.

Floods

Extreme weather conditions, such as floods and hurricanes, must also be considered. In areas that are frequently flooded (river deltas or low areas near the coast), it makes sense to build houses on piles above the recorded flood peaks. Many localities require this practice by law.

Gutters

Gutters are a sore subject with architects. They are generally ugly and freeze when clogged, which is practically always. Some architects think they were invented

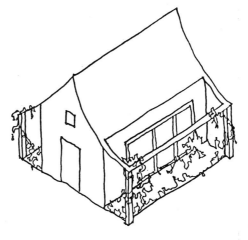

There are many creative solutions to gutter problems.

by itinerant and insensitive landscape contractors to protect foundation plantings. What to do when clients bring up the subject? There are several ways of handling the problem:

1. Build gutters into roof edges or combine them with a system of internal roof drains. However, building them in is expensive and a potential problem. If gutters freeze, expansion may force ice up through the shingles or other roof covering. This can happen as well with the simpler tack-on variety of gutters.

2. Select an attractive type of gutter, such as wooden ones or any of the available shapes other than the notoriously ugly extruded variety. Control the leaders by designing a straight drop to the ground or by using a chain to conduct the water to the ground.

3. If the architect chooses to eliminate gutters, he or she may consider landscaping devices such as a band of gravel at the base of the house to take the roof runoff. A look at Japanese architecture is instructive, as the Japanese have worked out a number of interesting and attractive ways to conduct rainwater runoff to the ground, including the devices mentioned earlier.

THE SMART HOUSE

If yours is a "smart house," it is possible to telephone from your car to your house on the way home so that your dinner will be hot when you get there, the lights on, and your favorite music playing as you walk in the door. It is similarly possible to computerize the operating systems of the house, with programming ranging from the simple to the sophisticated. Some of the more common features worth considering in a smart house are listed here:

• An automatic setback thermostat is an economical addition. It sets the heating or cooling at lower levels when it is less necessary, such as at night. Some thermostats are programmable for up to seven days, which permits owners of second homes to have their heat turned up automatically when they arrive for a weekend.

• Automatic light sensors that turn lights on when a person enters a room are commonly used in schools and offices. These devices turn lights off automatically at an interval after a room is vacated. They are a little spooky perhaps until you get used to them, but big energy savers, particularly in a house with children who tend to turn lights on, but not off. This kind of device is not advisable for use in bedrooms.

• The use of multiple controls can be desirable for sound and home entertainment systems. Such controls offer the ability to switch off or mute sounds from several sources.

• Intrusion alarms are reasonably easy to use and not very expensive. They are particularly useful in second homes where the occupants are absent for extended periods. Security lighting and other devices can be controlled when the front door is opened by proper keying in of codes.

• Fire alarms are mandatory in most new construction and should be retrofitted in older construction. Properly installed and maintained, they can save lives.

• Garage door operators are convenient and safe. They are quite useful in inclement weather and in high-crime zones.

More sophisticated control devices, unrelated to safety or security in the home, should be discussed with your client. Most are complicated to operate, expensive, and will someday require repair. Note that it is difficult to find the advanced repair skills needed to fix many of these devices among the ranks of workers who build houses. Engineers are employed to operate such systems in large office buildings and residential complexes.

A total design concept includes furnishings. (Quinones/Bieganek house, East Hampton, NY)

FURNITURE AND FURNISHINGS

The furnishings of a house are important to the comfort of the inhabitants and to provide visual pleasure. The architect should be familiar with the many kinds of furniture available. House furnishings range from valuable antiques to simply made shelves that you can ask a carpenter to nail up using framing lumber. Because household help is an increasing rarity, there is a growing interest in built-ins that do not have cavities around, below, or behind them.

Increasingly, the interior design profession has taken over the furnishings and decorative aspects of house design. Although this is a talented group, the architect should be involved in the total design process if possible. The architect has shaped the space of the house, by and large, and colors, floor coverings, furnishings, objects, pictures, and window and door treatments are part of the total design package. Your

*Consider designing the furnishings.
(Farese house, Montauk, NY)*

interest should be voiced early in the design process. If the client has a decorator or interior designer, it will be up to you to work together harmoniously. Suggest that you would like to provide full design services and that some working method needs to be determined. Because egos are often involved, it may be wise to divide responsibilities into specific areas of control, such as furnishings, fabrics, and window treatments. Above all, it is important for design professionals to work together. The following paragraphs discuss a number of key aspects of interior design.

Sources

It may be difficult for the architect in a small office to keep track of the many sources available for interior design. Fabric suppliers' sample books alone could fill many shelves. First the architect should decide whether it's possible to do this work. If not, he or she should interview interior designers to find someone whose approach is compatible with the end goals of the house design. The client should be alerted to the strategy and brought in at a stage where the selection has been narrowed to two or three people. The client can work with the interior designer at the appropriate time and select from up-to-date materials in the various showrooms.

Plan interior surfaces and finishes early in the design process. (Gropp house, Quogue, NY)

Furnishings Plan

When the schematics are presented, create a furnishings plan. Many clients lament that there is no place to put furniture in a contemporary house. Even if the architect's sympathies lie with underfurnished Japanese tea houses, most clients make it plain that they will not consider sitting on the floor.

Creating a furnishings plan will help the architect to understand the space more completely and will probably assist in window and door placement. It will also help in communication with the client, because most people seem to understand furniture placement better than the more ephemeral aspects of space.

Design Furnishings

Consider designing the furnishings yourself. It takes some knowledge of ergonomics, the science of the dimensions of the human body, but that's not so complicated. If you decide to design furnishings, as did Frank Lloyd Wright, Le Corbusier, and many other architects, it will be necessary to find a good cabinetmaker and upholsterer to work with. The operative rule is the same as with builders: Work with

With openness the goal, no window treatment is desired. (McConomy house, Sewickley, PA)

them and listen to them when they make suggestions. If you've selected an experienced and sympathetic collaborator, he or she will help you along the way.

Walls, Ceilings, Floors

The walls and the voids within them, plus the ceilings and the floors, constitute the interiors. Unlike some apartments, in which the interiors consist of a bland box with a few holes and doors punched in them, the custom house should have good interiors at the time of completion and not need a lot of "decorating."

Aspects of the in-place architecture should be shown to the client in the form of interior elevations. These drawings are normally done to show the contractor where trim and electrical outlets will go during construction. They can then be used to present colors and decorative aspects to the client.

Interior Finishes

It is important to start working on interior finishes early, because many items require lead time. Suppliers do not carry stock, which would tie up their money in inventory. Many interior items such as tile and fabrics are made overseas, so still longer lead times will be necessary. On the other hand, if you are working with a client who has difficulty visualizing the spaces in the house, it may be better to wait until the house is framed out and rough finishes are in place before interior selections are made. Remember that most clients have difficulty in visualizing a space. Patience is necessary.

Interior Surfaces

Design interior surfaces that are practical as well as attractive. A look at interiors designed by Arts and Crafts movement architects Greene and Greene or Charles Rennie Macintosh is instructive. Chair rails, trim strips, picture moldings, and wainscots were commonly worked into an overall scheme of interior decor. Color renderings were usually presented to clients showing a unified scheme of wall color, material, lighting, fabric, and furnishings. Because these interiors were meant for

Window treatments: shutters (De Vido house, East Hampton, NY)

Sunken sitting area features contrasting floor covering. (Sara house, Greenwich, CT)

intense living, the designers tried to show the possibilities of rugged finishes on areas of wear, such as the wall below a certain height. They then worked their scheme into a unified whole by carrying horizontal lines of material and moldings around entire rooms and throughout the house.

Built-ins

Built-ins should be provided for most storage areas. These have many advantages over more movable types of storage. They look orderly, and they hide the sometimes messy things of daily life. Most built-ins can be handled by the builders of a house or by cabinetmakers. There are also many companies that sell economical and attractive built-ins. If using stock built-ins is the best way to fulfill your client's needs, plan the space necessary to accommodate them within closets or along walls.

Window Treatments

Window treatments are an important part of any interior scheme. If the house you've designed has sun protection built into the structure, it may not be necessary to provide window coverings, but most people want them anyway for reasons of privacy. The choices include blinds, often called *venetian* for reasons few can remember, shades of all descriptions, curtains and drapes, and built-in movable shutters. Some shutters can be louvered to permit sun control and the passage of breezes. Shutters can be recessed into the wall, folded up, or hinged, like doors. If you are using shutters or foldup panels, it's important to plan where they go in the open position. A whole wall of glass without protective overhangs will create a hothouse without some sort of sun control.

It's important to think about window treatments early in the design process, inasmuch as the use of blinds or shutters may require deeper interior window recesses.

Shades can also be recessed within pockets at the tops of openings, as can drapery tracks or horizontal blinds. Louvered panels or insect screens can be recessed into side pockets. Some window treatments can be controlled electrically, an amenity that your client will appreciate if large areas are involved.

*House on piers above the dunes
(Kleinman house, Napeague, NY)*

The intrusion of window treatments in the open position within a space is a consideration. Your client will think you are a genius if you remember that casement winding devices commonly stick out far enough to conflict with blinds in the fully extended position. The solution to this common problem is to use compact winding devices, available on request, or deep window recesses.

Floor Coverings

Floor coverings should be thought of at an early stage when the finished floor is being specified. If the floor is tiled, for example, areas for seating or for other purposes can be made warmer and more inviting with an area rug. The selection of the actual rug can wait, but it is good to plan on it early and to ask the client to budget for it. If the specified floor covering will be carpet, the color and fabric should be selected before the walls and ceiling are finished, as all the colors must tie in together.

Wood floors and their finishes loom equally large in the selection process. Wood comes in a wide array of colors in its natural state, and these colors can be accented or muted with paints and finishes. Patterns can be stenciled or painted on wood and rendered relatively permanent with a hand finish, such as polyurethane.

There are innumerable combinations of woods and tiles, woods and carpet, and patterns made from floor covering materials. The visual density of a pattern should be considered within the overall context of a room, and unity, as well as variety, must still be achieved in a well-organized design.

Kitchens and Baths

Because they include expensive surfaces, fitted cabinets, and a great many electrical and mechanical hook-ups, kitchens and baths are the most costly spaces in any house.

Both kitchens and bathrooms require convenient, built-in storage space, which is best integrated with the space needed for applications and fixtures. These particular living areas house activities in which liquids are used; therefore, the counter and wall surfaces require special attention for easy maintenance.

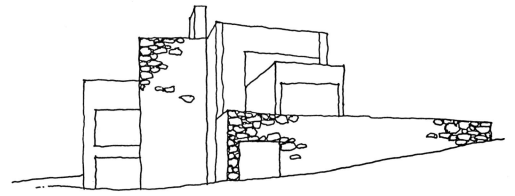

Natural stone was abundant near the site of this house, and it made a cost-effective, attractive material. (McCombe house, Riverhead, NY)

Cleanliness in a kitchen is particularly important for the health of the occupants. In planning, walls, counters, floors, and all surfaces should be devoid of dirt-catching crevices and porous joints and should be easy to clean when food is spilled and spattered in the course of cooking. The surfaces themselves should be durable.

Light and bright colors and finishes are appropriate for kitchens and baths. Here are areas for which the client may enjoy participating in design and planning.

Maintenance

Maintenance, always an important consideration, is influenced by the location of the house. For instance, a house at the beach where occupants track in sand from the outdoors may not be the best place to specify wall-to-wall carpets. In this environment, a harsher surface would be appropriate, because it can be easily swept or vacuumed.

Easily wiped surfaces for counters and sills are usually a plus. Natural materials, such as wood, tile, and stone, age gracefully and require little upkeep. They usually cost more than painted Sheetrock, however, and that factor will have to be weighed. Certain wall finishes can pose a maintenance problem, particularly in high traffic areas or those that children frequent.

LANDSCAPE AND EXTERIOR DESIGN

Depending on its design, the exterior of a house or house grouping can become an integral part of the house itself. Some house sitings can stand aloof of the site, looking over it and surmounting the topography, as in a house on piers. Apartments within larger buildings are often above the landscape, and the landscape becomes the view rather than an integral part of the living space of the house.

Historically, there were different ways of treating a landscape. In Chinese garden design, the exterior landscape was very much to be lived in. Separate buildings were distributed within a domestic site, frequently surrounded by walls, and within this site configuration were the elements of the garden: paving, plants, building, and water. The Japanese treated the garden as something to be seen from viewpoints

Raised or sunken exterior levels can change spatial perceptions. (Trosin house, Saltaire, NY)

within the house or adjacent to the garden. Except for larger stroll gardens, in which the garden was experienced by walking through it as well as observing it from inside the house, the Japanese looked at but usually didn't live within their gardens.

The modern landscape is more a part of the house because of the accessibility of larger pieces of glass and the use of movable, well-weatherstripped window walls. It is important for the architect to plan the garden as part of the overall design scheme. If there is no budget for extensive landscaping at the completion of the house construction, and there frequently is not, the architect can suggest to the client a master plan, drawn up as part of the design process, for later implementation.

If the architect is not conversant with the materials and plant characteristics that are a part of landscape design, it is a good idea to work with a landscape architect or designer. Leaving such an important component as landscape design to the mercies of the local nursery is to be avoided, although exceptions can be made if the local nursery has a competent and sensitive designer in its employ. Most do not. Assuming the house is carefully and beautifully designed, the landscape should enhance that design. Foundation planting usually conceals bad house design.

Garden Organization

Assuming there is access to the garden, visually or via sliding wall or doors, there are ways of arranging exterior space to work visually with the house spaces and extend them into the landscape or garden. Besides the visual and functional extensions of house space into the landscape, such as overhangs, porches, and walls, the material of the landscape can relate directly to the house spaces.

Enclosed Areas. By enclosing the garden within the walls or rooms of a house as a courtyard, it is possible to create outdoor rooms for living. An exterior enclosed space, such as a porch or a veranda, becomes a visual part of the house, provided glass or a movable wall enables the visual link to be made. These outdoor rooms can be punctuated by features such as plants, water, and outdoor sculpture.

Hedges. Hedges are planar structures; they can be clipped or left in a natural state, but their primary attribute is their wall-like character. Because this intrinsic char-

Roofed colonnade (Turchin house, East Hampton, NY)

acter is related to the walls of a house, hedges can extend house walls visually, define vistas from the house, or provide a backdrop for the focus of exterior space, such as a piece of sculpture or a fountain.

Sunken or Raised Levels. It is possible to alter the sense of space within a house by raising or lowering the level immediately outside the house perimeter. For example, a sunken garden immediately outside the house produces a sense of loftiness within the house. It also makes a small garden seem larger, because some of the immediate foreground of the garden is cut off from view by the floor plane of the room. A raised garden outside the house wall limits the view within the house space and makes it seem smaller, although raised portions of a garden on a small scale can give the impression of a small hill or unique feature within a larger outlook.

Groves and Orchards. The numerous plants within a grove or orchard can give a house space a sense of expansiveness. The scale of these plant materials can be manipulated by pruning or shaping, thereby enabling the designer to use them as visually important elements. Plantings can be regularly or informally placed in a grove or orchard. In a total design wherein house and garden are working together, the groupings of the exterior plant materials will become part of the house design.

Terraces, Decks, Paths, and Other Hard Materials. In general, plant material such as ground covers or grass does not react well to continual usage as a walking surface or as a place to put outdoor furniture. A wide variety of good-wearing surfaces are available for such use. In the selection of these surfaces, texture and finish should be coordinated with the surfaces within the house. A similar material, such as slate, indoors and out, serves to blur the difference between the two realms and extends one into the other. A contrast, such as a carpeted interior space and a decked patio, will heighten the visual difference. Paths that meander or extend interior space in a visual line can also direct interior space and give focus to a room.

Water. Water is a great material to use in extending and enhancing interior space. It can be arranged to be partly inside as well as outside a building. Reflective and fluid, water can be manipulated to make soothing noises, turn corners, suggest hidden recesses, or may simply be used as a pool for recreation. It is the main element

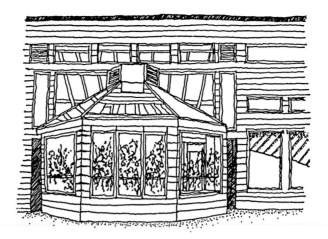

A greenhouse can bring nature into a house. (Mercer house, East Hampton, NY)

in the design of ponds, water lily pools, streams, wetlands, and fountains, attracting birds and other wildlife to these areas.

Alleys. Enclosed exterior spaces that are long and narrow can be usefully classified as alleys, or *allées* in the classical sense. These can usefully or grandly extend interior spaces. When the defining walls of an alley are skewed or combined with level changes, dramatic visual effects can be achieved from within the house through the creation of an artificial perspective. Renaissance garden design employed many visual tricks to fool the eye, both within the garden and as seen from the rooms looking out into the garden.

Bringing the Outside In. In addition to courtyard schemes that enclose gardens, it is possible to build room spaces that are indoor gardens as, for instance, within an attached greenhouse or within a glass-roofed atrium. When the life cycle of plant material is enclosed in a house, the house itself becomes a kinetic environment of plant growth, movement, and regeneration, which parallels the cycles of the people within.

PROJECT: HOUSE AT VERSAILLES, *France*

Architect: Auguste Perret

- This house is not in the modernist tradition espoused at the time of construction by Le Corbusier but, instead, attempts a more classic composition of simple openings and wall planes.
- The windows are composed vertically, giving the house an appearance of solidity and volume.
- A simple cornice caps the house mass.

Garden side of house.

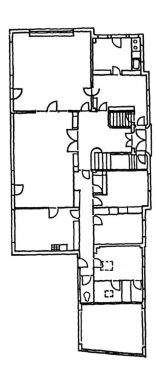

Ground floor plan.

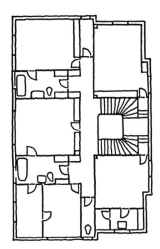

First floor plan.

Section.

PROJECT: SEMIDETACHED HOUSES, *Lyökkiniemi, Westend, Espoo, Finland*

Architects: Gullichsen, Kairamo, Vormala Architects
Erkki Kairamo, Aulikki Jylhä, Vesa Huttunen

- This project features paired single-family houses.

- Living spaces are oriented to a view and to the sun.

- Each house has a relatively closed entrance facade with a shielded private garden court on the first floor.

- Basements are partially above grade to provide additional living space.

- Walls abutting side yards are relatively windowless to ensure privacy from neighbors.

Garden facade showing an expanse of glass toward view.

Vehicular approach leading to entrances.

Exposed steel framing in an interior.

Interior stair and wood ceiling.

Exterior rear view of building at dusk showing paired houses.

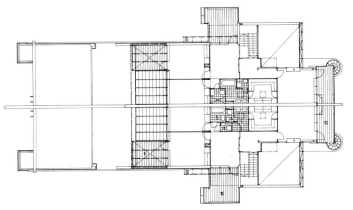

Second floor plan.

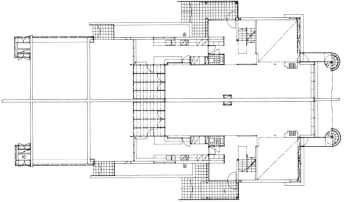

First floor plan.

PROJECT: QUINONES-BIEGANEK HOUSE, *East Hampton, New York*

Architect: Alfredo De Vido, FAIA

- Spatial interest is provided within a simple composition of two rectangular volumes by skewing a central circulation/porch/entry spine.
- Gables accent the arrangement of differing columns through the use of color on the exterior and a change in roofing material between the skewed and rectilinear parts of the house.
- Interiors are simply detailed, allowing emphasis on the geometry of the space.
- Sculptural elements within provide focus at key points.

Entrance approach.

Rear of house.

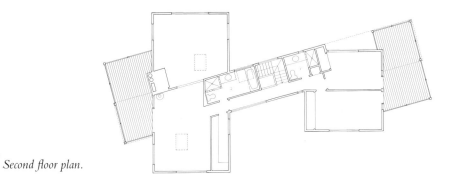

Second floor plan.

Living room looking toward woods.

Fireplace and entrance column serve as transitional elements between single- and two-story space and as foci for the living area.

Entrance approach with columns.

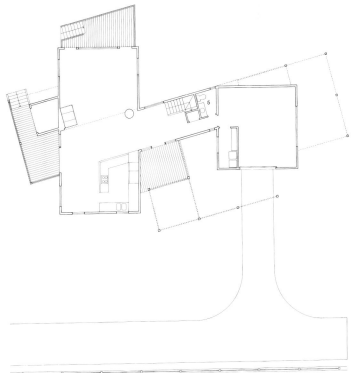

First floor plan.

PROJECT: FULLER HOUSE, *Scottsdale, Arizona*

Architect: Antoine Predock, FAIA

- This is a desert house, composed of a series of pavilions, each of which has its own character and finish.

- The design progresses east to west, with spaces ordered by daily routine.

- Environmental considerations dictated adobe construction, with small, deeply recessed openings for protection from the sun.

- Landscape planning features water in pools, channels, and fountains.

The house, sited in the rugged southwestern desert.

In a court featuring a circular pool and a water channel, rocks are placed to reflect the surrounding landscape.

Interior of pyramid pavilion is lit effectively from above.

Deep window recesses are capped by beamed ceiling in living room.

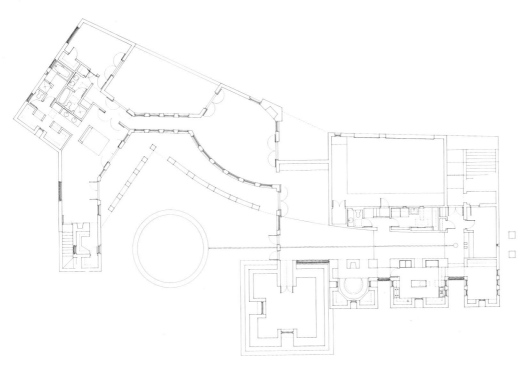

Plan.

PROJECT: BUILT-FOR-SALE HOUSE, *Long Island, New York*

Architect: Alfredo De Vido, FAIA

- This house has an adaptable plan that would appeal to a broad group of potential buyers.
- The interior has areas of fixed glazing overlooking areas below that extend the spaces visually.
- Finishes are carefully detailed to align with window and door openings.

Entry.

Rear of house.

Exterior of front of house.

Elevation.

Interior looking toward rear of house.

Interior looking at upper bedrooms, which show fixed glazing overlooking the living area.

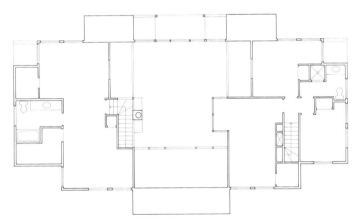

Second floor plan.

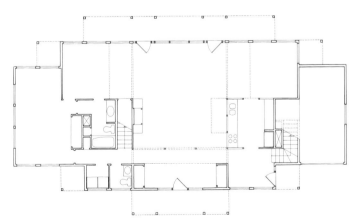

First floor plan.

PROJECT: ALAMO CEMENT HOUSE *(Carrarro House), San Antonio/Austin, Texas*

Architects: Lake/Flato Architects

- A portion of an existing cement plant that had been demolished was rebuilt and recycled to form the main structure of this house.
- In addition to the building, other elements were salvaged—stairs, railings, bricks, and a forge.
- New construction was set within this industrial framework to form a collage of cement plant parts and natural construction materials.

View of building group.

Living structure showing kiln recycled as an inglenook for the fireplace.

Within, exposed steel frame is used as a sunshade.

Industrial details.

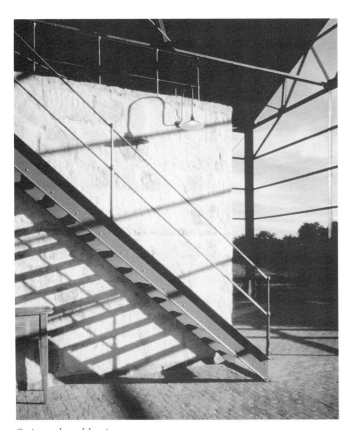

Stairs and steel bracing.

Plans.

PROJECT: DE VIDO HOUSE, *East Hampton, New York*

Architect: Alfredo De Vido, FAIA

- In this house, simple forms combine pitched and sloping roofs. They are clad on the exterior with shingles, a material commonly used on the East Coast.

- Extensive glass areas are balanced with expanses of blank walls that define space and allow the light from glass areas to provide light to the interior surfaces.

- Water features and outbuildings, such as a garden gazebo, extend the house visually.

- The landscape is closely integrated with the house.

View of the house, showing the pool.

Gazebo and pool.

A view of the side of the house showing the garden.

Living room.

Master bedroom.

Kitchen.

A view of the front facade.

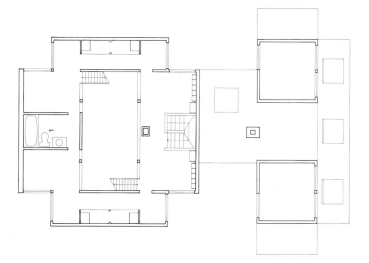
Second floor plan.

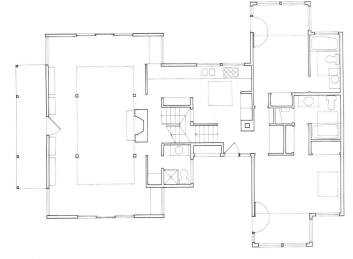
First floor plan.

PROJECT: GADICKE HOUSE, *Chestnut Hill, Massachusetts*

Architect: Jonathan Levi, Architect

- This house explores prototype construction details.
- Acoustically designed floor decks with a a lightweight concrete slab containing heaters.
- Special windows on friction pivots.
- A composition siding sandwich using flashed plywood and solid board technologies.
- A single interior vista connects the ground floor living spaces.

Detail of corner of house.

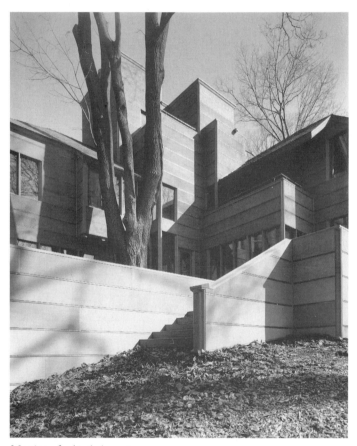

Massing of cubical elements.

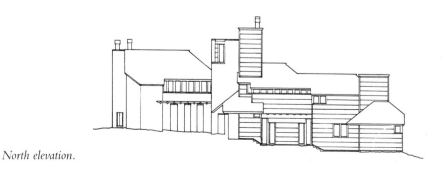

North elevation.

View from entrance showing integration of trees with house.

Interior.

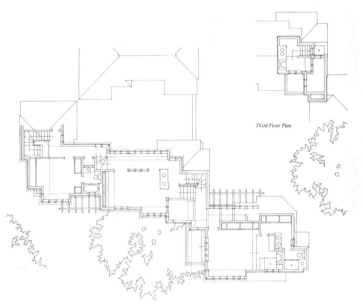

Ground floor plan.

Third Floor Plan

Second and third floor plans.

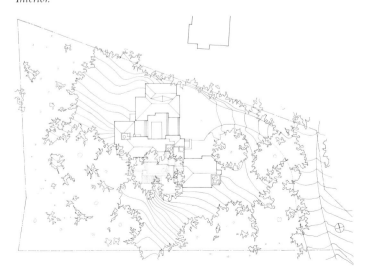

Site plan.

PROJECT: COOK HOUSE, *Oxford, Mississippi*

Architects: Mockbee-Coker, Architects

- This rural southern house has its roots in vernacular farm buildings.

- Nearby corrals house the owner's animals.

- The interior features a floor-to-ceiling aviary.

- Steep metal roofs unify the architectural composition.

- Stairs with hand-crafted handrail terminate in boulders at the floor.

Concrete block walls are topped by metal roofs with strong diagonal lines.

Facade showing a combination of building materials.

Contemporary furniture adds a note of whimsy to the interior.

Macaws at home.

PROJECT: CURUCHET HOUSE, *Argentina*

Architect: Le Corbusier

- This town house looks out on street activity and a nearby park but is designed to provide privacy and sun control.

- A structural grid supports the floors and roof. Walls within are placed freely to create dynamic spaces.

- The progression of spaces through the house has been designed to invite the eye, control the views, and surprise the viewer.

Street elevation shows sunshades and recessed spaces.

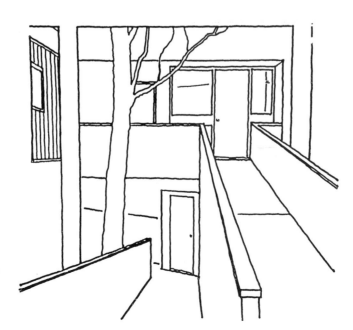

Ramp within provides an architectural sequence of vistas.

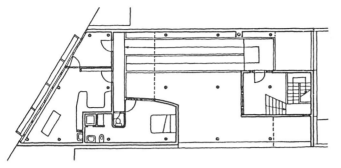

First floor plan.

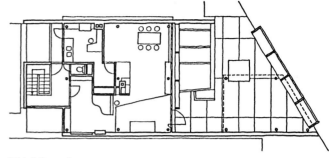

Third floor plan.

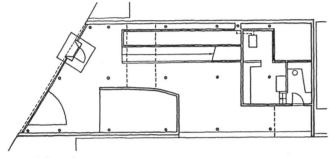

Ground floor plan.

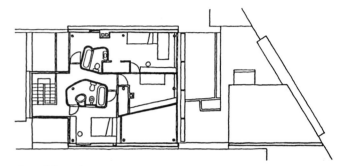

Second floor plan.

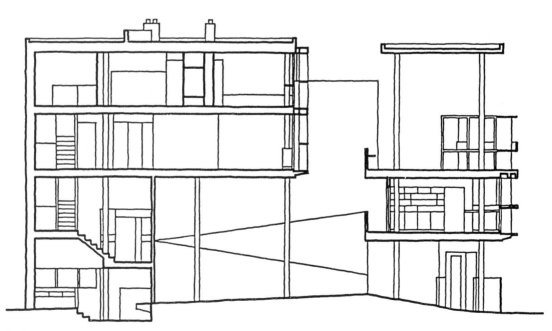

Section.

PROJECT: SCHLACHTENSEE HOUSE, *Berlin, Germany*

Architect: Peter Behrens

- The house is designed as an asymmetrical group of forms. The plan is conventional, but the exterior groups windows and presents forms in a modernist manner.

- Building material is reinforced concrete.

- There is a separate flat over the garages, accessed from the garage level below the first floor.

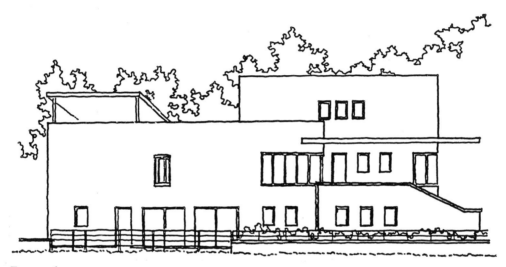

Entrance front.

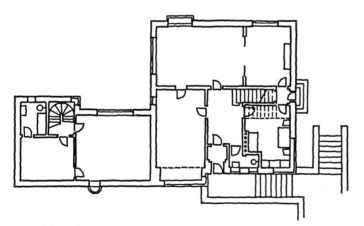

Second floor plan.

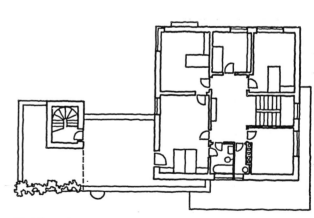

First floor plan.

3 | THE INTANGIBLES OF GOOD ARCHITECTURE

House design today inevitably uses the modern technologies and materials of today. Yet, whether the architect and the client wish to design a more classic house or a "high-tech" house, there is a natural way of building that employs intangibles such as good scale and proportion, harmonious blends of materials and color, proper balancing of light and shade, solid and void, hierarchy of dominance and background, and the uniqueness and rigor of the overall design. Some of these aspects are intellectual, some are aesthetic, others are emotional, and still others are the aftereffects of working out a design jointly with the client, because architecture, unlike the other arts, is social.

INTELLECTUAL CONTENT

There are many views of the intellectual content of architecture, some of which are arcane and mostly incomprehensible to anyone except those who have made an in-depth study of a particular school of thought or philosophy of building. There were, in some societies, quite specific outlines of intellectual content in building, such as the mysticism of Sufi Islam or the unreasoning doctrines of Zen, which challenge most Western minds. In Sufi architecture, for instance, the floor symbolized the earth on which life stands, walls signified the limits of defined space, and roofs were the sixth plane of the cube, which was static and thwarted expansiveness. Confucianism, the Tao of unreason, is another Eastern philosophy with its own set of building precepts, despite its avowed irrationality.

Western philosophy has been based in rationality for most of modern history. The intellectual content of Western architecture includes such concepts as coherence, integrity, and individuality.

COHERENCE

There ought to be a hierarchy of elements in a house. Normally, the entrance is an important feature, deserving emphasis. Windows are secondary to that in importance, yet deserve accent of some sort. They are vital to the occupants' ability to see out into the world and experience nature while being sheltered.

Hierarchy of entrance and windows

Unacceptable architectural pastiche

The system of accenting these elements ought to be coherent. It would probably be a joke to decorate one window in Greek Revival and an adjacent one in Gothic style. That might be successfully done by a talented designer, but to the uninitiated viewer the result would probably be incomprehensible. Some variation within a stylistic context is acceptable, however. For instance, ground floor windows were frequently adorned with more elaborate moldings and cornices, while those of the second floor and higher were smaller with simpler moldings. Dominant and subsidiary elements must thus be balanced among the diverse features in a house. Cloaking every element in comprehensible visual form is desirable.

INTEGRITY OF CONSTRUCTION

Unity in the constructional approach to a house will result in a more unified design. The Parthenon's beauty lies in its insistent arrangement of columns, lending it a particular order. This order is not the whole story, but it certainly is a part of the simple beauty of the structure, understood by lay people and professionals alike. The helical spiral of the Guggenheim Museum is a strong constructional form, adding its power to the bravado of the enclosed space.

INDIVIDUALITY

Despite certain common features of stylistic architecture, sometimes called the *syntax of design*, it's desirable to imbue each dwelling with individuality—the uniqueness of the individuals within. Failure to do so will inevitably result in the failure of the design, because the occupants will change the design as soon as the budget permits. It's important to get the syntax right: no Shingle Style revival for an avowed modernist, but rather an appropriate incorporation of the client's intangible desires into the house.

BEAUTY

Beauty of a classical sort depends on order in plan and elevation. Though some designers are able to take disjunctive combinations of materials and use skewed angles cleverly to form a unified whole, it does not ordinarily pay to celebrate confusion, disjunction, or disorder in residential spaces. Most architects cannot do this successfully, and the public does not usually understand excessive angularity or discord. Better, then, to stick to the classical norms of beauty as exemplified by the regularity of piers and windows of a Gothic cathedral, the strong centrality of a domed mosque, or the simple placement of a roof and four walls of a cottage. Simplicity is usually best.

Consider the house and site together.

THE SEARCH

When the architect approaches sources of design looking for canons of beauty, it is possible to address the search in a number of ways:

1. Look for analogies in terms of type. In house design, this is extremely difficult, because there are as many different types of house design as there are types of people occupying houses. However, some typology groupings can be made within sites, climate, and geographical restraints.

2. Look for a form that has beauty and work the design into it. This was an approach of Louis Kahn, who brilliantly adapted classic plans and forms he had studied in his travels to his building designs. According to some analysts, Le Corbusier used the shape of the horns of Indian cows as the basis for one of the roofs in his capital at Chandigarh. Certainly, his sketches of those animals closely approximate the subsequent forms of the architecture.

3. Quotation of well-known features in architecture enables the designer to recall acknowledged standards of beauty. For example, the order of a colonial entrance with its pediments and pilasters can be successfully quoted in modern architecture, while stopping short of actual replication of the source.

4. Pastiche is an undesirable way of applying accepted canons of beauty. The meaningless attachment of classical elements to an otherwise simple and functional house will usually look bad. It's possible to be ironic with this sort of visual statement, but the irony will usually escape the average viewer and have meaning to only a small group of architectural historians.

Relate the human body to the built form.

Houses can convey an interest in environmental awareness, such as by the way a house made with natural local materials is placed in the landscape or perhaps covered with it, as in an earth-sheltered house. Builders of large country houses at the turn of the century were interested in conveying a sense of culture. To achieve their intent they asked architects to use forms borrowed from Europe. Indeed, wealthier builders of country houses often bought whole houses or chunks of houses in Europe, dismantled them, and rebuilt them on New World sites.

In our more contemporary milieu, houses should incorporate some notion of their place on the site and some of the client's aspirations in building the house. It is appropriate, for instance, to build a house on the seashore with considerable glass expanses facing the sea and to give its form an overall strength to symbolize its ability to withstand the periodic fury of offshore winds. A house in the woods among tall trees might reflect its location and purpose best if the windows were oriented in a number of directions or if it were built vertically, to stand tall among the surrounding trees.

SCALE

Although the scale of a Blenheim Castle, built for the Duke of Marlborough out of gratitude by the nation of England after his victory over Napoleon at Waterloo, is impressive, it is meant to overwhelm the occupants and impress the visitor with their importance. Some builders of houses, both clients and architects, also seek to impress. This intent is valid enough, but the house at its completion should still hold enough humanly scaled elements to make the inhabitants comfortable living there. Some modern houses are so overwhelming in their single-purpose virtuosity that they are unlivable. Mies van der Rohe's Farnsworth house is a case in point. The completed house was the subject of a celebrated lawsuit in which the client claimed that the house was not habitable.

EMOTION

In addition to the intellectual content of buildings, which is not well understood by architects or by clients, there is an emotional content that, on a subliminal level, is understood by everyone. But, because this content involves feelings, it is often irrational and therefore hard to discuss. The following paragraphs provide some points for thought.

THE INTANGIBLES OF GOOD ARCHITECTURE

THE IDEA OF PEOPLE

Various forms within houses immediately show their relationship to the occupants. Windows and doors, by their size, relate to the size of the human body, assuming they are not oversized for some reason. Thick walls, staircases, and colonnades of a domestic scale all suggest human scale. Some Mannerist architects were fond of visual tricks, such as doors painted ajar on walls or trompe l'oeil effects that make short passages look longer. These tricks are fun and add humor to a house, but they only leaven the essentially serious design problems of relating the scale to the occupants. These people-related details convey the spirit of life, in contrast to the absence of detail in a funerary pyramid or a monolith without openings.

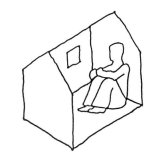

Nooks for people to claim

CARE IN DESIGN AND CONSTRUCTION

Craftsmanship of the sort shown in wood that has been polished to a deep, revealing gloss or in a carefully designed and unique set of hinges attached to an important door indicates that the architect and client have invested great care, time, and money in the design. Such details are surely an indication of their emotional attitude toward the building.

ACKNOWLEDGING SPECIAL SPACES

Particularly in renovations or additions to older houses, it is important to leave certain elements of the house intact, and even to embellish them, to show a sense of the history contained within. In new construction, the various people who will use the house should have their needs and claims on the building acknowledged in some way. For instance, a study used by one of the occupants as an exclusive sanctum might have wood walls, few windows, and a stone fireplace to reflect this user's personal desires. Another occupant's need for light and airy openness, as in a studio for painting or weaving, gives a house an additional level of meaning to the occupants.

NOOKS AND CRANNIES

Features such as bowed fronts, turrets, wide stair landings with seats, window boxes, and greenhouses all permit the occupants of a house to find nooks for enjoyable activities. Pets have this instinct; a cat finds a warm, sunny window sill to nap on, for instance. Provide a variety of opportunities for people to find their own places. In rooms with sloping ceilings, it is perhaps desirable to continue the slope to below-normal standing height of the average human occupant. Many people find this sort of space invested with cozy qualities that a uniform eight-foot ceiling does not create.

Tree-lined approach to house

SEQUENCE AND PROCESSION

The architectural promenade, as we walk or drive through exterior and interior spaces, is a time-enhancing experience. For instance, a Japanese garden may provide a route by which the visitor walks along a path, sensing the nearby sea by the sound of waves but not experiencing the view until it is time to wash the hands ceremonially, by stooping at the entrance to a teahouse. This is an example of creating a spatial experience enriched with a temporal quality and a feeling that it will take a bit of time to enjoy the place. Another example might be a relatively intimate entrance space with low ceilings and lighting, introducing a large living space with a view, a high ceiling, and dramatic lighting. Sequence and a climactic arrival have always been important in good architecture. Ecclesiastical architecture of all faiths is instructive on this point.

THE ARCHITECT/CLIENT COLLABORATION

Architecture is a social art because it is people oriented. It is not a mirror of an ideal or of some mythical or egotistical force, but rather of life. Le Corbusier stated that architects were not easel artists but, rather, were coordinators of life's activities within buildings. This means that the architect should coordinate the ideas and needs of the client in the design of the house. In so doing, the architect also imbues the spaces and forms with his or her artistic and functional convictions. This is accomplished as part of the give-and-take of a good relationship with the client.

CLAIMING TERRITORY

There can be several broad approaches to claiming territory from nature, ranging from the use of power and wealth to dominate a landscape, to a blending with nature. The human species has always claimed territory from nature for habitation. Such claims evolved from simple occupancy of natural shelters, such as caves, to more elaborate ones, such as palaces on the scale of Versailles. Examples of dominance over nature include the pyramids and most Palladian villas. In contrast, Taliesin and Villa Mairea blend with nature and seek to integrate their structures with the landscape.

THE INTANGIBLES OF GOOD ARCHITECTURE

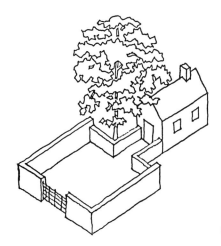

Claiming territory

Increasingly, we are interested in lessening the claims on nature by designing ecologically sound buildings that harmonize and work well with the natural world.

DIRECTIONAL SPACES

With your client, plan your design to give occupants of the house an image of where they are in the spaces and in relation to the objects in the house. An example of this aspect is the particularization that Charles Moore gave to many of his houses, in which views from and within rooms found goals, such as a piano, a well-loved object or work of art, or a carpet. Give the users of the space some place in which to act out life's roles.

A SENSE OF ORGANIZATION

Some sense of the organization of the house is desirable. For instance, you might treat the house as a single space divided into rooms differentiated by special needs. Extend the spaces into each other through the use of planned surfaces. Sheets of interior glass can be used to enable one room to flow into an adjacent one without intruding on the acoustical or visual privacy of each space, if such intrusion is undesirable. Indicate for the viewer the way beyond any point in the house.

Privacy norms have changed over the centuries. In Palladio's houses, there were few or no corridors, because in his day it was acceptable to walk through the various spaces regardless of what was going on in them. The spatial result was clear and sequential as one proceeded around and through the house. Because our sense of privacy is more restrictive, we must seek ways of providing spatial clarity and sequential effects, such as through the use of transparent or translucent materials and overlapping planes.

SHAPING FORMS TO CIRCUMSTANCES

In designing houses, originality can be drawn from the particularity of a given program, site, or client. Seek out the idiosyncrasies of human use and glorify them to lend interest to the house. For example, children like to slide down banisters, even though their mothers don't particularly want them to—this activity is a bit dangerous, and it scratches the finish as well. Although banister sliding is not a prime design goal, the shape of the banister itself certainly merits attention. It should be smooth, rounded, and easy to grip.

The cost of a house may be turned to advantage through the selection of materials or the discipline of keeping the budget low. For instance, it may be possible to design handsome, even elegant, spaces using inexpensive materials such as concrete block. Perhaps by selecting a colored or split-face block or by raking out the horizontal joints, the material can be made to transcend its low cost. Masonite cut into horizontal strips and lapped one over the other can give new scale to a material noted for its cheapness and inelegant appearance.

An irregularly shaped city lot can lead to the design of a triangular room possessed of great character. Kazuo Shinohara, a noted Japanese architect, once shaped an entire roof to echo the catenary of some high-tension wires above the house, from which he was required to keep a certain distance. It is not necessary to know this, however, to appreciate the elegant resultant form from without and the beautifully shaped room within.

PROJECT: MARVIN HOUSE, *California*

Architect: Edward Cullinan

- This plan consists of five glass-topped concrete towers placed beside a long gallery. The two-part plan places the service areas in solid cubicles in one-half of the house, and the social area in the other half, which is glazed and faces south.

- The house was owner-built. Therefore, details are simple and straightforward.

- A large valley in the roof divides the two halves of the house. Below the valley, a row of storage cabinets emphasizes the division.

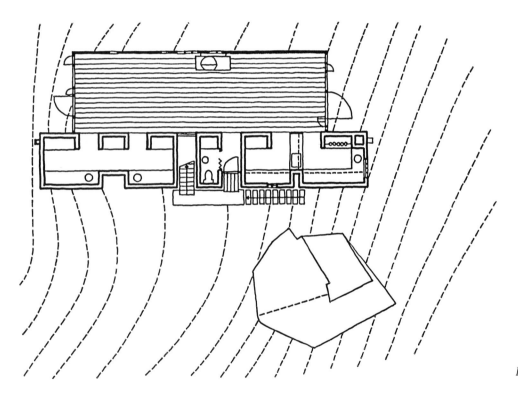

Plan.

View of house from below.

Section.

PROJECT: HOLLYWOOD DUPLEX, *Los Angeles, California*

Architects: Koning Eizenberg Architecture

- These houses were built for sale on a difficult, sloping, triangular site.

- Windows and doors were carefully positioned to provide privacy between the two units and adjacent houses.

- The plans were simply composed for economy of construction, with curved entrance walls defining terraces.

- The difference in level between the units enhances privacy.

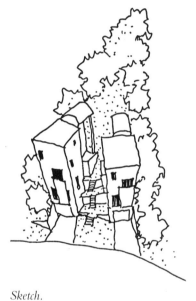

Sketch.

Garage and street side of the houses.

Terraces opening to the rear of the site.

Living room.

Living room looking toward the central stairs.

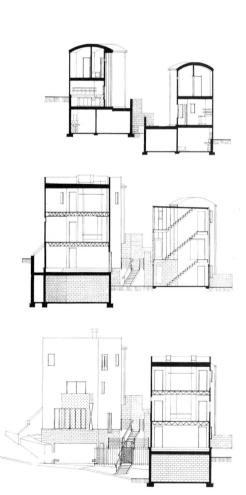

Sections.

Plans.

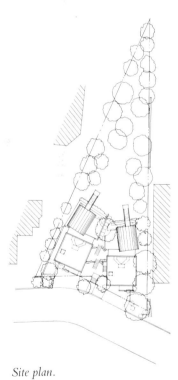

Site plan.

PROJECT: MATTHEWS HOUSE, *East Hampton, New York*

Architect: Alfredo De Vido, FAIA

- Materials are natural and easy to maintain—rough cut cypress boards for the walls and tile for the floors. Exterior wood shingles are a vernacular building material of the area.

- The two-story living space is divided into quiet areas by the tall brick fireplace and stairs that lead to the upper bedroom.

- Prominent lean-to roofs provide shade to the porch and entrance areas.

Tall roofs define the porch and complete the square plan of the house.

The house is sited high on a bluff.

The house from the land side.

The furniture plan can be rearranged to accommodate large gatherings.

The central chimney is the focus of the interior.

Massive cross beams span the corner space.

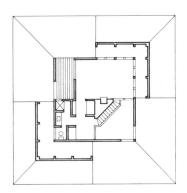

Second floor plan.

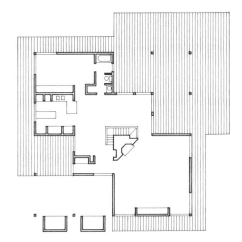

First floor plan.

PROJECT: GOODNOUGH HOUSE, *Seaside, Florida*

Architect: Walter F. Chatham, Architect

- This is a town house built in a community guided by planning and zoning regulations.

- It is an "upside-down" house, with living room, dining room, and kitchen on the third floor, from which views of the Gulf of Mexico can be seen. The upper floors are served by "elevettes" (a type of small elevator).

- On the exterior, a system of shutters protects inhabitants from the sun.

View of exterior showing shutters.

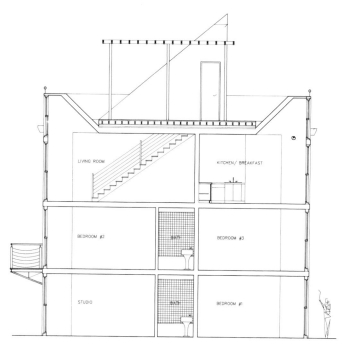

Section.

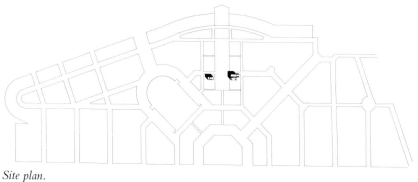

Site plan.

Dining room. Note cables from elevette.

Stairs from third-floor living room to the roof deck.

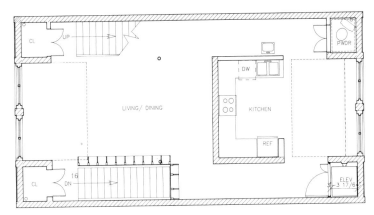

Third floor plan.

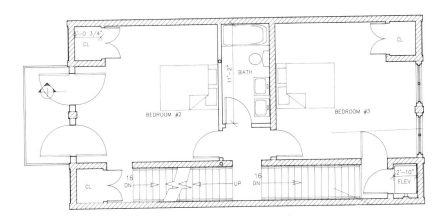

Second floor plan.

PROJECT: MOORE HOUSE, *Connecticut*

Architect: Alfredo De Vido, FAIA

- This earth-sheltered house utilizes timber and stone from its own site.
- The south-facing row of skylights bisects the middle of the house, providing light and sunshine within.
- Other windows face south as well, toward a view of a pond.
- Modular construction is used throughout.

House and roof construction.

View of house from pond.

Center skylight.

Living room.

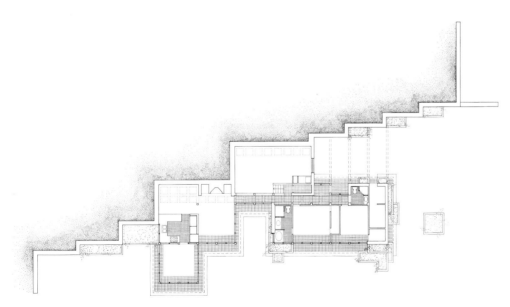

Plan.

PROJECT: LA LUZ, *Albuquerque, New Mexico*

Architect: Antoine Predock, FAIA

- Houses are clustered to save land for community recreation.

- Adobe construction and circular forms are intrinsic to the design.

- Each house is planned with two walled patios and is sited so that no adjacent house can interfere with its neighbor's view.

View looking over wall toward typical unit.

Pedestrian way showing walled patios.

Entrance facades.

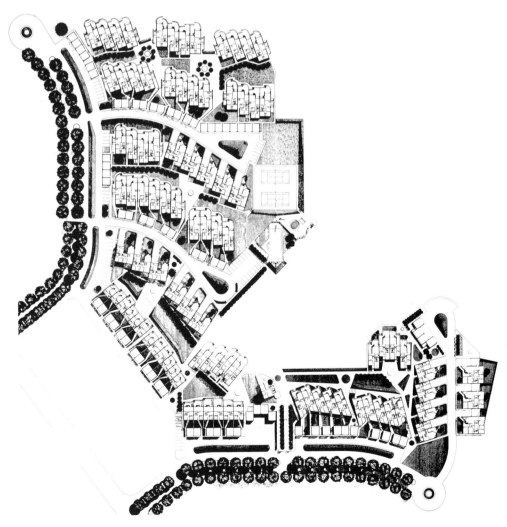

Site plan.

PROJECT: WIRTH HOUSE, *Waccabuc, New York*

Architect: Alfredo De Vido, FAIA

- Connected structures line up along a stone wall overlooking a view to the north. Additional glazing to the south permits solar gain.
- The exterior is clad in horizontal boards. The interior repeats the use of boards and incorporates stone and tile as well.
- Separation of living functions is achieved by zoning.
- Built-in furniture economizes floor space.

View from Lake Waccabuc looking toward the house.

Side elevation shows zoning of spaces.

View of living area from loft.

First floor plan.

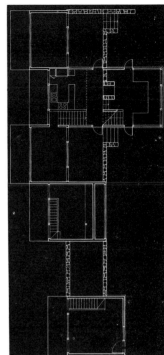

Second floor plan.

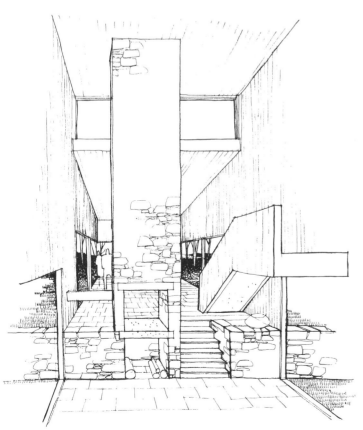

Sketch of interior looking toward fireplace and stairs.

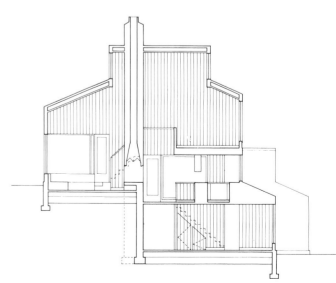

Section.

PROJECT: AUBURN COURT CONDOMINIUMS, *Newton, Massachusetts*

Architect: Jonathan Levi, Architect

- Condominium units are arranged to avoid an impersonal appearance of repetition, but the floor plans are based on an economical module.

- Board siding emphasizes the volume of the structures rather than their planes.

- This condominium grouping is built around a former rectory, still intact.

Condominium grouping.

Trellised walkway.

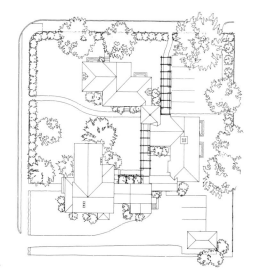

Site plan.

Archway to building court.

Interior.

Ground level plan.

Upper level plan.

PROJECT: VILLA AT GARCHES, *France*

Architect: Le Corbusier

- This house provides an important example of Le Corbusier's philosophy of architecture, utilizing free-standing columns supporting a cantilevered exterior wall in which strips of windows are placed. There is a roof garden, and the main body of the house is raised above the ground. Interior partitions are freely placed and often curved, expressing their nonsupporting function.
- The sections reveal an interlocking arrangement of free-flowing vertical space.
- A proportional system was used to design the plan and the facades.

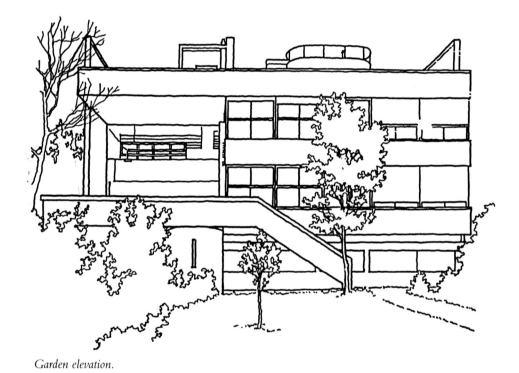

Garden elevation.

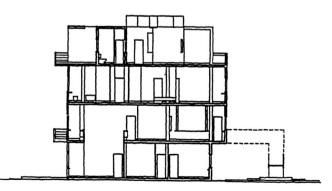

Section.   *Section.*

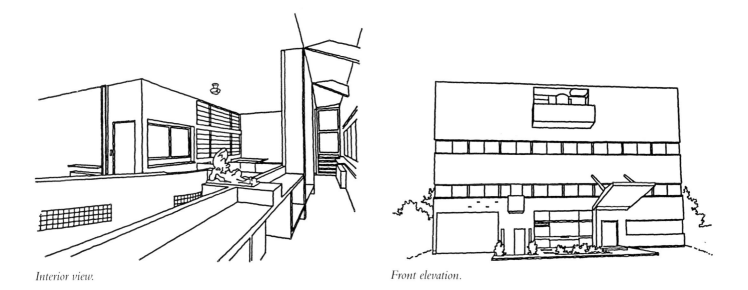

Interior view.

Front elevation.

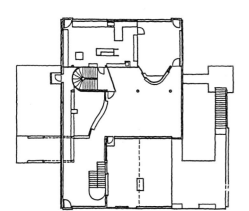

First floor plan.

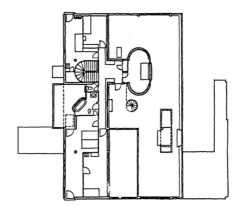

Third floor plan.

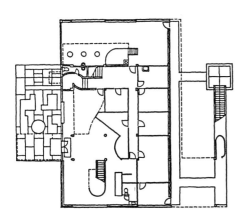

Ground floor plan.

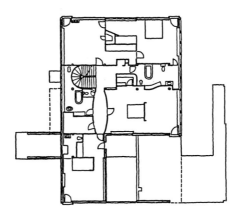

Second floor plan.

PROJECT: SUGDEN HOUSE, *Watford, England*

Architects: Alison and Peter Smithson

- This house utilizes external building materials typical of the London suburbs—brick and red tile.
- The spaces within are contemporary in arrangement, with a large, open L-shaped living/dining area.
- From the exterior, the asymmetrical pattern of windows reflects the internal planning.

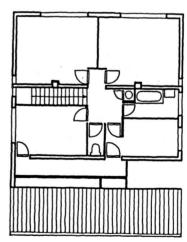

Street facade.

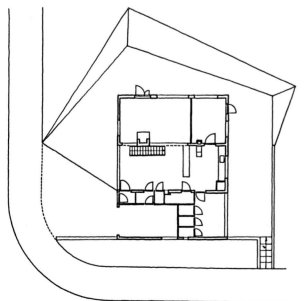

Second floor plan.

First floor plan.

4 |
THE ARCHITECT'S JOB

The architect's job is all-encompassing. If the house is to be built well artistically and functionally, it is necessary for the architect to think of all factors, whether or not they are obvious or pointed out by the client.

PLANNING THE SITE

The site is important. It can be ignored and the house placed on it or above it like a piece of sculpture. A house can enclose the site or reach out into it. A house can appear either confrontational to a site or as an organic part of it, working and integrating with the site.

FITTING WITHIN

The architect can set a house within a site, in effect, creating an earth-sheltered house. Although most people are not at ease living surrounded by creatures of the earth, such as worms and moles, the concept is quite ancient and the house quite livable. Some notable civilizations, such as the Chinese, native Americans of the Southwest, and early Greek and Anatolian people, have all lived within caves or hallowed cavities within the earth. Many houses are built against the earth, as in the hill towns of the Mediterranean region, using the earth as one or more of the walls. Frank Lloyd Wright was a strong proponent of using the earth in the construction of houses and advocated building them below the tops of hills, rather than on top of them.

Subject to the client's approval, the architect can use the site as part of the design, rather than ignoring, leveling, and clearing it of all natural features, as is often the case in builders' tract housing.

PLACEMENT ON

Another choice is placement of the house on the site as an object or as an addition to nature. History is full of such examples. Most Palladian houses come to mind, as well as the more modern approaches such as Le Corbusier's general placement of a house or group of houses above the landscape.

Reaching out to a wooded view (Rafferty house, Stratton, VT)

Most of the more successful examples of this approach are sculptural and have much surface area in the form of columns, arcades, recesses, or overhangs. This has some rightness to it, inasmuch as a simple block house set on a site, without transparency or with little surface modeling, can seem foreign and somewhat repellent to the eye. Think, for instance, of the effect of high prison walls on the outside observer, as in H. H. Richardson's Allegheny County Courthouse and Jail. That certainly is not the sort of place most people want to inhabit.

FACING OUT

Another approach, which might be considered a combination of the first two, is an organizational concept that is unidirectional or bidirectional. Common examples are row houses and multistory groupings of houses with common walls between dwellings. Groupings of houses on smaller suburban sites can be organized in the same way, fronting the slope of a gable roof to the street and front yard, and placing most glass areas so that they face the more private area of the backyard. As part of this approach, builders also place important features toward the street or public entrance as a welcoming or proclaiming feature. A house facing the public way can convey the intentions and general attitude of the owner. For example, most Greek Revival houses face the street, communicating the education of the owners and their sympathies with the glories of a past civilization.

ENCLOSING

More common in arid areas is the concept of the court, which provides tighter groupings of rooms and enables the enclosure of a sheltered, private space. Traditionally, the court, or enclosure, might be surrounded with arcades or deep overhangs to protect against the elements. Facades facing out from this arrangement were frequently blank or even forbidding. Think, for instance, of some Renaissance palazzi in an urban setting. In this instance, the clear intent of the builders was to let the public know that significant personages lived within and to keep out burglars. In

Row houses take a uni- or bi-directional approach. (Melone house, New York City)

modern times, most apartment buildings present relatively closed entrance floors. Urban chaos and widespread crime have much to do with this trend.

DESIGNING THE SPACES

Most spaces within houses are designed for particular purposes. Historically, house spaces were fitted into a box of some sort and assigned a function or set of functions. The configuration of these boxes was usually in response to the climate and its conditions.

Today we're no longer confined by weather or restricted by available building materials. It is possible to have flexible and imaginative configurations of space and room arrangements that make such space livable.

OPEN PLANNING

An open plan has many advantages, including easy passage from one space to another, good spatial vistas, and the possible multiuse of a given space, thereby achieving an economy of resources.

Extending Walls to Divide a Space

Spaces within a house can be subdivided by walls, solid or transparent, that enclose the rooms and extend through other spaces, often to the exterior. Mies van der Rohe was an advocate of such a system, using it to dramatic effect in the Barcelona Pavilion and the Tugendhat house in Brno, Czechoslovakia. This extension of walls to form space-dividing planes produces a rich interpretation of space, but at the sacrifice of privacy. The absence of doors means that sound will travel around the edges of walls into adjacent spaces.

Open planning (Drake house, Pound Ridge, NY)

Extending Space with Openings to Other Spaces

Even with a limited budget, there are ways of increasing spaces. Rooms can be opened to other rooms through the use of wider openings or by opening rooms to the exterior with the use of extensive glass areas. Common examples of this device are arches between living and dining rooms and patio doors.

Rooms can also be extended vertically. Spaces that are higher than normal convey a sense of grandness and the feeling that special things will happen therein. Light from high or unexpected sources can heighten the flow of space out and up.

Visual space can be borrowed from one room and given to another. For example, a piece of fixed glass between rooms or above normal door height can extend the roof planes or walls of both rooms. This spatial device can increase the apparent visual size of both rooms, while still preserving acoustical and visual privacy if the glass is above eye level.

Spaces Around a Large Space

It is important to provide a focus within a house. Frequently, this focus is the living room or family room, any space in which the social functions of the house take place. Some of the secondary rooms that relate to this large social space can be grouped around or on top of it, with the large space a focus for the other smaller spaces. The secondary spaces can be closed off from the large space acoustically with solid walls, transparent walls, or operable shutters and doors.

Spaces Within Spaces

Sometimes a particularly important function within a room can be emphasized by placing columns around it, or a special place can be set off by recessing the floor plane. Raising a portion of the ceiling over an area can also mark it as important. Visualize the cupolas of the main entrance hall in Jefferson's Monticello, for instance, or the baldichino over the altar in many sacred spaces.

ROOMS IN VARIOUS ARRANGEMENTS

Historically, patterns of room arrangements varied in response to the prevailing climate and topography. For instance, ranch houses in the Southwest faced out to the breezes, and small openings were sized to take advantage of the cooling effects of ventilation in the hot, dry climate.

In a Row Facing Out

On sites and with programs that require linear planning, rooms can be arranged to face a view of a selected private space. In modern times, such rooms are generally serviced by a corridor. In many earlier epochs, such as during the Renaissance or Medieval times, corridors were not used, owing to the lesser value

placed on personal privacy, although rooms were sometimes separated by anterooms or service spaces. People simply circulated through spaces to get where they wanted to go, no matter what was happening there. Those who have visited Versailles, for instance, may recall walking from one grand room to another. Commoners in those times fared no better; they frequently had to share space with livestock.

In a Row Facing Two Ways

As in the historical examples cited earlier, it is possible to design today's houses with living spaces facing in two directions simultaneously. This is done easily with end rooms, because the circulation space terminates there. There are multistory solutions to other arrangements, such as providing a private staircase in a room on the second floor or allowing the circulation to bypass a room while still preserving a view from that room in two directions.

Around a Court or Central Space

As in the kinds of space arrangements described for open planning, rooms can be formally or informally arranged around an outdoor place or an atrium that is either open or closed to the elements. Rooms can also be grouped around a core of service rooms, such as the kitchen and baths. Because there are many uses for service rooms, this arrangement has a certain logic to it. Disadvantages of this assemblage are the difficulty of getting natural light and air to the service spaces and intrusion from the functions of those spaces into the surrounding, perhaps more peaceful, rooms.

Grouped

Rooms are often arranged asymmetrically to take advantage of a site feature or to avoid a site disadvantage. Rooms grouped in this fashion can have picturesque informal qualities, because repetition of elements is avoided. Grouping can be effective on a sloping site, for instance, where the house is stepped to fit the site, or in the case of a very large house, where the design of all rooms within a single visual block would be overwhelming. However, if this arrangement is done badly, the visual effect can be chaotic.

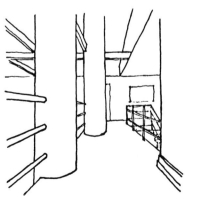

Open corridor as a circulation link between rooms (Fried house, Amagansett, NY)

Separate wings for children and parents, with a common living space in the middle (White Pine Road, East Hampton, NY)

Two-Part Plans

Binuclear plans were popular some years ago, before the atom bomb forever altered the term. Rooms for private functions, such as bedrooms and their service spaces, were grouped in one part of house, and social spaces, such as the living and family rooms and their services spaces, were grouped in another part. Variations on this theme of segregated house activities included placing the family room with the children's rooms, and the adults' room with the living rooms. The underlying theory was also binuclear, because families were the predominant grouping for which houses were built at that time. The arrangement certainly has much appeal even today, as it is based on a separation of lively social pursuits from quiet, more private activities.

Another variation on this theme includes the complete separation of spaces, or the use of pavilions. This arrangement works best where the climate allows people easy circulation between pavilions without encountering inclement weather. It is possible to find exceptions to this fair weather theory, as at Sissinghurst, a manor house in England, where meals were served in a separate house even in that frequently rainy climate.

Skewed Arrangements

Rooms can be planned with skewed walls, or rectangular rooms can be placed in skewed fashion to each other. This produces spatial surprise and vistas of rich informality. If visual chaos is averted, the effect can be picturesque. However, it is usually an expensive arrangement, in that builders must put materials together in an unusual way, which requires more careful management of personnel and materials.

ACCOMMODATING SERVICES

With the increase in machines and utilities that are now a necessary part of our lives, it is important for the architect to accommodate these services and integrate them visually so that they fit seamlessly within the design concept.

HIDING OR SCREENING SERVICES

Applying some aesthetic concepts can incorporate machines, wiring, and ductwork successfully within the spaces of a house. Because they are noisy, sometimes smelly, and visually imposing, it is more usual to hide or screen them.

Building Services as a Core

Accommodating the services in a core

Louis Kahn liked to speak of and design "servant" and "served" spaces. His intent was to differentiate the many kinds of service from the spaces in which people lived and worked. This approach makes sense, in that pipes and ducts work best when grouped, require fixing, and, in general, are not pretty to look at. Although the number of service elements, such as machines and the piping and ducting to and from them, is not as great in a house as in a laboratory building, nevertheless, the amount of space they require is considerable and their cost is a big part of the budget.

Services can be grouped in a room, as in a laundry or boiler room, or they can be put in closets. Manufacturers have made great strides in miniaturizing all kinds of mechanical equipment to make them fit within smaller spaces and to render them more efficient, thereby using less energy. Because machines are frequently used by the inhabitants of the house, they are often conveniently placed in such spaces as kitchens and baths. These spaces, in turn, are grouped as cores, because economies can be achieved through common piping arrangements. Most clients are familiar with the economy of stacked plumbing, for instance.

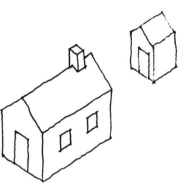

Services outside

Locating Utilities in Walls or in Other Spaces

Plumbing walls are commonplace. These walls behind bath and kitchen fixtures and appliances require a greater thickness to accommodate the necessary pipes and ducts. Because these pipes and ducts become clogged, leak, break, or otherwise require service, it's a good idea to provide them with service panels. This will lessen the possibility of having to rip apart expensively tiled finishes to gain access to a trouble spot.

Community Supplies

Many communities supply water and sewer services to their residents; some also supply steam. Practically all houses are furnished with electrical power from a public or privately owned utility. Some thought should be given to routing these utilities, because their connections to the house are often unattractive and utility personnel will require access for service and for recording meter readings. It is not a good idea, for instance, to locate the route to a meter through the flower garden. Although many

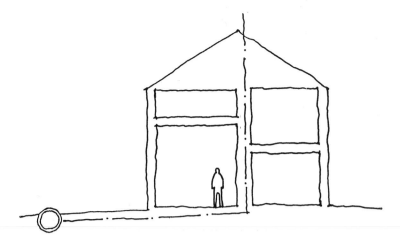

utilities prefer connections and meters to be highly visible and accessible, it is possible to negotiate with them and place the machinery in a compartment or enclosure close to the road traversed by the utility's service people.

Services Outside

Air conditioning, refrigeration units, and pool heaters are commonly placed outside the house, as are heat pumps. It is possible to locate heating furnaces outside the building as well, although most are not designed for outdoor use. One advantage to locating these machines outside is easy intake of air for combustion and venting of waste gases (heating and cooling of air frequently depend on combustion of fossil fuels.) Another advantage is lessening noise from these machines within the house. Bear in mind, however, that some communities require the enclosure of noisy machinery located outside a house where the sound is not audible to occupants of adjacent houses.

Services Above or Below the House

A time-honored location for many services and machines is the basement. Despite the fact that architects generally don't like basements, they are relatively inexpensive to build and can house many services. In addition, basements can provide great amounts of storage space. However, to suit the owners of the house, they must be dry. The two most common complaints about houses are wet or damp basements and leaky roofs.

If utilities and services are located in a basement or crawl space, easy access is both important and necessary. It may make sense to provide an outside entrance to this space so as to accommodate utility or other service workers.

Another good location for service machines and the connections to them is above the house, either in an open-air enclosure or simply out in the open. Attic spaces, semi-attics, and roof spaces above a hung ceiling are other good possibilities. Besides, providing an attic is frequently a good idea to accommodate later expansion. The first Levitt house built after the Second World War featured an unfinished attic

Community supplies

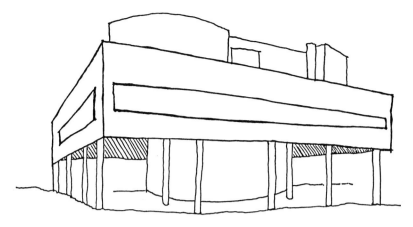

Services may be placed above or below the house. (Ville Savoye, France)

space, which held initial costs down and permitted future adaptation as additional living space. Indeed, the thoughtful inclusion of this amenity proved itself later in the life of the houses.

LEAVING SERVICES EXPOSED

Exposed machinery, wiring, and ductwork can be successfully integrated within a house design. This is not a concept for the average client, who will associate it with boiler rooms, basements, garages, and other utility rooms. Accommodating such integration successfully usually requires more work by the architect and builder, rather than less, because every connection must be considered aesthetically as well as functionally.

Decorative Approaches

Ducts, pipes, and machines are expensive and important. They are also subject to modification as new machines are added (few ever seem to be deleted). Some designers think they are also beautiful, as indeed they can be, and will make an effort to expose the machines. A prime example is Centre Pompidou in Paris. Although not a house, this building astonished the architectural world in the mid-1970s when it won an important international competition by exposing a vast array of ducts and pipes on the exterior of the building, thereby leaving the entire floor area within the building free for changing exhibition space.

On a residential scale, exposed heating pipe is commonly found in older houses, where the basic warm air transform between rooms was often accomplished by grilles. Although effective and inexpensive, privacy and cleanliness were problems. Many Victorian houses had a furnace in the basement that heated air in a chamber or plenum and simply let the warm air rise throughout the house.

Various kinds of ducts are currently available. In addition to the common sheet metal variety, there are more expensive, rigid, round ducts that can be decorative when provided with the proper air vents. Exposed ducts can also be painted to accentuate their function as utility elements.

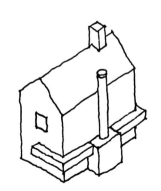

Consider the aesthetics of exposing machinery.

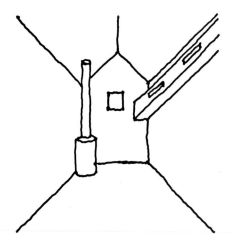

Revealing the mechanical systems

Control of Exposed Systems

It is important to remember that most workers believe that mechanical systems, ducts, pipes, and all such things are meant to be concealed. Because this concept is programmed within their minds, the designer of exposed systems is well advised to explain the concept to the subcontractors and make sure they understand and are willing to go along with it at the same price. For instance, exposed wiring must be in some sort of conduit, by code, and will require careful routing through the spaces to be served. This means that electricians must use extra care in placement of the wiring. But extra care usually means extra money, because it's faster to take the shortest route between service points by drilling through beams and concealing the wiring with later finishes.

Some distinguished designers, such as Frank Gehry, make a feature of exposed structure and services. A careful study of Gehry's work reveals that he does not allow contractors to put a structure wherever they like. On the contrary, the routing of all services is carefully controlled and requires more work by the architect to get it to look good than needed in the more conventional system of concealment behind finishes.

The more important lesson is that service elements within a house can be exposed, but should be controlled. This undertaking is expensive and time-consuming. It can also pose a functional problem, in that cold air conditioning or water piping can collect condensation and drip water onto finishes, furniture, and occupants below. The problem can be controlled by using more expensive insulated ducts or by insulating the pipes and ducts. This, too, presents aesthetic problems, because most insulation is ugly.

ARRANGING ARCHITECTURAL ELEMENTS

Architectural elements are symbolic as well as functional. This is particularly true when the architectural details are more elaborate than those strictly necessary to keep the elements out. The arrangement of architectural elements involves a great many

Windows are a fundamental design element. (Butler-Schnur house, East Hampton, NY)

choices that affect the "look" of the house and a system of ornament that will determine the patterning of the exterior and the spaces within.

WINDOWS AND DOORS

Windows and doors are human-scale-giving elements. Doors are the means by which people go in and out of buildings and rooms. Windows are the means of seeing out and in and providing ventilation. These elements can be solid or transparent, sliding or swinging, big or little, thick or thin, welcoming or forbidding, pompous or humble. They are a means of interaction between people and the world. Along with the creation of space, they are among the main elements within a house.

Placement

Windows and doors are a means of communication with nature and the outdoors. Depending on the climate, they can be small to protect against extreme heat or cold or large to welcome sun, view, and breezes. They are also fundamental, architectural elements, as they can be arranged to create an intangible rhythm of architecture.

In early houses windows tended to be evenly spaced. Symmetry was commonplace throughout the world, whether in a Renaissance palazzo, a Georgian house, or an early American colonial. In Asia, there were similar even spacings throughout Indian, Chinese, and Japanese houses. Regular spacing of windows proclaimed a sense of order within the house and promoted a feeling that the lives within were well regulated and prosperous. The urge to regularize buildings in one fashion or another is basic to most human conditions.

The size of windows and doors in the past frequently indicated the importance of the spaces they opened into. Consider just one example: The typical European or American townhouse might have had steps up to an important level that contained the grand rooms of the house, those in which the owners displayed their best possessions and upon which they lavished the most decoration. Ceilings were frequently higher there than on other floors. Above and below, windows were simpler and smaller, in keeping with the less important spaces behind them.

Windows and doors are a link to the outside. (Minton house, Copake, NY)

It should be remembered that in earlier periods glass was scarce or heavily taxed (as was the case in the American colonies), so large areas of glass were expensive. They were also impractical, because single glazing was the only option and weather stripping around the edges was primitive. Windows represented a great loss of heat and were a source of drafts. In modern times, technological advances permit more extensive areas of glass. Today we have double and triple panes of glass to fill window areas. We also have all kinds of glass block, fiberglass, and many new exotic types such as "smart" glass, which senses weather changes outside and renders itself more or less opaque to shield the inside from excessive heat buildup from the sun.

The designers of houses must work closely with the site and the client to decide on the optimal spacing, size, and location of the windows and doors.

Special Shapes

With advances in technology that enable larger pieces of glass to be set in walls, architects have begun working with special shapes. Circular windows have been around for a long time. They are frequently used to accent a wall or to fit within the sloping edges of a gabled roof high in the facade. Sometimes, as in round Gothic church windows, they are filled with a sortie. "Palladian" windows are in vogue at present. The term has been broadly applied to cover round-headed windows, with or without subdivisions.

Trapezoidal windows proclaim whimsy or indicate that the space inside has a special shape that is reflected in the facade. Other shapes are possible, such as triangles, ellipses, rhomboids, stars, crosses, and innumerable others. Most unusual shapes are custom-made and, therefore, expensive. Care must be taken to integrate these shapes within the rest of the architectural composition.

Ornamentation

Windows and doors can be ornamented to accent their importance in the hierarchy of house elements. Main entrances are a traditional choice for embellishment, as they are the primary means of entering and leaving the house. In the preautomotive era, this was a simpler affair. The front door was often the only entrance, it was frequently in the center of the facade, already a position to which the eye gravitated, and there was a vocabulary of decorative elements at hand with which to embellish the opening. Decoration was available for the area around the door, and the door itself could be paneled to further emphasize its importance. Windows followed suit, with those on the important floor, generally the ground floor or slightly above the ground level as in most Palladian villas and other early examples, given prominence.

In early modernism, a strict, clean, sweeping-away-ornamentation vocabulary was advocated by the leaders of the profession, and with it, the hierarchy of importance became blurred. Perhaps the interest of these designers in a more egalitarian arrangement was also at work. In some examples, placement and proportion became the means of composing the facade. Experiments were made with the golden mean, based on early Greek and Roman systems of proportioning classical facades.

Unfortunately, these systems or vocabularies of design ignored basic human urges to embellish the openings in house facades. In some cases, the owners and occupants added decorative features to bring some difference and distinction to their homes. This remains a problem in multiple-unit housing, where it is difficult for a person to find his or her own entrance in a row of identical doors. Owners make efforts to claim their entrances with distinction by painting them different colors,

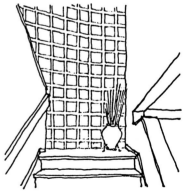

Glass blocks as a stair wall allow light in without compromising privacy. (Wright house, Guilford, CT)

Detailed entrance (54 Willow St., Brooklyn, NY)

installing new hardware, or just adorning them with wreaths. Even in apartment houses, where permitted, occupants may install different types of windows or distinctive window treatments, ranging from colored or swagged curtains to various types of venetian blinds and shutters. Inevitably, the occupants will make a house their own, and windows and doors are the most frequent sites for expressions of individuality.

Vehicular entrances pose problems for the contemporary house designer. Many people enter a house through the garage, be it to the side of the house or below it, with space for one or two cars, or part of a vast subterranean space in an apartment building. This is an awkward problem, because garage doors are not humanly scaled and are not easy to decorate. Garage door manufacturers do provide assorted paneled and ornamented designs, but the size of the door is practically unsolvable. This is a design area requiring attention, not only outside the garage, but also inside, since people may have to look at the door before entering the house.

TRANSITIONS

House design is ultimately a matter of the arrangement of spaces, so the designer must think about transitions between interior spaces and between those interior spaces and the outdoors. These transitions can be functional, as with the desirability of an airlock between inside and outside so inclement weather will not greatly affect the main spaces within the house. Or they can be symbolic, such as the space between major rooms that prepares the user for the experience of entering an adjacent space.

EXTENSIONS OF SPACE

There are many ways of extending spaces visually, both inside and out. The following paragraphs offer some suggestions.

Overhangs

Overhangs serve useful purposes, such as keeping the weather away from the walls and protecting the windows and doors. They also provide shelter if you're

The main entrance is clearly expressed below the largest opening. (Morton house, Middletown, NJ)

groping for your keys in the rain. In Japan, the area below an overhang was traditionally regarded as symbolic space, serving as a transition between in and out. The visual aspects of overhangs are important, requiring some design texture for viewing from below.

There are many examples of overhangs being treated as exposed structures. Visually rich, such a treatment produces a light-looking edge. It also has some advantages in cold climates, inasmuch as the roof ventilation slot can be positioned at the wall line rather than at the edge. This keeps the source of ventilation closer to the area that requires it—the heated portion of the house.

The aesthetic implications of overhangs constitute a subject of some interest to architects, because the addition of overhangs significantly alters the volumetric appearance of a house when it is composed of discrete groups of elements. But an argument can be made against them, because overhangs add to the cost of the roof by extending it. Countering this argument is their undoubted utility in protecting walls and windows. It is possible to construct effective and attractive houses either with or without adding overhangs.

Porches

Among the space-extending and welcoming devices of house design are porches. These were traditional in many cultures, providing a well-ventilated outdoor living space protected from the elements. They also offered a shaded area from which to view street or outdoor activity. Their counterpart in today's multistory housing is the balcony.

Most important, porches provide a welcoming transitional space, similar in effect to overhangs, but with a look of transparency. They can convey various moods. Two-story porches can be surrounded by tall, imposing columns, proclaiming to the outside world that the house is an impressive, well-designed one and that the owners are important. If the porch is a one-story affair surrounding a large house, it can create the opposite effect, proclaiming the occupants to be neighborly and welcoming. That type of porch space presents a more domestic face to the outside world.

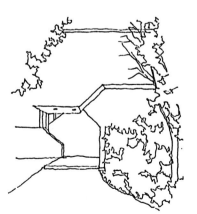

Entrance overhangs (Cohalan house, Bayport, NY)

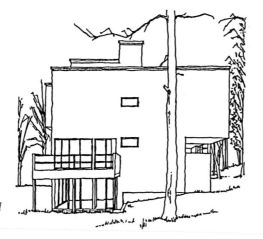

Corner overhangs (Vuolo house, Lloyd Harbor, NY)

Vestibules and Service Spaces

A room leading into a house from the outside is a functional transitional space. Not only does it provide an airlock to keep extremes of temperature and air movement out of the house, but also it serves as a preparatory space, anticipatory to the experience of traversing the rest of the house. It extends the mood of the space beyond. A vestibule or service space can have a simple, low, functional ceiling or a high, spacious, well-decorated one, depending on the budget and the sense of arrival desired in the house. Usually larger, grander spaces go well with houses of the same type. Some transparency is usual, but a sense of surprise can be achieved by having the space closed with doors or by placing a short flight of stairs within it. Great monumentality can be achieved by elaborating a level change, as in the Laurentian Library by Michelangelo. The entrance space in this building contains a set of stairs that is so sculptural in itself that the library space beyond is somewhat anticlimactic.

Service spaces and transitional rooms can also be placed between rooms. These were commonplace in large houses and palaces, where they were used as dressing or bath chambers. Today these spaces can be used in the same way or as enlarged closets.

CORRIDORS

Corridors are often required in modern houses, because most people want privacy in bedrooms and baths. Corridors can be treated simply, modulated with decorative devices such as pilasters, opened to views via windows, or well lit with skylights or artificial lighting. They can be used as art galleries, with appropriate lighting, or can end in pleasing views. The eye can be fooled by aligning the walls to converge, thus making a short corridor look longer. That sort of visual trick was common in Italy and France during the Renaissance and the Enlightenment.

Corridors can be widened into living space, as in Biltmore, the house designed by Richard Morris Hunt in Asheville, North Carolina. Or they can be glazed and mirrored to reflect a landscape, as in the Hall of Mirrors in the palace of Versailles. These examples may be grandiose extremes, but they are instructive.

INTIMATE SPACES

Small spaces that are hidden away, have low ceilings, or are connected with a fireplace or a window add appeal to houses. For example, a window seat at a stair landing can be a pleasant spot for people to sit and rest on the way to another floor. If it's a sunny spot, it can be a pleasant place to read a book or enjoy the view. Deep window recesses provide intimacy and convey a feeling of protection to the occupants. Colonial houses, where spaces were small in general and usually of a multipurpose nature, contained sleeping alcoves that were sometimes curtained. A low-ceilinged alcove in a contemporary intimate space can be equally appealing.

Fireplace alcoves, called inglenooks, were commonly provided in old houses as warming spaces. In times when central heating was not available, low-ceilinged spaces were fitted out with benches or surrounded with wingback chairs facing the fire, so that its radiant heat would not be dissipated into the larger room beyond.

ROOMS

House design is a matter of arranging spaces and rooms into a meaningful whole. The space can be discrete or flowing, shaped or four-square, light or dark, big or small.

Arrangement of Rooms

The rooms within a house can flow one into another via open arches or free-standing space dividers. Some rooms obviously demand privacy; bathrooms and most bedrooms fall into this category. Yet even bedrooms can be part of a grouping of flowing spaces if internal acoustical dividers are used like operable doors and panels. A study of Japanese houses is instructive. Here designers frequently employed a series of rooms that could be closed off from each other with sliding panels. In those houses, as

Transitional entry space (Frocht house, East Hampton, NY)

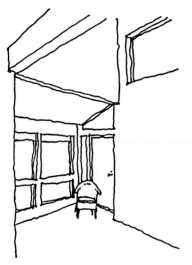

A recess creates a small, sunny space. (De Vido house, East Hampton, NY)

well as in Chinese houses, decorative panels above the sliding doors permitted ventilation between rooms. However, because these were openwork, there were obvious acoustical drawbacks.

Determining degrees of openness is a social decision to be discussed with your client. Some extroverts will find an open arrangement quite suitable; others will require maximum privacy. There are spatial considerations as well. Small, closed rooms will make some people claustrophobic. If the overall budget does not permit any large rooms, the house may seem cramped.

Limits of Spans

The size of a house's rooms is limited to the type and capabilities of its structure. Every room has width, length, and height. A room's ceiling is determined as part of the design process, and a decision must be made on how to cover the space enclosed. In ordinary lightweight wood construction, limits are imposed by the length of timber available. The most economical method is one that uses the shortest span and, therefore, the lightest structural members.

There are other ways of covering the space, such as using a larger beam at the ridge of the roof and affixing smaller members to it. This structural system is frequently employed where a shaped ceiling is wanted, commonly called a "cathedral" ceiling. Rooms of other shapes are possible, such as octagons, diamonds, parallelepipeds, and rooms with niches at one or more sides. Unusual shapes define a space as being special or ceremonial. They are more difficult to build and, therefore, more expensive. The impact of such a room as a visual climax is lessened if the concept is used more than once in the same house.

The designer should think about structure while working out room arrangements and shapes. A good engineer who can visualize space is invaluable and should be consulted early in the design process.

Spatial Variety

Some spatial variety from one room to another is desirable, particularly in rooms that are similar in function. For example, the bathrooms in a house may be similar in appearance—all have the same kind of fittings. Some designers gain variety by using different colored fixtures and tile. It is also possible to gain rich variety by shaping the spaces differently. One bathroom might be skylit, another might have a polygonal shower stall, and still another might have a window on each side of the vanity.

Bedrooms can also be varied with the use of a simple device such as a bay window from which the view can be a feature, a small balcony, or an oversized

window overlooking a private, enclosed garden. The goal is to give these rooms some individuality for the occupants' enjoyment. Barrackslike arrangements of rooms have never been popular—even in the barracks.

Light

Light is the most important intangible ingredient of architectural space. In fact, it is only through light entering a room that it can be seen and experienced. A dark cave has no architecture except that which can be touched and smelled.

A bedroom with an interior balcony overlooking a multistory living space (Frocht house, East Hampton, NY)

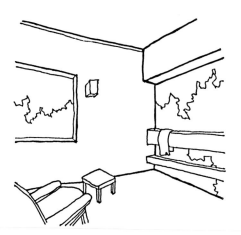

An outdoor room provides partial shelter but retains an outdoor feeling. (West house, East Hampton, NY)

Forms in light and the penetration of light into space are the essence of architecture.

The light that enters a room can be soft, as through a gauzy curtain; from a deeply recessed source, as on a fully moonlit night; sharp, as through a flush piece of glass when the sun is brightly shining; or pellucid, as on a bright winter day with the sun low in the sky. Light can also be modulated and controlled through the use of blinds, shades, or curtains.

Light can be brought into a space from unexpected sources, such as high in a room or from behind a vertical element such as an interior chimney flue.

Focus

Focus is important to give interest and purpose within a house. Rooms or groupings of rooms can have direction and focus on a particular view or feature. In primitive societies, figures of gods and goddesses to be worshipped were placed in niches. In other societies, niches displayed works of art. A fireplace, as an all-important source of heat within a house, was a frequent focus. In rooms in which the view and the fireplace are dual foci, some designers have successfully placed the fireplace in front of a whole wall of glass. If the fireplace is an open type with a minimal flue, it will not block the view and may even enhance it, as the flames can be seen against this natural background.

It is possible to have multiple foci within a room, as in a central space surrounded by other rooms. There can also be a space within a space, as an aedicula.

MATERIALS

The materials selected for room finishes are important determinants of spatial quality. Many aspects of function and cost contribute to the selection of materials.

Unified Materials

Wood can be used on all surfaces in a room. Wood floors generally require a finish to fill the pores, although the Colonial house had unfinished pine boards that were periodically scrubbed.

THE ARCHITECT'S JOB

Symmetry of a window grouping focuses the eye. (White Pine Road, East Hampton, NY)

In fact, rooms can be finished entirely in unfinished wood. This is a rich natural material that ages well and provides a unified color palette in the warm range. Although it is more expensive to buy and install than wallboard, it can provide a cost savings over the years. Natural wood indoors needs little maintenance, whereas wallboard requires painting every four to five years, depending on wear.

The designer can always use wallboard throughout a space or room. This material can be all of one color or painted in different colors from one surface to another. Some architects have experimented by leaving wallboard in its natural unpainted state, with only the joints spackled. However, most clients will not accept this look, because it appears as if the contractor quit in the middle of the job.

Masonry can be used throughout a room to good effect. Exposed brick or concrete masonry units, which come in different colors, are fireproof and durable. The joints can be tooled in various ways. Poured concrete can be handled in a rich variety of ways, ranging from a smooth finish created by steel or finished formwork to rough formboarded concrete or concrete that is later hammered or sandblasted. For masonry used as part of a unified palette of materials, there are many kinds of tile available, as well as economical ways to handle poured concrete floors, such as applying sponged or polyurethane finishes. Ceilings can be vaulted using tiles or poured-in concrete employing shaped or flat forms.

Some clients like masonry houses and request them. Some people, who may have listened to the story of the three little pigs, are culturally inclined to think that a masonry house is better built than a wooden one. Many parts of Europe have a vernacular tradition of masonry houses.

Contrasting Materials

The use of contrasting materials most often helps to focus the direction of a room. For instance, a fireplace wall may be built with exposed brick whereas the rest of the room is painted wallboard. Brick can also be juxtaposed with stone, although these textures may possibly clash. Some fireplace walls have stone placed randomly within the brick, a combination that is usually assertive, although the use of stone

The fireplace, as an important source of heat, has long been a natural focal point. (Wright house, Guilford, CT)

quoins, or borders, around brick can work well. All decisions concerning these choices involve cost as well as aesthetics.

Contrasting materials can be harmonious and work well together in a limited color range. For instance, a softly textured wood in the beige range can work quietly with a sand-textured paint on wallboard.

Floor finishes most frequently contrast with wall and ceiling finishes, because floors take more wear than walls and ceilings and require a harder, more durable material.

Unusual Materials

It is possible to use unusual materials or common materials in an unusual way. For instance, plywood sheathing that is manufactured from chips of wood can be used as a finish material. Although not designed for an exposed use, it can be finished handsomely and look quite expensive, despite its humble origins. Raw, low-grade plywoods require special fastening to make them look special. A designer must be careful to specify a common material for finished use, however, because carpenters will not automatically understand that it is to be the finished material.

Other common inexpensive materials that can be interesting are ordinary corrugated metal, painted or left unfinished; various kinds of fiberglass, flat or corrugated; treated metals of all kinds; and old boards salvaged from a demolished building. Well-weathered barn boards can be very handsome if properly used. Sometimes, however, they cost more than new boards just because of their age.

Natural and Synthetic Materials

Most building materials are manufactured in some fashion. Even a house built of fieldstone and unfinished wood will have had some work done to its materials at

In designing furniture, consider the comfort instead of stiff, angular seating.

the local stone yard or sawmill in terms of shaping or cleaning. Synthetically finished materials are usually subjected to more processing in the mill or factory and are frequently finished with paint or other preservatives. Some materials, such as the whole range of synthetic countertops, are wholly manufactured from plastic or petroleum derivatives. The designer should select materials on the basis of their cost and durability. Natural materials generally weather and age well. Most plastics will never be as good as on the day they are installed.

MOVABLE ITEMS

Within any house are always a number of movable items: furniture, household objects, art, and collections. These are often personal things that the owners feel more strongly about than the house itself. They represent the specific pieces of the world that the owners have gathered. They provide human scale and add personality to the house.

Furniture and Built-ins

Furniture should be anthropomorphic if it is to be comfortable. However, much of it is not, for reasons that are not clear. It may have to do with preconceptions about what a chair should look like, or with traditions or ease of manufacturing. Customs have changed over the centuries. For instance, ancient Romans took their meals reclining on their sides, a position many doctors say is more healthful than the constrictions of the sitting position. Reclining chairs are generally more comfortable than upright models; witness the quiet success of operable recliners cherished by many TV couch potatoes. In contrast, Neils Diffrient, a distinguished industrial designer, has designed a series of chairs for work and relaxation that not only permit adjustment to various positions, depending on the task, but that are visually appealing.

The house designer can design furniture. An advantage to this enterprise is that the furniture design will usually fit the context of the house design. However, this is a difficult task that should not be taken on without some knowledge and study of the human body and what constitutes a comfortable position. Many distinguished

Arrange furniture to take advantage of space and views. (Drake house, Pound Ridge, NY)

architects have attempted furniture design with varying degrees of success. Gerrit Rietveld designed many pieces of furniture, all interesting to look at, some very comfortable, and all in the same design idiom as his houses. Rudolph Schindler did the same, leaving unfinished end grains exposed in much the same way he did with his houses.

Assuming the main job is not the design of furniture, it is important to decide where the various pieces will go. A furniture plan is a good idea at an early stage to make sure there is an arrangement that will work with the view, if any, or the foci of the rooms, and to see whether there is any conflict with travel patterns through the rooms. Some rooms, such as dining rooms, are rather straightforward. They must accommodate the width of the dining table, plus the depth of the chairs pushed up to the table, plus the circulation necessary to get around the chairs. It sounds simple, but there are a surprising number of dining rooms that do not work because they are dimensionally deficient.

Built-ins are frequently a good idea, but seating should be designed with the comfort of the body in mind, *not* with appearance as the main criteria. Built-in bookcases and bunk beds are space savers and also eliminate the necessity of cleaning beneath and behind them. Again, they should be dimensionally correct. Dimensions should be coordinated with the client. It should be noted bed making is very difficult with bunk beds surrounded by walls on three sides. This should be pointed out to people who have never had a set of bunk beds.

The design qualities of the furniture selected for the house should be coordinated with the design of the house. Chrome and leather chairs generally look better in a house of modernist design. The Barcelona chair by Mies van der Rohe, for instance, never looks better than it does in a building of his design, where the design idiom of the enclosing structure matches that of the chair.

Fabrics and colors should be coordinated with the clients. If there is an interior designer on the job, try to work with him or her. Explain to the client that the end result will be better with such collaborations.

The curved tabletop fits the bow of the exterior wall (Drake house, Pound Ridge, NY)

Household Objects

Modern life is full of gadgets and things, ranging from a wide assortment of kitchen machines to TVs, hi-fis, VCRs, faxes, and other electronic devices that arrive on the scene almost daily. They should all be accommodated in some way, neatly. In a materialistic age, all of us have a great many things, and a lack of storage space for them is a constant complaint of homeowners.

The responsible house designer should, therefore, spend considerable effort in asking the clients what they have and where it will go. Ask them to estimate, if possible, the required linear feet of hanging space for clothes and shelving for clothing storage. Then make these spaces convenient. Research the latest storage systems and get to know at least as much as the local closet company, which will tell your client that it will fit out the closets after the architect leaves the scene.

Kitchen design is another interesting area and a very important one. Try not to foist your personal ideas about kitchen planning onto the client. Although kitchen

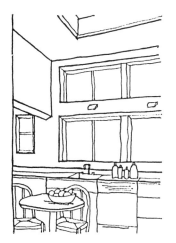

Kitchen habits are personal, and the design must be worked out with the client. (De Vido house, East Hampton, NY)

habits are personal, there are certain rules of thumb that should not be violated. It behooves the designer to know these and work them out with the client.

Inquire as to where other objects are to be placed in the rooms of the house. For instance, it's important to know that a client has a grand piano, which requires a lot of space away from direct sunlight.

Art

Providing for art within a house design requires some fairly subjective decisions. It's best to find out about a client's artworks early on, because some modern pieces are large, and, in the case of sculpture, heavy. It must be gotten through doors to reach its intended space. It must also be exhibited in the proper light to set off its characteristics. For example, an ancient Chinese sculpture should be illuminated from several sources to highlight its surface texture, shape, and beauty. A two-dimensional painting should be lit from above, and the source of light should be at some distance from the painting to avoid scalloping or creating unwanted highlighting of the painting's texture. If the client is greatly interested in art and has or plans to have an extensive collection, it may be a good idea to work with a lighting consultant.

Climate and sun control are important considerations. Works of art on paper, for instance, should not be in direct sunlight. They should not even be subjected to high levels of artificial light, which will in time render the paper brittle and yellow it.

Humidity and temperature control are also important for many works of art. Each specific case should be researched and incorporated into the design.

Collections

Collections of any sort lend personality to a house. The designer should find out what is to be displayed and inquire whether any other collections may be added in the future. Sir John Soane designed his house in London as a future museum, with accommodations made for lighting his collection of books, architectural fragments and castings, and paintings. Despite the sheer quantity of personal memorabilia, it is a very livable house that does not give one the sense of being in a museum. Charles Moore's

Plan for collections of art and books.

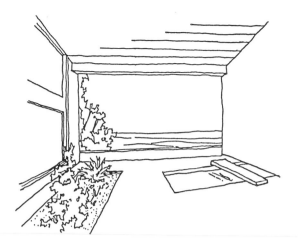

Enclosed garden area (Palmer house, York, PA)

various houses had the same feeling. Long an admirer of Soane, Moore designed niches, shelves, and stairs on which his large collection of folk art, fragments, and books could be displayed. The niches and shelves for these pieces were visually at ease with the objects.

Gardens represent collections of another sort. The ensemble of the garden, composed of plants, shrubs, trees, paths, alleys, vistas, ornaments, and furniture is another area of design requiring attention not only within the garden but from the house. The architect must consider how to frame or control views, as well as the temporal experience of moving through the garden.

PROJECT: NEW FARM, *Haslemere, England*

Architect: Amyas Connell

- For this house, a fan-shaped plan gives rooms individual orientation.
- The structure has 4-inch poured concrete walls, with structural columns pulled within the rooms, reflecting the Corbusian idea of free facade treatment.
- The stair wall is clad in glass and serves as a visual focus for the building.

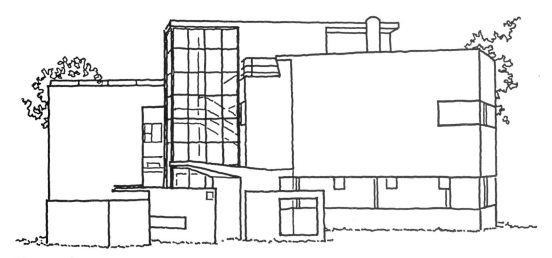

View toward entrance.

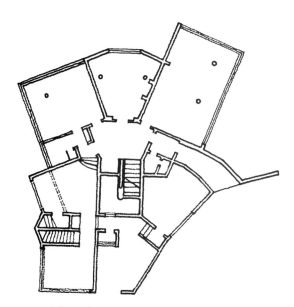

Ground floor plan.

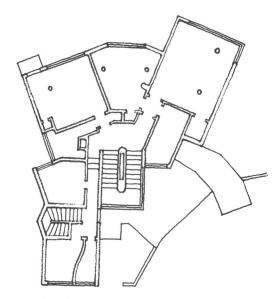

First floor plan.

PROJECT: HOUSE, *Easton, Maryland*

Architects: Wesley Wei Architects

- This two-story house integrates architectural forms such as the stairs, table/landing, hanging fireplace, curved roof, weathervane, and unique window cuts.

- The stairs connecting the two floors provide a focus. The architectural promenade up and down the stairs offers views of the interiors and the garden.

Exterior of curved roof.

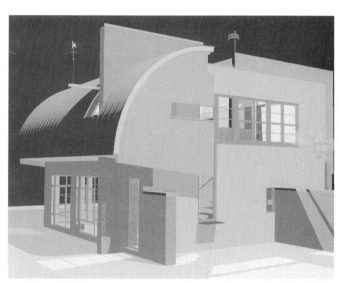

Computer drawing.

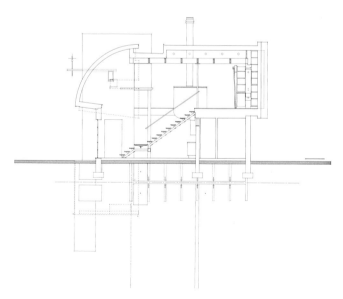

Sections.

Axonometric view.

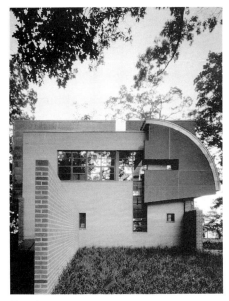

Exterior.

Roof and weathervane.

Stairwell with architectural features.

Second floor with fireplace.

Second floor looking toward stairwell.

Ground floor plan.

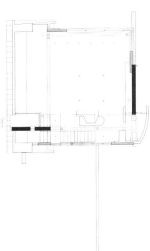

First floor plan.

PROJECT: SHEEHY HOUSE, *East Hampton, New York*

Architect: Alfredo De Vido, FAIA

- The elongated plan is zoned for separate quarters for parents and children with a second-story bridge connecting the two.
- The focus of the house is a two-story living room, with many windows opening onto views of the surrounding woods.
- Space is "borrowed" from adjacent rooms through the use of internal glass.

Horizontal siding emphasizes the long, low aspect of the house.

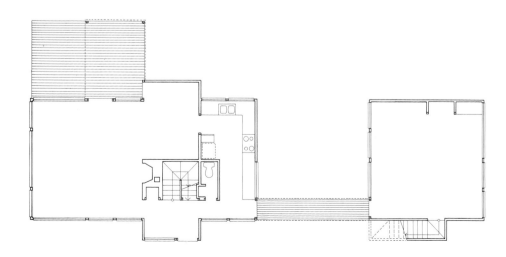

Lower level plan.

A skylit bedroom.

The master bedroom overlooks the living room.

Large-paned windows allow a view of the landscape.

An open-air terrace is framed by free-standing beams.

The house is set in a stand of mature pines.

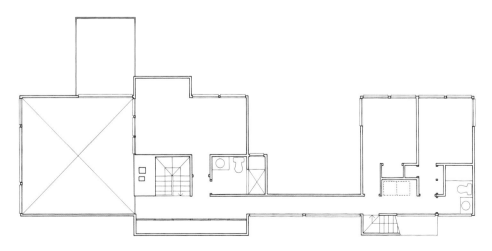

Upper level plan.

PROJECT: CHANDLER HOUSE, *Mason, Texas*

Architects: Lake/Flato Architects

- The house, set on a series of prominent limestone bluffs, was designed to make a strong visual connection with the natural setting while preserving the beauty of the landscape.

- The linear plan works with the steep grades and prevailing breezes.

- Overhangs, built from recycled oil field rods, are cantilevered to shade the house and terraces.

Limestone buttresses echo the rugged countryside.

Sunshades control solar gain.

House sits atop bluff.

The core of the house is simply gabled.

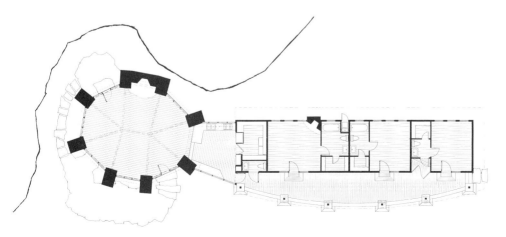

Plan.

PROJECT: WRIGHT HOUSE, *Connecticut*

Architect: Alfredo De Vido, FAIA

- The emphasis in this house is on the separation of the spaces and functions within through the use of color and volume.

- Glass areas are multiwindowed to maintain the visual integrity of the walls.

- The spaces within have thick walls for insulating purposes. The walls are shaped for visual effect.

Entrance steps.

Side window showing the chimney.

Rear of house.

Living room wall.

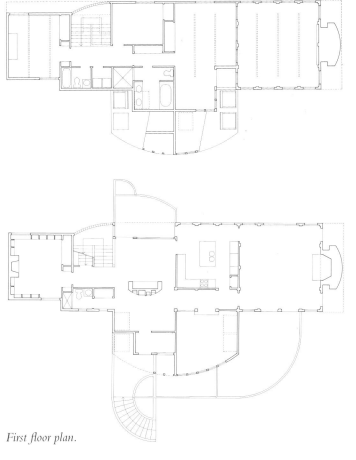

First floor plan.

PROJECT: HOUSE VILLANGOMEZ, *Ibiza. Spain*

Architects: Francisco Javier Palleja, Salvador Roig, Jose Antonio Martinez Lapeña, and Elias Torres

- A single floor plan arranged in the form of an L opens onto a patio oriented toward the sea.
- The patio is bounded by walls with openings through which one can glimpse the immediate environs, pines, and shrubs, and, in the distance, the seascape.
- Walls are thick, stuccoed, and provided with small windows that are protected by exterior louvered shutters.

View of court showing planting pockets.

Exterior of court wall.

View from court toward pines, detail of louvers.

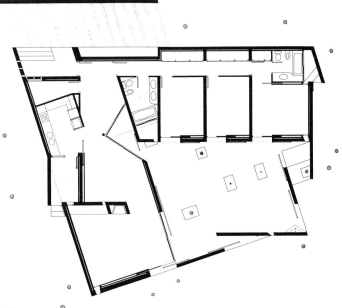

Plan.

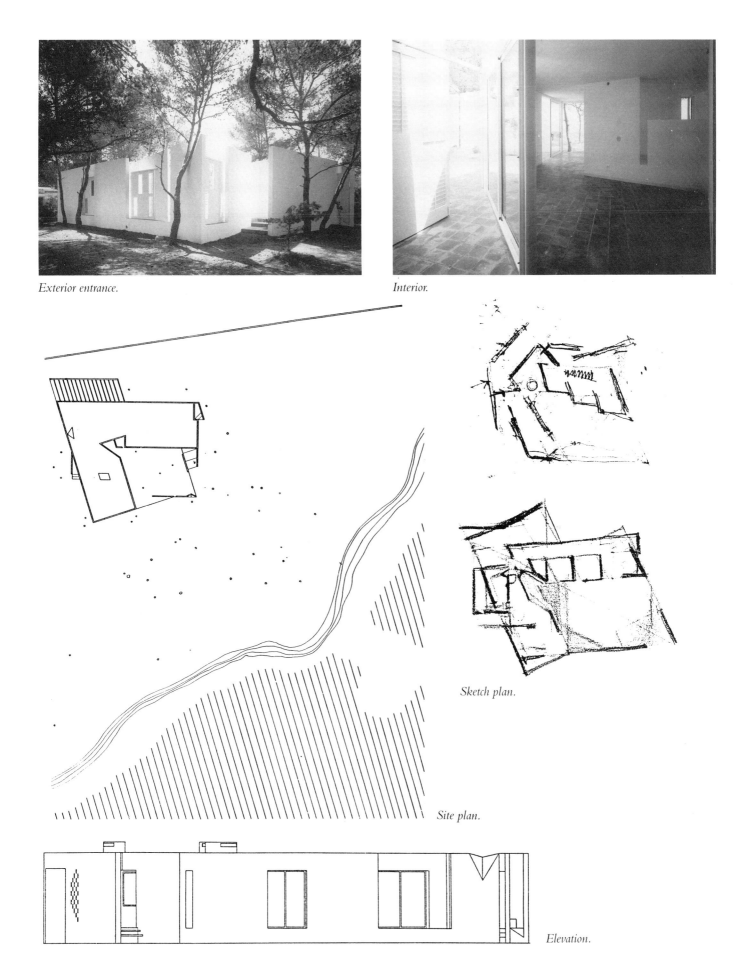

Exterior entrance.

Interior.

Sketch plan.

Site plan.

Elevation.

PROJECT: APARTMENTS, *113 Bis, Rue Oberkampf, Paris*

Architect: Frederic Borel, Architect

- Individual apartments achieve personal character through a variety of shapes, views, and spatial arrangements.
- The overall design of the apartment building has a distinctive style.
- An enclosed garden enhances the concept of individual houses within the metropolis.

Center of building.

View from the street.

Sketches.

Elevation/section.

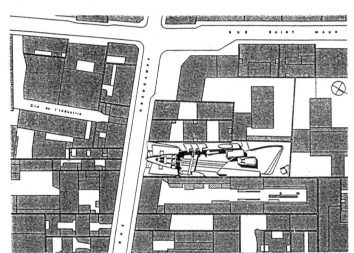
Bedroom.

Site plan.

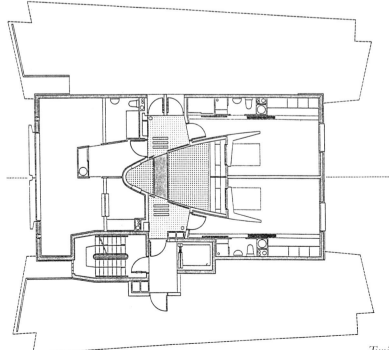
View of garden court.

Typical floor with apartment plans.

PROJECT: PUGIN HOUSE, *Seaside, Florida*

Architect: Walter F. Chatham, Architect

- In this townhouse, the plan places the "core" elements along party walls to serve as buffers against noise from adjacent houses and, at the same time, to keep the middle a free space.

- Color and pattern are integral to the interior design scheme.

- Windows are recessed to provide protection from the sun.

Exterior.

Living room.

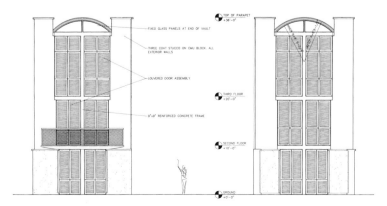

Elevations.

Stair hall.

Exterior windows and doors are louvered.

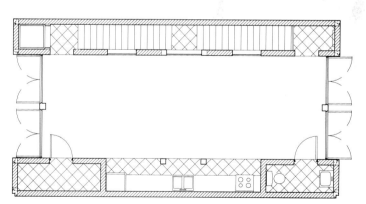

Third floor plan.

PROJECT: 222 COLUMBIA HEIGHTS, *Brooklyn, New York*

Architect: Alfredo DeVido, FAIA

- A Landmarks Preservation District within New York City is the locale for this project, which contains a triplex, a retail unit, and a condominium. The structure was designed to harmonize with the adjacent row of Renaissance Revival houses.

- The design uses a grid of regularly spaced window and door openings, accented by profiled cornices, sills, and belt courses. A separate entry is set back on the side.

- The spaces within are organized openly, using two stories in the larger spaces that flow into one another.

Entrance and side facades.

Living room.

Promenade view.

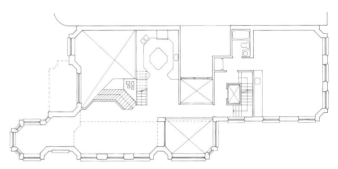

Plan of triplex second floor.

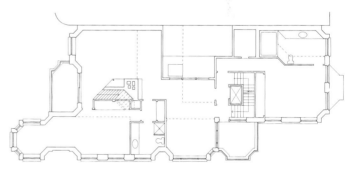

Plan of triplex first floor.

Details of cornices and belt courses.

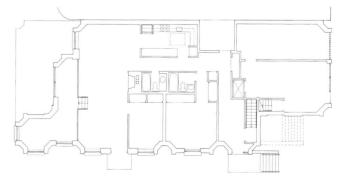

Lower level condominium and entry plan.

PROJECT: MERZ HOUSE, *Switzerland*

Architects: Atelier 5

- In the tradition of Corbusian modernism, this house uses a linear progression of rooms turned to the view. A service wing is perpendicular to this wing.
- Imprinted in the concrete used for construction is the texture of the board forms. The house is in sharp juxtaposition to the landscape.
- A roof garden capping the living wing is the culmination of the progression of spaces through the house.

Entrance showing service wing to the side.

Roof garden.

Roof garden.

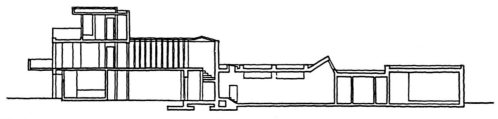

Section.

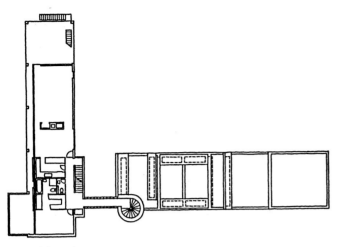

Second floor plan.

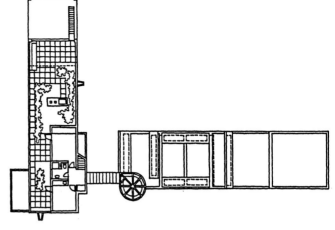

First floor plan.

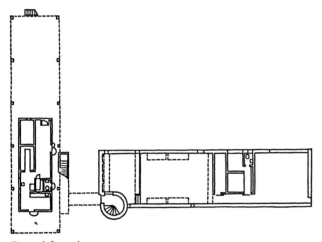

Ground floor plan.

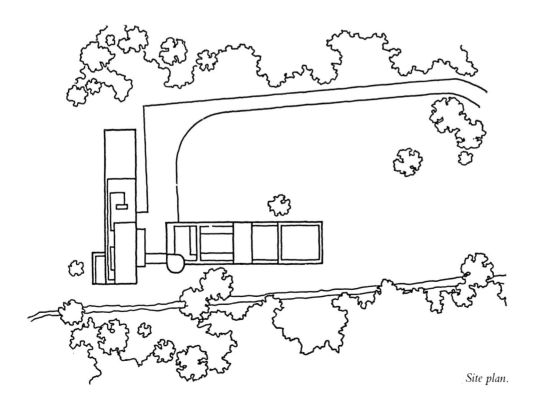

Site plan.

PROJECT: HOUSE AT BINGIE POINT, *Australia*

Architect: Glenn Murcutt

- This house is industrial in style, built of glass and corrugated metal.
- The plan is linear and basic.
- Within, the house is straightforward and open, with lightweight partitions and unadorned finishes.

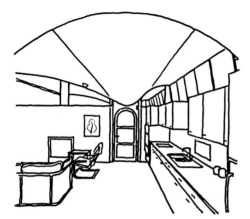

Interior of dining/kitchen area.

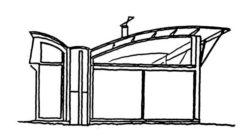

End elevation showing unusual roof structure.

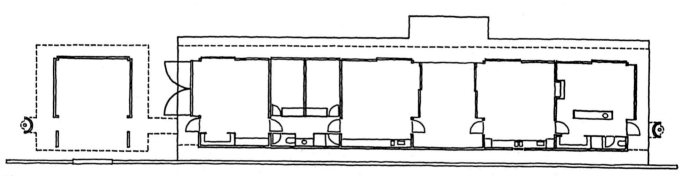

Plan.

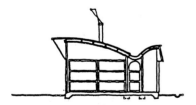

Section.

Long view of house facing sun.

5 | THE DESIGN PROCESS

The starting point for determining the scope and cost of a house is the *program*. Although factors such as the site, building codes, legal requirements, and community input affect the program, the most important components are the client's ideas and needs. The architect is supposed to guide the project through all phases and ensure that the budget will be respected while also seeing to it that all the client's needs and aspirations are fulfilled.

THE PROGRAM

The client's program may be a statement of the number of rooms needed, or it may be a few vague images. Or the client may include detailed requirements, such as square footage, room sizes, materials to be used, and ideas for layouts. The program will probably include a cost ceiling, which is an important consideration.

COLLECTING DATA FROM THE CLIENT

Start out by asking the clients if they have a file of clippings or a written program concerning the house. If not, give them your brochure, if you have one, or show them your portfolio and ask them to react positively or negatively to various aspects of your past work.

If you are new to house design, ask about houses your clients have seen and liked. You might also take a drive with them to look at houses or ask them to send you shelter magazines or books, with their comments noted on various pages.

It's helpful to have your clients' programs in writing. If they don't readily agree to give you all the information you need in a tidy package, giving them a checklist may be a useful alternative. If a checklist intimidates or appears tedious for them to fill out, or if clients seem reluctant to set their thoughts down on paper, it may be better to ask your own series of questions and take notes. Taking notes is important because it is unlikely otherwise that you'll remember all the details later. It also communicates to clients that you are making a serious effort to understand their desires.

If your clients are builders, they will lay out very specific ideas and construction techniques based on their backgrounds. However, they have come to you for your ability to organize their disparate and sometimes conflicting needs, and they may not be aware of some time- and cost-saving techniques.

TYPICAL PROGRAM
- Living room
- Dining area/room
- Kitchen
- Entry/foyer
- Family room
- Library/den/studio
- Master bedroom
- Master bath
- Additional bedrooms
- Baths
- Powder room
- Basement, if any
- Garage
- Shop
- Attic, if any
- Laundry room

Floor Plan
- Number of stories
- Bedroom separations
- Views from individual rooms
- High ceilings
- Entry and its relationship to other spaces
- Secondary entry/garage/kitchen
- Fireplace
- Traffic patterns

Space Utilization
- Work spaces (kitchen, elsewhere)
- Storage (closets, kitchen, bath areas)
- Room uses (primary/secondary)

General Considerations
- Rooms in relation to sun/views

- Outdoor relationships
- Informal/formal
- Maintenance
- Type of heating
- Solar installations
- Exterior spaces for outdoor activities—deck, barbecue, games
- Pool—now/later?
- Pitched roof/flat
- Exposure of structural elements
- Busy/simple walls
- Detailed with cornices/moldings
- Texture
- Energy efficiency—good insulation, windows
- Coziness/warmth

General Character
- Formal
- Feeling of space
- Relation to outdoors
- Sense of sheltered enclosure
- Variety of spaces
- Neighboring houses and relationships
- Garage as part of house
- Elegance/retreat
- Interior furnishings: sofas and chairs, tables, desks, artworks
- Charm
- Casualness

Entrances
- Front door conspicuous and conveniently located
- Entrance and relationship to street and drive
- Parking area
- Comfortable entrance hall/greeting area with coat closet and guest bath convenient to kitchen, living room, and private areas
- Kitchen door near driveway for groceries
- Various doors to decks and garden as appropriate
- "Mud room" entrance
- Access to living level from basement, if there is one

Kitchen

- Separate eating area

- Family social center

- Sunshine

- Space, work island, and cabinets

- Working layout: refrigerator-stove-sink relationship

- Ability to delegate dinner preparations (so people can work independently)

- Entrance to living room: open/closed doorway

- Access to deck/patio

- Phone in kitchen: place to sit, take notes

Dining Room

- Separate?

Dining Area of Kitchen

- Is there to be a kitchen dining area?

- Separated from kitchen work space: generous space for table

- Lighting from outdoors

- Kitchen table as place to read newspapers, write shopping lists, peruse cookbooks, etc.

- Size of chairs

Living Room

- Spacious/intimate areas

- Fireplace as focal point

- Areas in room: central seating, gaming, fireplace, dining area, piano, art collection

- Importance of natural light

Study

- Library

- Desk, sofa, comfortable reading chairs

- Large?

- Fireplace

- Retreat

Fireplaces/Stoves

- Fireplace in living room

- Elsewhere

Bedrooms

- Master: Large? Private bath? Dressing area?

- Morning sun? Sitting area? Writing table? Phone?
- Closets
- Other bedrooms: Shared bath? Separate bath? Size? Reading areas? Window seats? Number?
- Closets
- One room will probably have twin beds and so should be a little larger than others

Baths

- Large or fancy?
- Functional? Convenient with good lighting and storage space for towels, linens, medicines

Other Considerations

- Is master bedroom on same floor as other bedrooms?
- Adjacent bedrooms separated?
- Closet walls or bathrooms to separate bedrooms and ensure privacy
- Should library/study double as guest room, replacing one of the additional bedrooms?

Storage

- Generous and convenient as possible: coat closets, utility closets, kitchen/dining storage areas, place for folding chairs, games, etc.
- Wood box for fireplace
- Linen closet
- Clothes closet
- Storage rooms
- Garage

Basement

- Desirable/not?
- Space for workshop
- Possible shower, sauna, hot tub
- Finished/unfinished?
- Freezer/extra refrigerator
- Storage areas
- Mud room
- Gym, games

Garage

- One or two cars?

- Storage?

Grounds

- Future pool/pool house
- If pool, access to shower in main house?
- Grass/ground cover
- Vegetable garden
- Cutting garden
- Natural/formal landscaping
- Ground water problem?

BEYOND THE OBVIOUS

Of course, it is important to know the room count and approximate sizes. Of equal importance and much harder to discover is the client's attitude to sensitive issues, such as aesthetics, relationships of rooms to one another, attitudes toward mechanical systems and maintenance, room shapes, colors and textures, and the overall house form. For example, it is possible to draw simplified house shapes with a flat roof, a curved roof, and a gabled roof and ask which one the client prefers. You will undoubtedly have ideas of your own on these subjects, but it is best to elicit those of the client.

SOME GUIDING QUESTIONS

- Unless the clients have indicated which houses they like or dislike within your own portfolio, ask them if there are built houses or any in books or magazines that they like.

The clients may want to visit houses you've designed. This is fine, but time-consuming and a bother to the owners. If it would advance the process of developing the program, arrange a visit beforehand with your previous client. Explain to your present clients that they shouldn't try to project themselves into the house or houses to be visited, because such houses, like the one you're designing for them, are client and site specific.

- Ask about space. Within the good examples that you've elicited, is there some quality of space that your clients like? Is it bigness? Smallness? Idiosyncratic? Low ceilings? High ceilings? The contrast of low to high?

- Ask about style. Are they looking for a traditional house in some eclectic style such as Colonial? Or are they simply using that word as a description of the typical Colonial plan of center hall, two stories, with bedrooms upstairs and family spaces downstairs?

- Is there some aspect of the Colonial style they particularly like, such as multipaned windows and more wall surface than window? There may be some other aspect of Colonial, such as steeply pitched roofs, that they like. Be sure to probe deeply.

- In questions about style, avoid evangelizing. Remember that you are on a learning mission at the beginning. You may later attempt to lead the clients in your own stylistic direction, if that is what you want to do.

- Ask about materials. Point out their relative costs and maintenance qualities.

- You've already determined preferences as they relate to cost and practicality. You might now present materials as an aesthetic. For example, how do the clients react to rough, textured wood and beams? To hard materials such as marble and metal?

- Ask about color. Do the clients like color or a neutral palette? Are they aware of the psychological effects of color? Are members of the household (children, for instance) going to pick colors for their own room or rooms?

- Ask about noise and acoustics. Does anyone in the household play a musical instrument? What about loud music from a stereo or TV? How important is acoustical privacy?

- Ask about light. Do the clients like a lot of light from natural sources during the day? How much artificial light is desirable at night? Just in certain areas? What about lighting fixtures—concealed or surface mounted?

- Ask about room and wall shapes. Do they like angled walls? Curved walls?

Don't spend too much time on this information gathering, because you'll need more data as the design process moves along.

DETERMINING A REALISTIC BUDGET

After you are completely familiar with the clients' wants and desires, determine whether the program and your clients' cost ceiling are realistic for the type of house desired. Any estimates you make at the point are not binding, but rough calculations will establish the range within which you will be working. Don't reject this first estimate out of hand because it is more than the clients say they want to spend. In some cases, a client will give a deliberately low figure at the outset, but reserve the option to make upward adjustments if so desired. In any case, your relationship with a client will benefit if you are straightforward about costs from the beginning. Before you proceed with the design, you must know whether the clients will compromise on the program or on the budget if the two are at first incompatible.

Your first estimate will be based on your knowledge of the cost of materials and labor. Don't forget to add the architect's fees to the total, unless that's already agreed to as a separate sum. A realistic estimate also takes time into account: the cost of a house will increase by the rate of inflation during the construction period. Never base a first estimate on the lowest bid of your last job; costs almost certainly have risen since then, and each project must be considered independently.

If, at this early stage, the budget is out of line, ask the client what can be eliminated or deferred. Cutting room sizes across the board can help, but not as much as deletions of specific costly items such as a bathroom, guest room, or library. As an alternative, some functions can be combined, for example, a library/study can be designated to serve also as a guest room. Materials can be changed as well. Projected materials, such as stone, extensive wood walls, and completely tiled walls in the bathrooms may have to be changed to inexpensive Sheetrock. First projected costs are rarely, if ever, below the projected budget. But it is better to face budget realities early.

It is you who must take responsibility for keeping the program and budget in line. Resist the client's requests for additions, alterations, and substitutions of materials when they will affect costs. Many architects feel that denying the client's wishes will make them appear difficult to work with. They therefore incorporate all client suggestions into their design, hoping that they can somehow manage to conjure up a balanced budget in the end or that the client will come up with the additional money. It makes better sense to help the client keep costs down.

Be on guard: Amendments and expansions may balloon a program beyond recognition—and beyond the means of the client. However, don't bother to revise the

The site itself can provide clues to the overall design, scale, and views of a house. (Drake house, Pound Ridge, NY)

budget for every minor change. Inform the client, as you go along, of how the changes will affect expenses. Then provide a formal update of the estimate about halfway through the design phase—perhaps at the model stage, if you're making one—and again when the project is ready to be turned over to a contractor.

If you think that the contractor's bid will be out of line with the original budget because the scope of the project has increased since the outset, prepare the client by suggesting that the extra bedroom or more expensive building material be a bid alternate. Keep all such estimates clearly separate so that the client can then make an informed decision based on this information.

MORE GUIDING QUESTIONS

• Is the budget flexible?

• Has inflation been considered?

• Will the time schedule affect costs?

• What is included in the budget: just "bricks and mortar," or site development and utility costs as well? Have fees for lawyers, surveyor, and architect been budgeted separately?

• Has the client figured the cost of financing and is it available?

• Is your fee to be settled initially, or will it be part of a flexible building budget?

• Has the client balanced first costs against operating costs of mechanical systems? The reason to ask this question is to determine whether some aspect of the budget should be raised in the interests of saving future operating or maintenance costs. For example, electric resistance heating in the northeastern part of the United States has a low initial installation cost, but high operating costs later on. On the other hand, the cost of electricity in many Rocky Mountain states is inexpensive owing to the availability of hydroelectric power. When these considerations are factored in, the budget might be adjusted.

• Will site conditions, such as the need for a well or a long access road, affect costs? Have large items been budgeted separately? What about utility costs?

• Where is the client's money coming from? Is most of it from the bank, and will that affect the contractor's payment schedule? Is any of the "up-front" money, such as your fee, to come from the bank? Does the client know that banks will lend money on a percentage of the total project, including fees and land?

• Is the land paid for?

• Are there any special procurement procedures for building the house, such as the client's having a friend in the lumber business or a relative who is a plumber?

ENVIRONMENT

An important part of the design process is the study and understanding of the environment and the site within the environment. Along with the data collected from the client and the budget information, the site and its physical and human factors are important determinants of the final product.

FITTING IN

All houses are located within an overall environment. The geographical location, called the macroclimate, is basically a function of temperature and precipitation, humidity indexes, and prevailing winds. The microclimate includes the house in its local setting, be it on the shore, on a mountain or hill, or in a valley. Both climates have an effect on the energy needs and protective structure required for a house or grouping of houses, which the architect should consider during the design process.

Topographic surveys help one understand the site.

Fitting the house to its location gives it a sense of place. The house should look as if it is part of the region. Houses can be designed that are inappropriate to their climatic conditions, but the cost of operating such buildings is high, energy is wasted, and the occupants may be uncomfortable within. In some cases, the occupants of a building may modify the form because they do not think it works in the prevailing climate or in the regional vernacular. Witness the sad modification of Le Corbusier's group houses at Pessac, France. An attempt to build low-cost housing was almost immediately modified by the occupants, who added fake pitched roofs to Le Corbusier's sophisticated flat roof. His concept fit within his five principles of architecture. Unfortunately, the occupants did not know or care about his design philosophy.

Both overall and site-specific climates affect the form of a house and the selection and treatment of materials. For instance, consider roof shape. Flat roofs work well and look good in hot, dry climates. Pitched roofs are frequently appropriate in temperate and rainy climates. Not only do such selections affect the working of the structure, they also look better, because the regional vernacular probably already recognizes these climatic factors and has a visual set of forms that fit the climate. That's why adobe houses look out of place in temperate climates. Steeply pitched chalet roofs look equally out of place in a desert.

Materials also perform better when selected appropriately. Stained or natural wood that is allowed to breathe performs better in a humid climate, such as the seashore, than painted wood that seals in moisture.

THE MACROCLIMATE

The macroclimate is a basic consideration in studying a site. Study it carefully to determine the following restraints and possibilities.

Topographic Survey

Get a topographic survey of the site to determine the natural flow of rain and snow and runoff. If it is too expensive to order a topographic survey from a local sur-

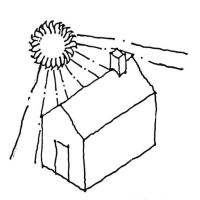

Analyze how the sun will affect the design.

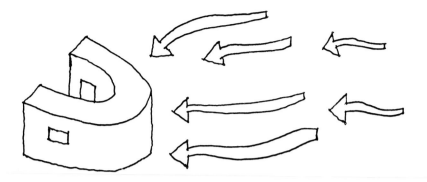

Wind direction can influence design.

veyor, others are frequently available for very little money, such as the series drawn by the U.S. Coast and Geodetic Survey. These are sectional and cover the whole country. Although these surveys are drawn at a large scale, their accuracy is good enough to give a broad picture of the land slopes. There are also companies that have flown over broad areas and can furnish surveys based on their work, which are quite accurate. Any surveyor you ask will know of these companies.

The Sun

Analyze the direction of the sun and how its rays fall on the projected house and specific spaces within the house. Note that the path of the sun and its position in the sky are different in summer and winter. Sensible, properly sized overhangs can keep out heat-generating summer sun and allow entry of valuable winter sunshine to warm the interior.

Also analyze the sun's shadow patterns with regard to the natural features that will be retained, such as a fine stand of trees. If the house is situated among the trees, the sun will not be able to warm the house in winter. On the other hand, the trees will serve as natural shading to keep the house cool in summer.

Wind Direction

Determine the prevailing wind direction in the various seasons to enable you to choose a careful location for the house on the site. It is optimal to catch summer breezes and avoid winter winds.

Temperature

Measure the temperature in different parts of the site. The area on the leeward side of a wind may prove to be warmer than that on the windward side, because the pockets of air collected there will be warmed by the sun. There may also be depressed areas that will be warmer in the winter and cooler in the summer. These areas are well known to animals, such as deer, who seek natural hollows to shelter themselves from icy winds in winter. These same hollows can be cooler in summer owing to the mod-

Natural vegetation gives clues to local humidity.

erating temperatures of the surrounding earth. Also consider the effects of vegetation on temperature and altitude.

Humidity

An important clue to the humidity of a site is its natural vegetation. Sites can harbor moisture resulting from subsurface conditions, such as layers of clay. The prevalence of certain species that thrive in wetlands, for instance, ferns, will indicate such conditions.

Ground moisture levels are a good indication of humidity for practical considerations, such as dry basements. A common homeowner complaint is the presence of moisture in the basement, which can render it useless. Study of site humidity will help in determining such conditions and how to orient and place the house properly to avoid a wet basement.

Precipitation

Rain and snowfall are contributors to the overall humidity of a house and its site. An obvious clue to the effects of precipitation is the location of puddles on the site immediately after a heavy rainfall. Similar indications can be noticed after a snowfall and subsequent thaw. Where the snow does not thaw quickly is sometimes an indication of where it collects and may cause problems. For instance, a house in a snowdrift area will be a solid obstruction that will cause deeper snowdrifts. House locations in Alpine areas are worth studying, because mountain people have long lived with the problems of heavy precipitation.

Natural Vegetation

Study the natural vegetation, and consider how the building will work within it. If the site is low, some of the natural vegetation may reveal subsurface conditions that will require a careful, conscious design. For example, wetlands species thrive in low, marshy ground. Not only is it bad ecologically to build in this kind of terrain because it destroys wildlife habitats, but also the house will suffer from dampness. It's

Heavy rain and snow contribute to the humidity of the house.

best, therefore, to avoid building houses in wetlands or low areas that collect water, inasmuch as these are important to the well-being of the land as a living part of the earth.

Natural Disasters

If a site is subject to extremes of sun, wind, rain, or seismic stresses, try to figure out which spot on the site is the most protected or the safest. For example, if the house is located next to a steep, unstable embankment, an excess of rain can produce mud slides that will destroy the house and injure the occupants. In brushy areas subject to fire, locate the house at a distance from the flammable brush, if possible, or design it to be fire resistant. Wind- and seismic-resistant design features are necessary precautions in areas where these natural cataclysms occur.

THE MICROCLIMATE

Most houses are not located on sites large enough to permit unlimited selection of orientation and optimal choice of position and viewpoints. These sites, often in semiurbanized areas, are big enough to permit single-family houses on individual plots, or small groupings of two to four connected dwellings on one piece of land. Such sites require investigations similar to those necessary for sites in natural landscapes, but additional thought is needed in regard to the presence of neighbors.

Effect of Surrounding Houses

Consider the effect of the surrounding houses on the proposed location of the house you are designing. Plot the path of the sun, and see where shadows of the adjacent house fall on your site. Some communities have "pyramid" laws that require setbacks sufficient to provide unobstructed access to the sun for each house. Wind patterns are also affected. Note the prevailing winds in relation to natural phenomena and provide for them accordingly.

Privacy

One of the most important considerations in a built-up area is privacy. Attention must be given to the location of all areas of the house that will be adjacent to neighbors. One early task is to study the disposition of spaces within the proposed house to maximize privacy. Consider alternate locations close to setback limits. Consider as well courtyard configurations for the house itself, which can guarantee a secluded, private outdoor area.

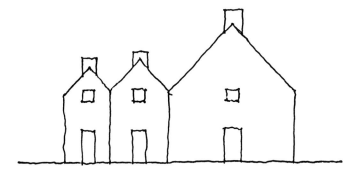

Consider surrounding houses when designing.

No Neighbors

Where there are presently no neighbors to a site in a built-up or suburban locale, it is desirable to consider where adjacent houses will be built. Frequently, planning regulations show what the setbacks will be, giving the architect a quick picture of the location of the adjacent house. However, not many regulations reveal where the living areas of the houses will be, so it is necessary for the architect to do some planning to anticipate the future.

Think about the various possible locations of the house on the site. For instance, the house can be placed as close to the rear setback line as permitted. Although this will provide a larger-than-usual front yard, it will probably guarantee that rear living areas do not abut similar areas in the houses to the left and right. Consider a skewed placement of the house as well, or skewed wings in the house. These can provide long views that are otherwise difficult to achieve.

Regulations

Regulations of the town or city in which the site is located are more stringent in built-up areas than they are in rural localities. These should be carefully scrutinized and observed. In any case, it is a poor idea to try to subvert these regulations. Even if they seem needlessly restrictive or bureaucratic, failure to follow them will inevitably lead to problems with the authorities. If there's an important feature on the site, such as a magnificent tree or vital wetlands, a request to modify the regulations to permit another siting for the house so as to preserve it will probably be approved by the local authorities, who are usually interested in such preservation.

Site Features

Site features such as drives and walkways should be given thought early in the site planning process. The vehicular and pedestrian approaches to the entrances can enhance the sequential experience of the architectural promenade. Consider forming the driveway in curves or in a loop if there is sufficient space. Although most people

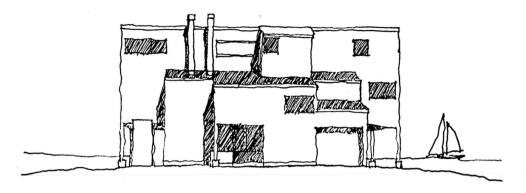

A house oriented toward ocean and views, away from road (Kleinman house, Napeague, NY)

arrive at a house by car, vehicles are sometimes left in the street or roadway. The front path is therefore an important consideration, not only from the street, but also from the driveway to the front door.

Thought should be given to the location of on-site parking. If a two- or three-car garage is included in the program, the garage will take up a considerable amount of available site space. Allowing sufficient space to maneuver in front of garage doors will take up a greater area than the garage itself. The garage doors are an important feature that often become the major view of the house from the street. Many people leave their vehicles in the drive in front of the garage doors, only infrequently putting them inside. The position of these spots is a difficult site planning problem that should not be left to later stages in the design process.

Surfacing materials for vehicular traffic ways should also be considered. Porous materials are available that simultaneously stabilize the ground and permit plant growth.

Landscaping

Landscaping is an important, yet often neglected, aspect of house design. The front garden, serving as the entrance to the house, can be made inviting through the use of selected plant materials or a low fence. In fact, features such as fences and hedgerows can be added to enhance privacy. Consider the streetscapes of Martha's Vineyard and Nantucket, where low fences beautify both street and house and are welcoming to passersby. If the house is located in an arid zone, consider the use of low-maintenance or low-water-use plant materials. Some sites are limited as to the amount of available water, so it is wasteful to provide water-intensive plant materials in such areas.

Above all, avoid traditional and sterile schemes such as the typical front lawn and foundation planting. Natural landscaping should be a prime consideration. Before construction begins, important existing plant material should be tagged and the contractor instructed to protect it. If a planting obstructs other site considerations, it can be removed, wrapped in burlap, and kept alive until the house is completed. Then it

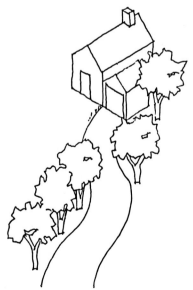

Driveways should not be an afterthought.

Landscaping should be an extension of the aesthetic of a house. (La Rocca house, East Hampton, NY)

can be suitably relocated to enhance the site. Even large trees can be moved with machinery designed for such purposes.

LARGER STRUCTURES

When the house is part of a larger entity, such as an apartment building or group of houses that fit together, the architect does not have as much control over the basic orientation and positioning of openings. In fact, the building in which the house or apartment is located may already be constructed, in which case the designer is limited to the selection of finishes and moving nonstructural walls. If the building has not yet been constructed, but exists only on paper, the architect usually has more latitude in the number of changes that can be made. Some housing schemes have been proposed in which a system of supports, or platforms, was provided for the design and construction of individual, distinctive houses. However, few of these schemes have been realized, owing to the reluctance of communities to permit widely disparate houses to be built within a structure requiring fire exits and other safety provisions.

If the house site or apartment is within a larger structure, the following site investigations should be made:

- Where is the public space in relation to the house or apartment? Is the point of entry fixed in reality or by regulation? Does it make a better dwelling to move the point of entry?

- Are there any options to change the windows, exterior private area, or balcony? Can balconies be enclosed to make additional living space if the client wants it or if it is needed and desirable? Study the exterior finishes and their suitability. If the structure is not yet built, work up a list of possibilities to discuss with the client and all required reviewing agencies.

• Consider thermal comfort in regard to prevailing sunlight and winds in relation to the features provided in the existing structure or those planned for construction. If you are working within an existing building, find the location of the plumbing and ventilation stacks for other units. It's highly unlikely that you will be able to change these without many approvals and much expense. Normally, it's not worthwhile to try. Of importance is what you can do to make a better house, perhaps reallocation of space and provision of thermal buffers such as planting areas adjacent to the house, or conversion of the balcony for greenhouse use if permissible. Study the rerouting ducts or piping within the space that is controlled by your client without approvals. Sometimes this aspect can be the key to a better plan.

• An addition or subtraction to the allocated shape or existing footprint of the house or apartment may be possible. If adjacent units are vacant or will be vacant soon, explore the possibility of various combinations with those units. If your client does not need so much space and could use the money to greater advantage in renovating or upgrading a smaller space, it may be that a portion of the site or unit can be sold to an adjacent owner.

CONTEXT

All sites are part of a larger whole, whether natural or manufactured. Historical stylistic context is subjective and the source of much debate. Less contentious is the appropriateness of the house within its cultural, aesthetic, and situational context. The contextual use of materials and the fitness of the design to the location and sense of place give the house a timeless design quality. In a townscape, it is possible to fit houses with their neighbors through the selection of facing materials, type of roof, and arrangement of windows. The design does not have to be a slavish imitation of the older one next door, but instead can be evocative of the surroundings and fit within them.

Establishing Relationships

There are several considerations in relating a house to its context:

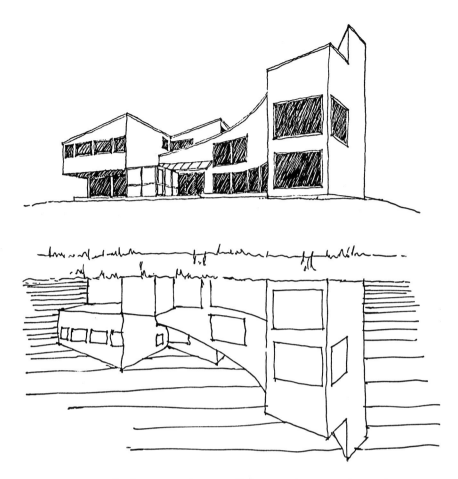

House curves to embrace pond views.
(Aksen house, Stamford, CT)

•   Design the house so that it will fit into the natural or urban surroundings. For example, you can fit a house into a thickly wooded site by unitizing the elements of the house among the trees to take advantage of views. Use materials that will relate the house to its surroundings. Brick might be a suitable material for a house in an area where brick is available and widely used.

•   Related to the disposition of house spaces and elements are the sizing of openings and the units of materials that give a sense of scale to the occupants of the house. Openings should be people-related as to their size and placement and should be designed accordingly. Bricks and fitted boards have a basically domestic scale that large pieces of cut stone do not. The latter material is more appropriate to the scale of large public buildings than to that of houses.

•   A harmonious relationship of the house with the natural or urban site can be achieved by sizing the house or group of houses to

A beach house has special foundation conditions, and pilings are frequently necessary. (Wertheimer house, Bethany Beach, DE)

fit the neighborhood. A three-story stack of houses around an elevator will not harmonize with a street of low, one-story bungalows; nor will a pink stucco house with a row of white painted clapboards.

The architect should take a long view of the future of the building to be placed on a site. Inevitably, the building envelope will be adapted to use throughout the period of private ownership, and its success as a work of architecture will depend on its harmony with the site and within its context.

THE ARCHITECT'S ENVIRONMENTAL CONSIDERATIONS

The environment of the site should have a profound effect on how an architect chooses to construct a house. The following paragraphs discuss questions regarding the environmental impact on the architect's choices.

Roofs

What is the best shape for the roof? Should it shed water, as in a gable, or collect water, as in a butterfly? What should be done about collecting the runoff, no matter what the shape? Are gutters best, or perhaps a collection strip of gravel that will absorb the runoff without spattering the side of the house or flooding the plantings? If the roof is flat, should it pitch gently to a drain? Should the roof have a parapet? Should it be of thick, dense material to absorb heat without transmitting it directly into the house during the hot part of the day, or something lighter with an air space below it to permit ventilation?

Walls

What is the most appropriate material and construction for the walls? Should they be open to catch breezes, as in tropical countries that are hot and humid, or should they be well-insulated, thick walls with small openings to keep out winter winds and extremes of cold? Should they be of locally made materials, such as brick or wood, or are there other considerations, such as fire protection, if wood is chosen? In this instance, a combination of materials such as a veneered wood frame may be the best possible answer.

Foundations

What about the foundations? Does the house require pilings because of unstable soil conditions or the possibility of high winds? Are there special requirements because of earthquakes or other severe natural phenomena? Should there be a basement, crawl space, or slab on grade? In damp climates basements tend to be useless unless they are carefully waterproofed and dehumidified. Slabs on grade can be appropriate in warm climates where there is no frost and foundations do not have to be deep. They can also be equipped with radiant heating, required in cooler climates, which can be quite comfortable at the same time.

Ceilings

High ceilings are appropriate in hot areas, low ceilings in cold areas. Shaping ceilings to allow the passage of warm air to a high point where it can be exhausted is a good technique. It can also be used to recirculate warm air in cold weather if the peak is provided with a mechanical means of sending the air downward. There are also methods of venting spaces without mechanical means through syphonic venting systems. These are based on the simple physical principle that hot air rises; replacement air can be sucked in at the bottom of the space to create natural interior breezes.

Doors

In tropical climates doors are frequently equipped with louvers to allow breezes to pass through. However, louvers are not so suitable in cold weather, because cold air can infiltrate through the louvers and cause drafts. For this reason, in cold cli-

A large, high-ceilinged living room (Vuolo house, Lloyd Harbor, NY)

mates doors must be carefully weather-stripped to prevent the great heat loss caused by open cracks around doors and windows.

Windows

Windows have been mentioned previously in respect to their size in warm and cold climates. The architect should also consider their ability to open and close tightly or loosely, depending on the climate. Windows can be insulated in various ways. In addition to weather stripping, which is important, double and triple panes of glass can be specified. There are ways of treating the cavities between the layers of glass to help transmit desirable solar radiation, and reject radiation of other types. Recent developments are moving toward "intelligent" varieties of glazing that react to the specifics of local weather conditions. For instance, the glass may react by blocking out the direct glare of intense sunlight. These more exotic types of glass are still quite expensive for residential use, but costs are coming down.

Movable shutters should also be considered by the architect. These were commonplace in earlier times when protection from the elements was an important consideration. Sometimes the ease with which we can now control the interior climate of a building makes us forget some of the simpler, more economical devices that moderate temperature, such as shutters and movable glazing.

PHASES IN THE DESIGN PROCESS

Once you are confident that you know the site and the program, the budget is in order, and you have all the legal/zoning limitations in hand, you may begin work. The best rule of thumb is to work closely with the client through all phases of the design process, thereby building a strong interactive relationship based on trust.

KEEP IN TOUCH WITH THE CLIENT

Of paramount concern is to exercise a steadying influence on clients by keeping them advised of how changes will affect their budget. It is also important to

The climate helps determine the number and size of windows. (Minton house, Copake, NY)

discipline yourself in the area of design; beware of decisions and ideas of your own that will result in a broken budget. If you feel that a particular feature is essential to produce a distinctive design but will cost extra, discuss it honestly and thoroughly with the clients.

There are a number of reasons to keep in touch with the clients while you are working on the documents, which include the following:

• Frequent communication allows clients to feel that they are a part of your efforts.

• Showing clients what you are doing lets them know that the money they are investing in your services is well spent. It is surprising how many clients are unaware of how much work architects do.

• Making clients aware of all the design decisions that are part of the process avoids the possibility of having them say they "didn't know it would look like that."

Once you have signed, or come to an agreement with the client and received a retainer, you may proceed with the work along the following lines.

OFFER EARLY CONCEPTS OF THE DESIGN

Simple schematic drawings or perspectives will show the general massing, window location, and orientation of the house. Bubble diagrams are fine, but they tend to be too abstract and generalized for the average client to react to.

The clients may ask you to come up with several broad conceptual ideas. This is a reasonable demand, but be wary about presenting so many diverse ideas that confusion will be the end result. It's a good idea for the architect to review a great many ideas in studying options, but the presentation of these ideas should be limited. Presenting too many broad options to clients will probably indicate that you are unable to make up your own mind. The clients have come to you for your ideas as a professional in response to their problems. Indicate your recommendations in a positive, responsive way. If you do present several broad directions, try to emphasize the one you think best and why.

When you present the early concepts, listen carefully to the clients' reaction. The chances are good that this will give you better insight into their programmatic and visual thinking than earlier conversations. For the first time, the clients will see visual material relating to their project. They will certainly take a keener interest in this material than they did in the unrelated exploratory material shown earlier to outline the program.

These early concepts should be presented soon after you get the job. Although you may be busy with other work, the clients are keen to proceed and it is a mistake to dull their appetite for the project by letting it sit for a lengthy period.

While moving briskly on this phase, bear also in mind that this is the most important phase conceptually. Be critical of your own work (not in front of clients, however). Ask yourself whether there isn't a better idea you haven't thought of yet. Resist falling in love with the first lines you put on paper. Have a mini-competition with yourself; then pick out which ones you think best. Resist putting your concept into a predetermined design that you think beautiful. This approach is actually common among architects historically. Eclectic architects in the past always used (and still do) previously selected models as their pattern to some extent. This approach has validity, provided your selections from historical and contemporary scenes are good.

The way you present these early concepts is important. Many techniques are available, ranging from hand-drawn sketches to computer imaging to sketch models. The following paragraphs give some suggestions for schematics.

DO SCHEMATICS WITH SOME, BUT NOT ALL, DETAILS

If your initial presentation shows building massing, don't indicate busy textures that will detract from the form. Concentrate on openings, shapes, and plan relationships. For example, it is good to show plumbing fixtures and cabinet outlines in the schematic plan, but don't get too fussy. Above all, remember the closets and other necessary functional items. Clients find the early-stage inclusion of the more mundane aspects of the house reassuring. It indicates to them that the architect has paid attention to their needs and will continue to do so.

REVIEW AND REVISE THE INITIAL CONCEPT

The wise architect recognizes a client's poor response. Rather than pursue an idea that clients do not like, it pays to look at different ideas. For example, you may have proposed a certain configuration that faces rooms toward a view without adequately discovering the clients' strong feelings about it. Or you may have proposed a pitched roof and find that the clients prefer a flat one. Use the initial schematic meeting to further advance your knowledge of the program. Above all, be flexible.

REFINE THE INITIAL CONCEPT

If your schematics are generally acceptable, incorporate client comments and refine the drawings to set the overall project direction. It is easier to make changes at this early stage than when working drawings are more advanced. Take time now to examine every aspect of the concept critically. Architects tend to like their initial concepts too much. Often, design flaws, or ugly elements that show up in the built project, were quite obvious in the schematic stage. Ask yourself, for example, whether there is a better way of designing wall intersections or room shapes. It's also very good practice to ask yourself whether there's any way of economizing on the design. Can complicated and expensive roof shapes be simplified without sacrificing design quality? Do the bedrooms have to have so many windows or skylights? Be disciplined and rigorous in your evaluation of the initial concept.

Once schematics are generally accepted by the clients, proceed to the preliminary stage. Some architects, and probably all lawyers, will think it a good idea to get a written approval for the schematic phase. For bigger projects, it's a very good idea. However, because house design is such an interpersonal relationship, it may be off-putting to request formal legal sign-offs at this point. A better way might be simply to bill the client at the completion of this phase, while moving seamlessly into the preliminaries.

CREATE ADVANCED PRELIMINARIES

Many people find it difficult to visualize space and form. The presentation of a series of sketches or a model, or both, will help both client and architect. Remember also to look at these materials critically as you are preparing them. If you have a model, observe it at eye level, rather than from a bird's-eye vantage point. If you are confident that your design is acceptable, it may save time to do the preliminaries on your working drawing sheets. Then, if they are acceptable, the same drawings with some elaboration can serve as contract documents.

SUGGESTIONS FOR PRELIMINARY DOCUMENTS

- Do good drawings. Drawings that are crisp, descriptive, and attractive help to sell the design. Consider adding color, through the use of pencils, pastels, or watercolors. Nothing builds confidence in a client's mind more than truly professional drawings.

- Be sure to select the best view when doing the drawings.

- Show vegetation and the surrounding context to set your design in its place.

- Avoid axonometrics. Very few clients understand them. They normally show bird's-eye views and can frequently be confusing if there are many breaks in the design. For pitched roof houses, such drawings are very misleading.

- Consider mounting the drawings on a board or pinning them to a wall. Architecture is a performing art as well as a visual one. If the clients see you care enough about introducing your ideas in a careful, dramatic presentation, they may pay closer attention to them.

- Models are very useful, but be careful about making one too early in the process. It may reveal detail that needs more design work. On the other hand, you may be quite facile at doing quick-sketch models so as to expose those unworked-out details. If so, go ahead with them, but set a time limit—for instance, one day per sketch model.

- A preliminary model can take longer. Consider sending this out to a professional, because building a model can take up a lot of your time or that of your staff.

- If you assign the construction of the preliminary model to an outside professional, you won't be able to work with the design while it is being built. However, if model making is part of your design process, it may be better to do the work in-house.

DO CONCISE WORKING DRAWINGS

After the architect has received the clients' approval, working drawings can be started. Here it is important to remember that most house builders know their craft.

They normally do not require or even welcome advice on every construction technique. Recognizing this, the architect should endeavor to set forth the design intent in the working drawings and to document everything the contractor needs to know to price out the job.

If you are doing the job on a cost-plus basis, it is not necessary to document everything at the outset; it may be more appropriate to defer the selection of some finish items until the clients have a better feel for the look and scale of the house.

Realize that the end result is your primary concern. So it is safe to assume that you are not responsible for basic construction techniques, unless a certain detail is not important enough to merit specific erection procedures. In such instances, it is a good idea to research the detail and to get the manufacturer's specific instructions. For example, earth-sheltered houses are particularly demanding. The loads are enormous and the roof is constantly wet. To make houses of this type even more formidable, otherwise qualified contractors have little or no experience with them, and their fund of practical experience will not help as much as with conventional construction.

Suggestions for Contract Documents

Here are 15 points to help you prepare working drawings.

1.	In preparing working drawings, show dimensions once. Do not repeat the same dimensions on sections, elevations, and plans. Otherwise, if changes are made during construction, the chances for mistakes are multiplied.

2.	Use as few sheets as possible. Not only is a large number of drawings costly to reproduce, such a quantity is also bulky for the contractor to handle and can cause confusion on-site.

3.	Put the specifications on the drawings. Avoid presenting a thick specification book, which frequently goes unread. Specifications on the details or typed as "stick-ons" as part of the drawing set are handier and easier to refer to.

4.	Draw dimension lines to the point being dimensioned. Do not dangle them far from the point to be clarified. That makes it difficult for the contractor to see what is called out.

5. Use a hierarchy of lines, but not too many. The cut line of the outside walls should be heaviest. Cabinet or built-in lines, or lines within walls, should be the next weight. All dimension lines should be the same weight.

6. Use short diagonal lines at dimension points, rather than arrows; they are less work and clearer. Make these heavy so they can be read even if the point is light. Run them in the same direction for both vertical and horizontal dimensions.

7. Put section markings on plans and elevations using a standard symbol.

8. Use a simple cross-reference system that calls out the sheet number and the number of the detail on it. Use this system on all plans, sections, and elevations.

9. Label extensively but concisely. Use language that is direct and simple; for example, "Install 1" x 4" trim" rather than "1" x 4" trim to be installed here."

10. Do not draw unnecessary detail on the plans and sections. Assuming they are small scale, which is usual, it is unnecessary to show interior and exterior finish lines within wall sections. The contractor learns of the finishes from the details and finish schedules.

11. Draw typical details and wall sections at a larger scale, say, 1" = 1' 0" or $1\frac{1}{2}$" = 1' 0". Key them into the plans and smaller-scale sections and elevations. Do not duplicate details by drawing a lot of wall sections that vary only slightly. Ask yourself whether it is really necessary to vary such detail in the first place.

12. If the house is small, consider showing structure on the basic plans. If the structure is large, it may be desirable to show separate framing plans. In this case, make reproducibles of the basic plans before they are noted and dimensioned; this avoids redrawing. CAD (Computer-Aided Design) is particularly useful.

13. Consider showing electrical items on the base plans. The value of this inclusion is that the relationship of electrical items to window and door openings is clearly shown. However, if you think this will make the drawings too "busy," use reproducibles of simplified plans, as with the structure.

14. If you do separate electrical, mechanical, and plumbing drawings, make sure they are clearly coordinated with the architectural drawings. Most mechanical and electrical contractors will assume you have done this.

15. Be sure to put plumbing riser diagrams, electrical load calculations, door and window schedules, and equipment lists on the drawings.

MODULES

Modules (a series of standardized units for use together) are nothing new. They have been used from classical to modern times. The module's main advantage is as a means of planning and communication. It can also enhance creativity: Witness Wright's innovative house plans in which he used various kinds of geometric modules. Wright used them to communicate exceptionally difficult plans to builders in the designs of his Usonian houses.

THE ADVANTAGES TO USING MODULES

When designing, the architect should consider the use of a module. In renovation work this is frequently impractical, but use of a module in new construction will enhance communication between all parties (architect–owner, architect–staff, architect–contractor). It will also provide an orderly framework on which to base design decisions.

There are many reasons to use modular design. The advantage of working with modules is simplification of the architect's task and ease of communication. With modular standards, an ordering of the building elements occurs. Although this ordering is not necessary, it is desirable from constructional and aesthetic viewpoints.

Interoffice Communication

If the architect creates a conceptual design in a modular fashion and has explained to staff members the principles of the kind of modular design being employed, it will not be necessary to supplement visual material with lengthy verbal or graphic dimensions. Modular design facilitates computer-aided design (CAD) as well, since computers work on a digital, modular basis.

Communicating with Clients

If you explain the modular system to clients, emphasizing that it will save them time and money, they will work with you in the use of the module. That will simplify your work and cut down on small but time-consuming requests from the clients. For instance, if you've explained the advantages, the client will not request an extra 6" in the bedroom, but rather an extra 1' 8" or 3' 4", which will be easier for you to integrate into the design. In answer to a possible question about the extra dimension costing more money, you can explain that it will take some additional material, but small incremental changes in modular dimension have a small effect on overall costs.

Communicating with the Contractor

The use of modular construction techniques indicates to the contractor that you know the elements of the building and how they go together. This, in turn, will probably result in lower bid prices. For example, if a contractor studies the drawings and sees that the architect's dimensions, rather than using the modular standards, call for trimming all vertical studs 6" from a stock length, he or she will have to assume that is your intent and figure his prices accordingly. But that may discourage the contractor, because it means that he or she is being asked to do a lot of extra and perhaps unnecessary work.

Be sure that you explain the whole modular system to the contractor. Do not assume it is evident from the drawings. If the contractor knows your planning module, he or she will have a better understanding of the way you dimensioned the drawings. If an error has crept into your drawings, a contractor who understands the system may pick it up and correct the error without bothering you. In addition to making your job easier, you will also bias the contractor to your way of thinking and enlist him or her as part of your team in achieving a smoothly flowing job and pleasing, well-constructed end result.

CREATING USABLE PLAN MODULES

A workable major module is 10', subdivided into 3' 4". Half of a 3' 4" module is 1' 8", which makes 5' 0" when combined with 3' 4". Use this module at the centerline of partitions and explain it to all parties. Most clients accept its use when you explain that it will save money in terms of greater contractor efficiency and ease of communication. Contractors like this idea because it enables them to understand how the architect arrived at the placement of walls.

Plan modules do not have to conform to the sizes of stock material panels other than being able to fit stock doors and windows and in relation to masonry that works within a 3' 4" module. (Some years ago, designers of prefabricated houses advocated a 4' module, because various wallboards and panels were made in this width. However, wallboard is now made in longer lengths, which are placed horizontally.) In addition to the basic 3' 4" module, other modules can be used.

Smaller/Larger

Smaller modules are possible. For instance, within a rectangular grid, it is possible to combine 3' 0" modules to make a 9' 0" major module. However, use of this module results in small rooms and corridors. For example, a 3' 0" center-to-center module for a corridor nets approximately 2' 8" clear by the time wall thickness is deducted from both sides. Although this space is acceptable, it is not comfortable, and disabled persons will surely find it difficult to negotiate around corners. The recommended 3' 4" module nets a clear corridor of 3' 0", which is better.

The same applies to room sizes. Rooms of 10' 0" (3 modules) or 11' 8" (3½ modules) or 13' 4" (4 modules) yield more comfortable spaces than the corresponding 9' 0", 10' 6", and 12' 0" rooms based on a 3' 0" module.

Larger modules can also be reviewed by the architect, such as 4' 0", half of which is 2' 0". This unit has both advantages and disadvantages. One advantage is that it can be used with 4' 0" building materials, such as wood paneling and wallboard. The problem with using a module to accommodate these materials without cutting is that it does not take into account wall thicknesses, which are variable. The type of finish must also be taken into account.

Polygonal/Circular

In addition to rectangles, modules come in a variety of shapes, such as circles, hexagons, diamonds, and triangles. However, these require workers with an unusual talent for geometry. Some have the requisite skill, but most will find the use of exotic modules puzzling. The architect is advised to proceed with caution in the use of such complex modules. Frank Lloyd Wright used unusual modules, but he had the contractor lay out the module on the concrete slab as a guide. He also had an apprentice on duty at the construction site, who served as an on-site supervisor and interpreter of the drawings. All of this helped, and architecture has been enriched by such brilliant spatial configurations as the Hanna house in Palo Alto, California.

VERTICAL MODULES

The key to the success of a vertical module is establishing its value and economy. Builders understand vertical modules and know how to use them.

Wood Construction

Wood structural members used in platform framing come in various stock lengths. Structural beams used to frame floors and roofs come in various thicknesses and depths and in stock lengths that generally increase in 2' 0" increments. Structural members for walls, frequently called studs, also come in stock lengths. A commonly used length is the precut stud, which is 7' 8½". Although this is an odd length, it combines with a bottom horizontal member, called a sill or sole plate, and two top horizontal members called top plates. The cross-sectional size of these plates varies with the thickness of the wall, but they are generally 2" x 4" or 2" x 6" nominal dimensions; actual dimensions are 1½" x 3½" or 1½" x 5½". When these are combined with precut studs, the resultant dimension from top to bottom is 8' 1". This dimension permits the installation of finish material on the ceiling, generally ½" to ⅝" in thickness, and an overlay on the subfloor. The key idea behind this somewhat complicated set of dimensions is that the materials can be used with 4' 0" x 8' 0" wallboard (also called Sheetrock or gypsum board) or plywood paneling of the same dimensions. Because 4' 0" wide wallboard comes in longer lengths, 12' 0" and 16' 0", the panels are laid horizontally.

Another type of framing is balloon framing. This type uses longer lengths of studs and can be more economical. Second-floor joists generally rest on a ribbon strip let into the long vertical studs.

Windows and doors must be fitted within the vertical stud system. The vertical dimension of doors is commonly 6' 8" or, occasionally, 7' 0". It is also possible to use doors 8' 0" high, but they are not commonly in stock, are expensive, and have a tendency to warp. Headers for the most commonly used size, 6' 8", are fitted to take the load of the wall above the opening to be created for doors or windows. They can be two 2" x 4"s for an opening up to 3' or two 2" x 8"s for an opening up to 5'. Headers for large openings should be sized by an engineer or by the architect, using commonly accepted load tables or actual calculations for very large openings.

The height of the opening to accommodate a 6' 8" door will be 6' 10½" above the rough floor. This allows for the top piece of the door frame, which is between ⅝" and 1", depending on what has been specified or what has been used from a stock door or window company, plus the thickness of the finish floor. The floor-to-floor, or floor-to-roof, construction height is therefore established as a module, as are the uniform heights of the door and window openings.

Masonry Construction

Selecting and combining masonry units as modules means economical, fast construction. It is not efficient to call for cutting a row of brick around the entire perimeter of a building; there is rarely a good reason to do so.

The same general principle applies to masonry construction as applies to wood construction. Masonry units are generally multiples of 8" from center to center of the joints. This means that a vertical measurement of 2' 0" will accommodate three rows (courses) of nominally designated 8" masonry units.

There are many sizes of masonry units. Common brick, for instance, has a vertical dimension that fits three rows (courses) within one vertical row of 8" masonry units. Other sizes of brick fit vertically and horizontally in different ways according to their dimensions.

Masonry or brick can also be combined with wood structural frames; this is known as masonry veneer or brick veneer. The combination of the two types of construction requires coordination and may entail some compromise. For instance, ten courses of masonry units that are 8" high equal 80" in height, or 6' 8". This height can be coordinated with a backup wood veneer wall through the use of separate or combined lintels, or headers. Modular coordination of this sort has been well documented by the construction industry.

EXCEPTIONS TO THE MODULAR SYSTEM

Cabinets and many built-ins do not fit within the recommended 3' 4" basic module. Vanity cabinets, for instance, are 1' 10" to 2' 0" in depth. Clothes closets are convenient if they have 2' 0" clear hanging space behind the doors. You can make them deeper (front to back), but you will then be wasting space that might be better employed in the room. You can also make closets shallower, but many heavy garments and hangers will not fit properly.

Kitchen cabinets are also of different dimensions, because most appliances are stock sizes and designed to fit within a 2' 0"-deep base cabinet. Anything shallower will not take stock appliances, and anything deeper will waste space. However, a client may have good reasons for wanting a deeper counter, for example, to accommodate countertop kitchen machines or to have space to roll out dough.

In general, storage and work counters may not fit within the module recommended, but there are other modules within which they will fit. It is up to the architect to select the combination that best fits his or her working method and the client's needs.

METRIC MODULES

It should be noted that a 3' 4", the standard module dimension, is quite close to a meter, which is about 3' 3⅝" (3.28 m). Because many U.S. architects are working overseas and because practically the entire rest of the world uses the metric system, it may be useful for the architect to use an inch/foot module that is close to metric measure.

MODELS

The construction of a model at an advanced design stage can be of use to both the architect and the client, as well as to the contractor during construction. The model should be made of some material that can be easily changed so design modifications can be made during the working drawing phase, if necessary.

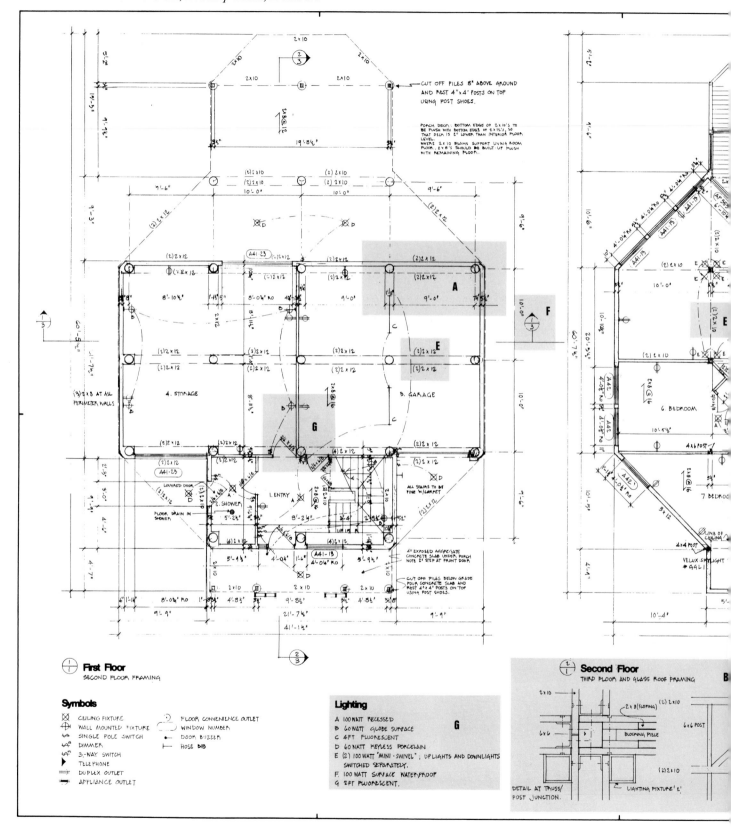

First Floor
SECOND FLOOR FRAMING

Symbols

- ⊠ CEILING FIXTURE
- ⊕ WALL MOUNTED FIXTURE
- S SINGLE POLE SWITCH
- S^D DIMMER
- S^3 3-WAY SWITCH
- ▶ TELEPHONE
- ⊟ DUPLEX OUTLET
- ⊟ APPLIANCE OUTLET
- ⊙ FLOOR CONVENIENCE OUTLET
- ② WINDOW NUMBER
- ● DOOR BUZZER
- ⊢ HOSE BIB

Lighting

- A 100 WATT RECESSED
- B 60 WATT GLOBE SURFACE
- C 4FT FLUORESCENT
- D 60 WATT KEYLESS PORCELAIN
- E (2) 100 WATT "MINI-SWIVEL"; UPLIGHTS AND DOWNLIGHTS SWITCHED SEPARATELY.
- F 100 WATT SURFACE WATERPROOF
- G 2FT FLUORESCENT.

Second Floor
THIRD FLOOR AND GLASS ROOF FRAMING

DETAIL AT TRUSS/
POST JUNCTION.

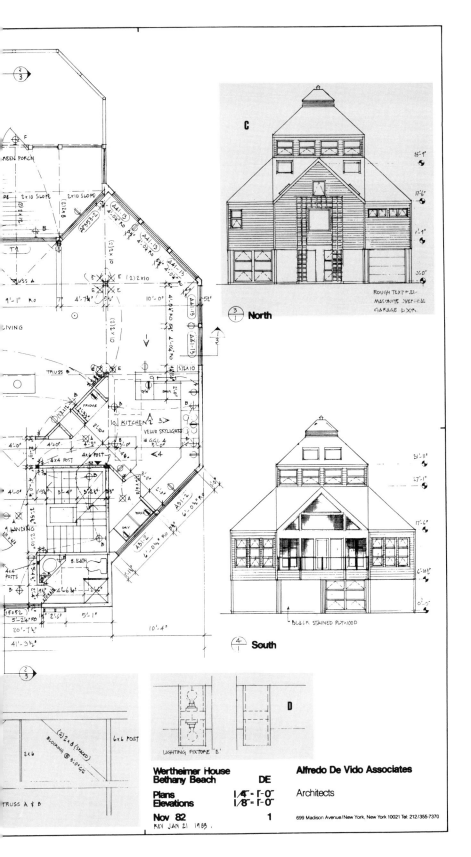

North

ROUGH TEXTURE EL.
MASONITE VERTICAL
GARAGE DOOR

South

BLACK STAINED PLYWOOD

LIGHTING FIXTURE 'E'

Wertheimer House
Bethany Beach   **DE**

Plans   1/4" = 1'-0"
Elevations   1/8" = 1'-0"

Nov 82   1
REV JAN 21 1983

Alfredo De Vido Associates

Architects

699 Madison Avenue/New York, New York 10021 Tel: 212/355-7370

This is a two-and-a-half-story wood house built in a floodplain near the ocean in accordance with federal and local regulations, which require placement of living areas above mean high water, on piers, with "knockout" construction below.

1. Plans/Elevations/Symbols/Lighting/ Structure

A. *Pilings as required are shown in location, but piles are not guaranteed to within close tolerances. To assure an orderly structure above, the piles are generously boxed in on the first floor (the knock-out floor) and the entire area is enclosed for use as a garage and recreation room.*

B. *Special structural details are shown.*

C. *Elevations for this house are shown at a smaller scale ($^1/_8$") than the plans ($^1/_4$"), because they are simple and show the basics required to build the house.*

D. *A special lighting detail is shown.*

E. *The structure for the second floor above is shown on the first floor, as the structure for the third floor is shown on the second floor.*

F. *Sections are indicated.*

G. *Wiring diagrams and fixture types are indicated, and references to the lighting schedule are on the same sheet.*

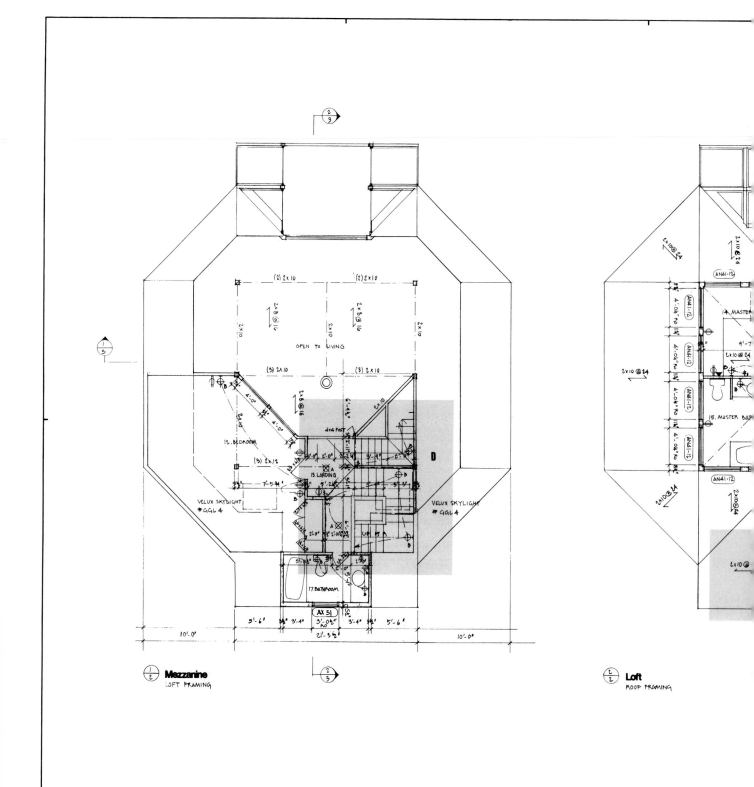

(2) 2x10   (2) 2x10

2x8 @16   2x8 @16

OPEN TO LIVING

(3) 2x10   (3) 2x10

2x10

2x8 @16

4x4 POST

12. BEDROOM

(3) 2x12

13 LANDING

7'-5¾"

VELUX SKYLIGHT   VELUX SKYLIGHT
GGL 4   # GGL 4

UP 15 R

17 BATHROOM

AX 31

5'-6"   3'-4"   3'-4"   5'-6"

10'-0"   21'-3½"   10'-0"

Mezzanine
LOFT FRAMING

2x10 @ 24   2x10 @ 24

AN41-12

AN41-12   4'-0" RO

14 MASTER

AN41-12   4'-0" RO   9'-7

2x10 @ 24   AN41-12   2x10 @ 24
             4'-0" RO

15. MASTER BA

AN41-12   4'-0" RO

2x10 @ 24   AN41-12   2x10 @ 24

2x10 @

Loft
ROOF FRAMING

2. Plans/Finish Schedule/Elevations

A. *Mezzanine and loft levels are shown at $1/4$" scale. Elevations, as on Sheet 1, are at $1/8$" scale.*

B. *A finish schedule is shown.*

C. *Roof pitches are shown.*

D. *Stairs in this split-level house are shown with the numbers of risers indicated. The stair arrows are shown in a consistent direction (up).*

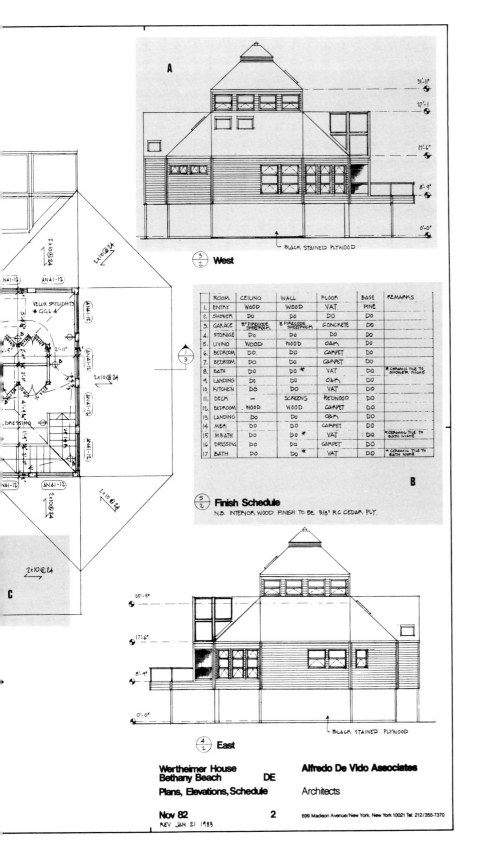

A

31'-11"
27'-1
17'-6"
8'-9"
0'-0"

└ BLACK STAINED PLYWOOD

(3/2) **West**

	ROOM	CEILING	WALL	FLOOR	BASE	REMARKS
1.	ENTRY	WOOD	WOOD	V.A.T.	PINE	
2.	SHOWER	DO	DO	DO	DO	
3.	GARAGE	⅝" FIRECODE SHEETROCK	⅝ FIRECODE SHEETROCK	CONCRETE	DO	
4.	STORAGE	DO	DO	DO	DO	
5.	LIVING	WOOD	WOOD	OAK	DO	
6.	BEDROOM	DO.	DO	CARPET	DO	
7.	BEDROOM	DO	DO	CARPET	DO	
8.	BATH	DO	DO *	V.A.T.	DO	* CERAMIC TILE TO SHOWER NICHE
9.	LANDING	DO	DO	OAK	DO	
10.	KITCHEN	DO	DO	V.A.T.	DO	
11.	DECK	—	SCREENS	REDWOOD	DO	
12.	BEDROOM	WOOD	WOOD	CARPET	DO	
13.	LANDING	DO	DO	OAK	DO	
14	M.B.R.	DO	DO	CARPET	DO	
15	M.BATH	DO	DO *	V.A.T.	DO	* CERAMIC TILE TO BATH NICHE
16	DRESSING	DO	DO	CARPET	DO	
17	BATH	DO	DO *	V.A.T.	DO	* CERAMIC TILE TO BATH NICHE

B

(5/2) **Finish Schedule**
N.B. INTERIOR WOOD FINISH TO BE 3/8" R.C. CEDAR PLY.

C

25'-9"
17'-6"
8'-9"
0'-0"

└ BLACK STAINED PLYWOOD

(4/2) **East**

Wertheimer House
Bethany Beach **DE**

Plans, Elevations, Schedule

Nov 82 2
REV JAN 21 1983

Alfredo De Vido Associates

Architects

699 Madison Avenue/New York, New York 10021 Tel: 212/355-7370

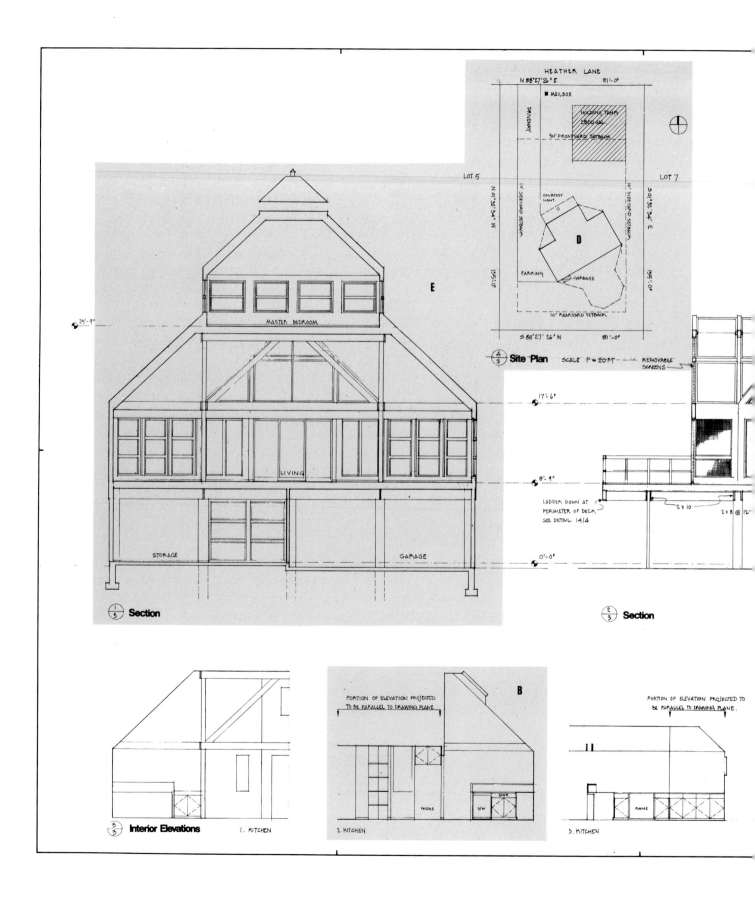

HEATHER LANE

N 88°27'26" E 81'-0"

■ MAILBOX

HOLDING TANK
2800 GAL.

30' FRONTYARD SETBACK

LOT 5   LOT 7

COURTESY LIGHT

D

PARKING   GARAGE

10' REARYARD SETBACK

S 88°27'26" W 81'-0"

⊕4/3 **Site Plan**   SCALE 1" = 20 FT ---- REMOVABLE SCREENS

E

MASTER BEDROOM

25'-9"

17'-6"

LIVING

8'-9"

LADDER DOWN AT
PERIMETER OF DECK
SEE DETAIL 14/4

2 x 10   2 x 8 @ 12"

STORAGE   GARAGE

0'-0"

⊕1/3 **Section**   ⊕2/3 **Section**

PORTION OF ELEVATION PROJECTED
TO BE PARALLEL TO DRAWING PLANE

B

PORTION OF ELEVATION PROJECTED TO
BE PARALLEL TO DRAWING PLANE.

FRIDGE   SINK

D/W   RANGE

⊕3/3 **Interior Elevations**   1. KITCHEN   2. KITCHEN   3. KITCHEN

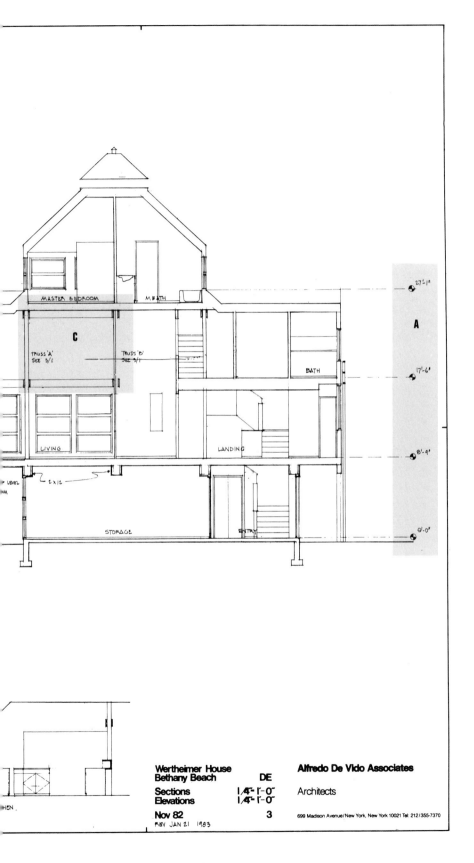

3. Sections/Interior Elevations/Site Plan

A. *Levels are shown with datum.*

B. *Interior elevations are shown where there are cabinets and special conditions, such as the relationship of skylights and roof trusses to the exterior roof.*

C. *The exposed structure is shown at the proper level.*

D. *The site plan indicates the setbacks and area for a septic field as required by code.*

E. *Sections are cut through the building at the most revealing spots to explain the levels and structure.*

MASTER BEDROOM   M BATH

C

TRUSS 'A'   TRUSS 'B'
SEE 3/1   SEE 3/1

BATH

27'-1"

A

17'-6"

LIVING

LANDING

8'-9"

LEVEL

2 x 12

STORAGE   ENTRY

0'-0"

KITCHEN

Wertheimer House
Bethany Beach   **DE**

Sections   1/4"= 1'-0"
Elevations   1/4"= 1'-0"

Nov 82
REV JAN 21 1983   **3**

Alfredo De Vido Associates

Architects

699 Madison Avenue/New York, New York 10021 Tel: 212/355-7370

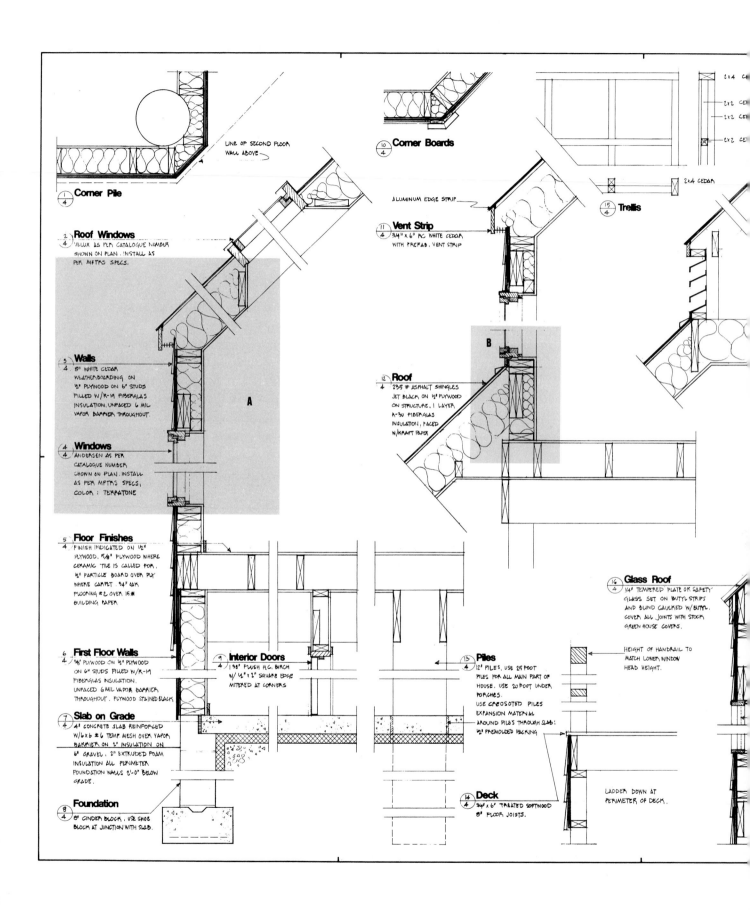

① Corner Pile
4

LINE OF SECOND FLOOR
WALL ABOVE

② Roof Windows
4 VELUX AS PER CATALOGUE NUMBER SHOWN ON PLAN. INSTALL AS PER MFTRS SPECS.

③ Walls
4 8" WHITE CEDAR WEATHERBOARDING ON ½" PLYWOOD ON 6" STUDS FILLED W/R-19 FIBERGLAS INSULATION. UNFACED 6 MIL VAPOR BARRIER THROUGHOUT.

A

④ Windows
4 ANDERSEN AS PER CATALOGUE NUMBER SHOWN ON PLAN. INSTALL AS PER MFTRS SPECS. COLOR: TERRATONE

⑤ Floor Finishes
4 FINISH INDICATED ON ½" PLYWOOD. 5/8" PLYWOOD WHERE CERAMIC TILE IS CALLED FOR, ½" PARTICLE BOARD OVER PLY WHERE CARPET. ¾" OAK FLOORING #2 OVER 15# BUILDING PAPER

⑥ First Floor Walls
4 ⅜" PLYWOOD ON ½" PLYWOOD ON 6" STUDS FILLED W/R-19 FIBERGLAS INSULATION. UNFACED 6 MIL VAPOR BARRIER THROUGHOUT. PLYWOOD STAINED BLACK.

⑦ Slab on Grade
4 4" CONCRETE SLAB REINFORCED W/6x6 #6 TEMP. MESH OVER VAPOR BARRIER ON 2" INSULATION ON 6" GRAVEL. 2" EXTRUDED FOAM INSULATION ALL PERIMETER FOUNDATION WALLS 2'-0" BELOW GRADE.

⑧ Foundation
4 8" CINDER BLOCK. USE SHOE BLOCK AT JUNCTION WITH SLAB.

⑨ Interior Doors
4 1'-3/8" FLUSH H.C. BIRCH W/ ½" x 2" SQUARE EDGE MITERED AT CORNERS

⑩ Corner Boards
4

ALUMINUM EDGE STRIP

⑪ Vent Strip
4 ¾" x 6" P.C. WHITE CEDAR WITH PREFAB. VENT STRIP

B

⑫ Roof
4 235 # ASPHALT SHINGLES JET BLACK ON ½" PLYWOOD ON STRUCTURE. 1 LAYER R-30 FIBERGLAS INSULATION, FACED W/KRAFT PAPER

⑬ Piles
4 12" PILES. USE 25 FOOT PILES FOR ALL MAIN PART OF HOUSE. USE 20 FOOT UNDER PORCHES. USE CREOSOTED PILES EXPANSION MATERIAL AROUND PILES THROUGH SLAB: ½" PREMOLDED PACKING

⑭ Deck
4 ¾" x 6" TREATED SOFTWOOD 8" FLOOR JOISTS.

2x4 CE
2x2 CE
2x2 CE
2x2 CE

2x4 CEDAR

⑮ Trellis
4

⑯ Glass Roof
4 ¼" TEMPERED PLATE OR SAFETY GLASS SET ON BUTYL STRIPS AND BLIND CAULKED W/BUTYL. COVER ALL JOINTS WITH STOCK GREEN HOUSE COVERS.

HEIGHT OF HANDRAIL TO MATCH LOWER WINDOW HEAD HEIGHT.

LADDER DOWN AT PERIMETER OF DECK.

4. Details/Outlined Specifications

A. *Typical wall sections are shown at $1\frac{1}{2}$" = 1'0" scale. Special details are included at the same large scale.*

B. *On typical sections, materials are indicated by hatching or stippling. The structure is shown to the builder's standards. Paragraph quotations are made directly next to the wall sections and call out "typical" walls, floor construction, slabs, roofs, and foundations.*

C. *Specifications are given in an outline format, citing quality standards and specific products by manufacturer and type.*

D. *Allowances for certain items, such as kitchen cabinets, carpet, and tile, are noted in dollar amounts. These are realistic estimates that will set the quality standard.*

E. *The time allowed for construction is noted in the outlined specifications. Although damages, in the event that the goal is not met, are not spelled out, a reasonable time limit on construction is set, which is understood by all concerned.*

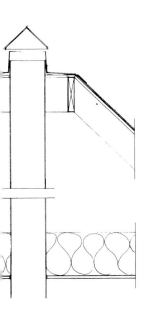

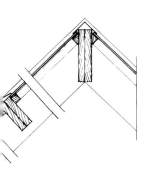

SPECIFICATIONS:

1. GENERAL REQUIREMENTS: Plans and specifications are cooperative. All labor and materials required to fully carry out the intentions of the plans and specifications are part of this contract, whether or not specifically documented. The contractor shall provide each item mentioned, indicated or implied to achieve the intended building according to the methods of best construction practice. In no event is any article, operation, method or material to fall below the standards set by FHA Min Property Standards for One and Two Living Units, latest edition, and all amendments to date. The contractor will comply with all State and local codes even in the event of conflicting requirements in the plans and specifications at no additional cost to the Owner. All equipment and materials to be installed according to manufacturers' recommendations and are to be new. The architect shall be the final judge of the quality of the workmanship, and reserves the right to reject any work he considers inferior.

2. SITEWORK: Pilings per drawings. Excavate as required for foundations, holding tank, electrical and mechanical work. Backfill well compacted. Comply with Town regulations.

3. CONCRETE: Minimum strength 2000 psi. Mesh reinforcing all footings and slabs 6" x 6" x 10/10 wire mesh lapped 6". Approved hardener, steel trowel finish. (Hardener - Sonneborn or equal.)

4. METALS: Aluminum all flashing, all anchor bolts, framing anchors and hangers galvanized. Zinc chromate primer all other steel.

5. CARPENTRY AND MILLWORK:
   A. FRAMING: Hamlock fir, construction grade, 1200 psi. Bridging blocking maximum 10' o.c. all floors and roof. 2' x 6" studs all exterior walls, except as indicated, block horizontally 8' o.c., where otherwise unbraced. STANDING FRAMING WESTERN SPRUCE 900 P.S.I.
   B. PLYWOOD: All exterior grade, 1/2" walls and roofs.
   C. ROOF AND DECKING: Asphalt shingles, jet black, 235#.
   D. BUILDING PAPER: #15 asphalt-impregnated felt, horizontally applied in long lengths. Lapped 6" all directions, extra strip 6" wide all door and window jambs.
   E. SIDING: 8" white cedar Weatherboarding. Corner boards per details.
   F. MILLWORK: Fabricate and install cabinets in Kitchen and Baths. Built-in shelving and closets per drawings.
   G. INTERIOR FINISH: Walls 3/8" rough cedar plywood. Cover joints with lattice.

6. MOISTURE PROTECTION:
   A. DAMPPROOFING: One (1) layer 4 mil polyethelene under all slabs on grade. All joints lapped 6", sealed and taped. Mopped waterproofing entire perimeter foundation. Perimeter rigid foam insulation.
   B. INSULATION: Fiberglass, R-19 unfaced all exterior walls. R-30 in roof, Kraft faced, 6 mil vapor barrier all exterior walls.
   C. SEALANTS: Silicone type, clear. Where opening more then 3/8" deep, pack with Neoprene joint filler to 3/8" of surface.

7. DOORS, WINDOWS AND GLASS:
   A. DOORS: Exterior doors, Pease, per catalog numbers. Interior doors and closet doors 1-3/8" hollow core luan. Screen doors - screening gray plastic.
   B. WINDOWS AND GLASS: All Anderson, catalog number per drawings. Insulating glass. Provide w/screens. Safety glass where required.
   C. WEATHERSTRIPPING: All windows and doors not factory stripped, Accurate or approved equal, top, sides and sills.
   D. HARDWARE: Furnish and install Schlage Plymouth hardware, brushed chrome, coated hinges.
   E. SCREENS: Provide for all operating sash.
   F. SKYLIGHTS: Velux installed per manufacturers' directions.
   G. CERAMIC TILE: Per Handbook for Ceramic Tile Installation, latest edition.

8. FINISHES:
   A. PAINTING: All Pratt & Lambert, Samuel Cabot, Minwax or approved equal. Interior doors: 1 coat stain, 1 coat polyurethane. Exterior doors: 2 coats oil base. Sheetrock: 2 coats latex flat. Interior wood finish on walls: unfinished. Trim and base: stain plus 1 coat poly. Exterior cedar is unfinished.

9. EQUIPMENT: Install kitchen and laundry equip. furnished by Owner, providing all necessary ducts, plumbing and wiring.

10. SPECIALTIES: Two (2) 24" towel bars, coap dishes, medicine cabinets, shower rods, paper holders to be furnished and installed.

15. A. HEATING, A.C.: Electric resistance baseboard throughout.
    B. PLUMBING: Furnish and install (American Standard)
       Two (2) Bildor recess bath 2267.375 w/1101.203 fittings.
       Three (3) Aqualyn 0476.028 lavatory w/Moen single lever faucet.
       Three (3) Cadet w.c. 2120.133
       One (1) Stainless sink Elkay (ILR-5422-DD) double w/Moen single lever.
       Two (2) Fiat shower receptacles with A/S 1204.320 fittings.
       All fixtures white.

16. ELECTRICAL:
    A. SCOPE: Adequate service for layout and complete wiring job. Conform to Local and State regulations and National Electric Code. Buried electric service.
    B. DISTRIBUTION: Circuit breaker type, Square D or approved equal. All labeled. 2 extra single-pole circuits, 6 extra double-pole circuits Meter concealed. Location approved by architect. Copper wire, plastic coated. Hook up water system and electric.
    C. FIXTURES: Install fixtures furnished by Owner. Switch plates 36" above floor.
    D. DEVICES: Pass & Seymour or equal. Murray panel. Leviton devices, silent.

TIME ALLOWED FOR CONSTRUCTION : SIX MONTHS.
ALLOWANCES :
1. KITCHEN CABINETS VANITIES AND TOPS $ 4000
2. REVERSIBLE TYPE PADDLE FAN $ 400
3. FIREPLACE, CHIMNEY AND HEARTH $ 1250
4. CARPET AND VAT TILE $ 3000

17/4 Screens
BUILD REMOVABLE SCREENS PER LOCAL BETHANY BEACH STANDARDS. LOCATE HORIZONTAL MEMBER AS SHOWN ON ELEVATIONS.

Wertheimer House
Bethany Beach   DE
Details 1 1/2"= 1'-0"   Specs

Alfredo De Vido Associates

Architects

Dec 82   4
REV JAN 21 1983

699 Madison Avenue/New York, New York 10021 Tel: 212/355-7370

WORKING DRAWINGS FOR A LARGE HOUSE

DUPERRAULT HOUSE, *Princeton, New Jersey*

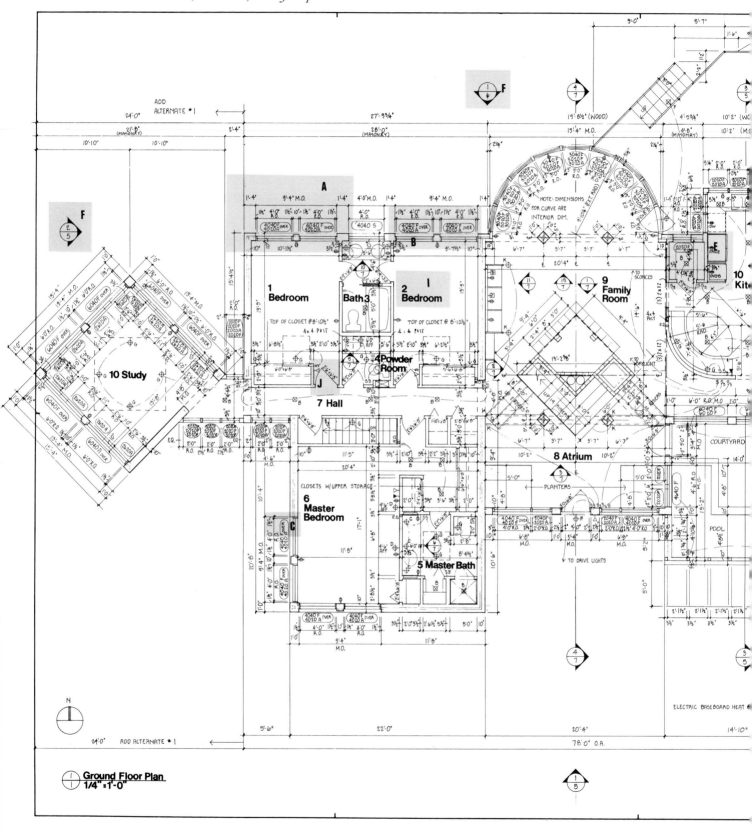

1 Bedroom

2 Bedroom

3 Bath

4 Powder Room

5 Master Bath

6 Master Bedroom

7 Hall

8 Atrium

9 Family Room

10 Study

10 Kit

Ground Floor Plan
1/4" = 1'-0"

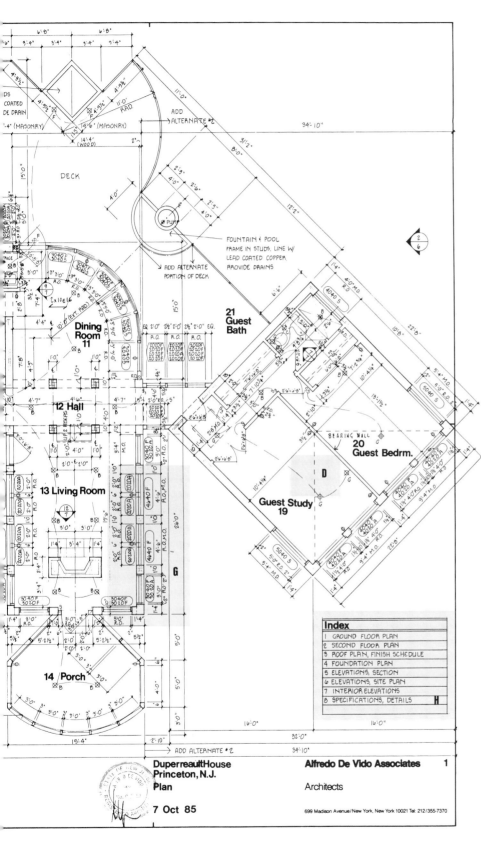

A one-story mostly masonry (concrete ground-face block and accent color glazed block) plus polychromed wood building with curved and clerestory volumes.

1. Ground Floor Plan

A. *Masonry openings are dimensioned for windows and other openings. Walls in between are dimensioned in multiples of the concrete masonry unit.*

B. *Window and door catalog numbers are called for on the drawings in targets.*

C. *Blocked-in areas around masonry openings are dimensioned.*

D. *Electrical work is shown, including fixture types.*

E. *Cabinets and appliance locations are shown and keyed to other drawings.*

F. *All sections and elevations on later sheets are shown with standard symbols, keyed in later sheets.*

G. *Dimensions are shown for smaller units close to the wall, progressing to overall dimensions further out.*

H. *An index of drawings is included.*

I. *Rooms are clearly identified to provide a basis for location of specifics during telephone conversations between architect and contractor.*

J. *Door sizes and swings are shown directly on the plan.*

Index

1	GROUND FLOOR PLAN
2	SECOND FLOOR PLAN
3	ROOF PLAN, FINISH SCHEDULE
4	FOUNDATION PLAN
5	ELEVATIONS, SECTION
6	ELEVATIONS, SITE PLAN
7	INTERIOR ELEVATIONS
8	SPECIFICATIONS, DETAILS

DuperreaultHouse
Princeton, N.J.
Plan
7 Oct 85

Alfredo De Vido Associates
Architects
699 Madison Avenue/New York, New York 10021 Tel: 212/355-7370

1

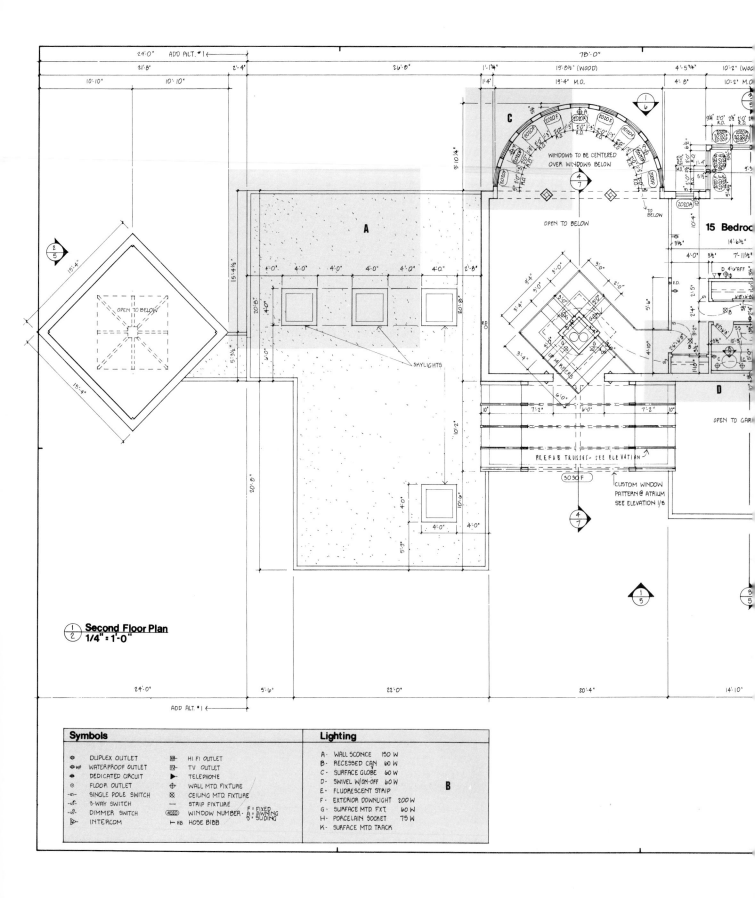

Second Floor Plan
1/4" = 1'-0"

15 Bedroom

OPEN TO BELOW

WINDOWS TO BE CENTERED
OVER WINDOWS BELOW

SKYLIGHTS

PREFAB TRUSSES - SEE ELEVATION

CUSTOM WINDOW
PATTERN @ ATRIUM
SEE ELEVATION 1/8

OPEN TO GARAGE

A

D

OPEN TO BELOW

Symbols		Lighting
⊕ DUPLEX OUTLET	⊞ HI FI OUTLET	A - WALL SCONCE 150 W
⊕wp WATERPROOF OUTLET	⊞ TV OUTLET	B - RECESSED CAN 60 W
⊖ DEDICATED CIRCUIT	▶ TELEPHONE	C - SURFACE GLOBE 60 W
⊙ FLOOR OUTLET	⊕ WALL MTD. FIXTURE	D - SWIVEL W/ON-OFF 60 W
—σ— SINGLE POLE SWITCH	⊗ CEILING MTD. FIXTURE	E - FLUORESCENT STRIP
—σ³— 3-WAY SWITCH	--- STRIP FIXTURE	F - EXTERIOR DOWNLIGHT 200 W
—σᴰ— DIMMER SWITCH	⟨4020⟩ WINDOW NUMBER	G - SURFACE MTD. FXT. 60 W
▷ INTERCOM	⊢ HB HOSE BIBB	H - PORCELAIN SOCKET 75 W
	F = FIXED A = AWNING S = SLIDING	K - SURFACE MTD. TRACK

B

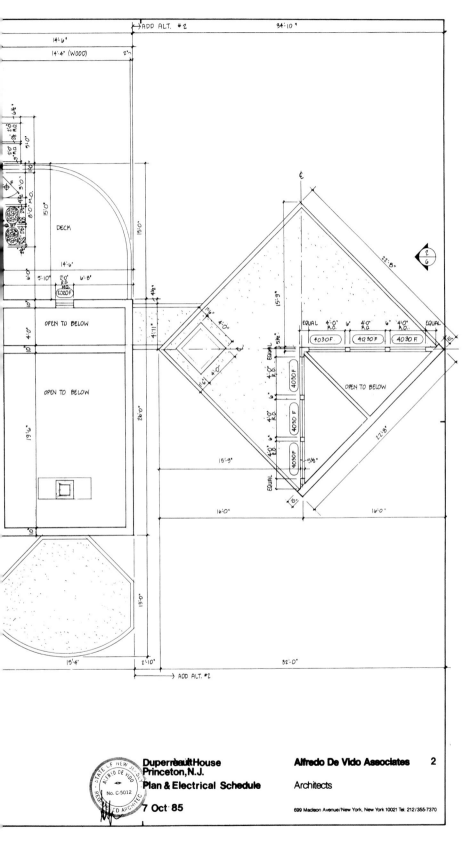

2. Second Floor Plan

A. *Outline of roof plan below area of section is shown, with the location of skylights and clerestories indicated.*

B. *A symbols list and lighting schedule are shown on this drawing, keyed to the standard symbols used on the drawings.*

C. *Dimensions are detailed for areas in which windows and clerestories are shown.*

D. *Line weights are heavier for walls that are sectioned. Roof edges and portions of the house that are not sectioned are shown lightly.*

E. *Dimension terminations are marked in the same way (with a short, dark "tick") and heavily indicated to show clearly where the dimensions end.*

DECK

OPEN TO BELOW

OPEN TO BELOW

OPEN TO BELOW

Duperreault House
Princeton, N.J.
Plan & Electrical Schedule
7 Oct 85

Alfredo De Vido Associates   2

Architects

699 Madison Avenue/New York, New York 10021 Tel: 212/355-7370

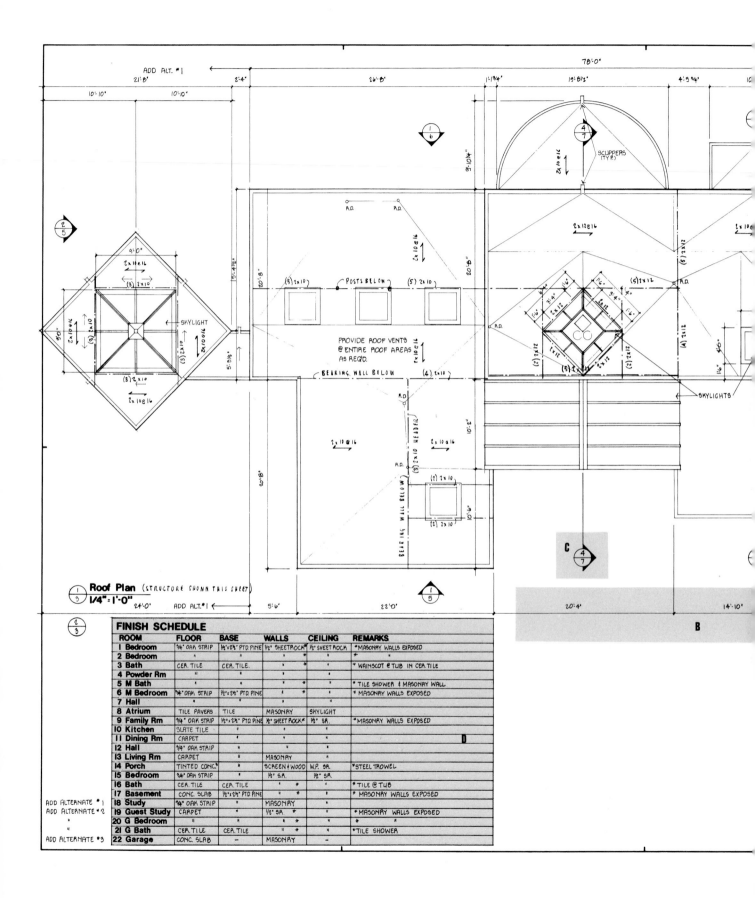

Roof Plan (STRUCTURE SHOWN THIS SHEET)
1/4" = 1'-0"

FINISH SCHEDULE					
ROOM	**FLOOR**	**BASE**	**WALLS**	**CEILING**	**REMARKS**
1 Bedroom	3/4" OAK STRIP	1/2"x2 1/2" PTD PINE	1/2" SHEETROCK	1/2" SHEET ROCK	*MASONRY WALLS EXPOSED
2 Bedroom	"	"	"	"	*
3 Bath	CER. TILE	CER. TILE.	"	* "	* WAINSCOT @ TUB IN CER. TILE
4 Powder Rm	"	"	"	"	
5 M Bath	"	"	"	* "	* TILE SHOWER & MASONRY WALL
6 M Bedroom	3/4" OAK STRIP	1/2"x2 1/2" PTD PINE	"	* "	* MASONRY WALLS EXPOSED
7 Hall	"	"	"	"	
8 Atrium	TILE PAVERS	TILE	MASONRY	SKYLIGHT	
9 Family Rm	3/4" OAK STRIP	1/2"x2 1/2" PTD PINE	1/2" SHEET ROCK	1/2" SR.	*MASONRY WALLS EXPOSED
10 Kitchen	SLATE TILE	"	"	"	
11 Dining Rm	CARPET	"	"	"	
12 Hall	3/4" OAK STRIP	"	"	"	
13 Living Rm	CARPET	"	MASONRY	"	
14 Porch	TINTED CONC.	"	SCREEN & WOOD	W.P. SR.	*STEEL TROWEL
15 Bedroom	3/4" OAK STRIP	"	1/2" SR.	1/2" SR.	
16 Bath	CER. TILE	CER. TILE	"	"	* TILE @ TUB
17 Basement	CONC. SLAB	1/2"x2 1/2" PTD PINE	"	* "	* MASONRY WALLS EXPOSED
18 Study	3/4" OAK STRIP	"	MASONRY	"	
19 Guest Study	CARPET	"	1/2" SR. *	"	*MASONRY WALLS EXPOSED
20 G Bedroom	"	"	"	* "	*
21 G Bath	CER. TILE	CER. TILE	"	"	*TILE SHOWER
22 Garage	CONC. SLAB	—	MASONRY	—	

ADD ALTERNATE #1
ADD ALTERNATE #2
"
"
ADD ALTERNATE #3

3. Roof Plan and Finish Schedule

A. *Slopes of roof drains and scuppers are indicated.*

B. *Overall dimensions coordinate with dimensions on lower level plans.*

C. *Sections are indicated as shown on lower levels.*

D. *The finish schedule is shown on this plan because there is room for it. It could be shown on other plans as well.*

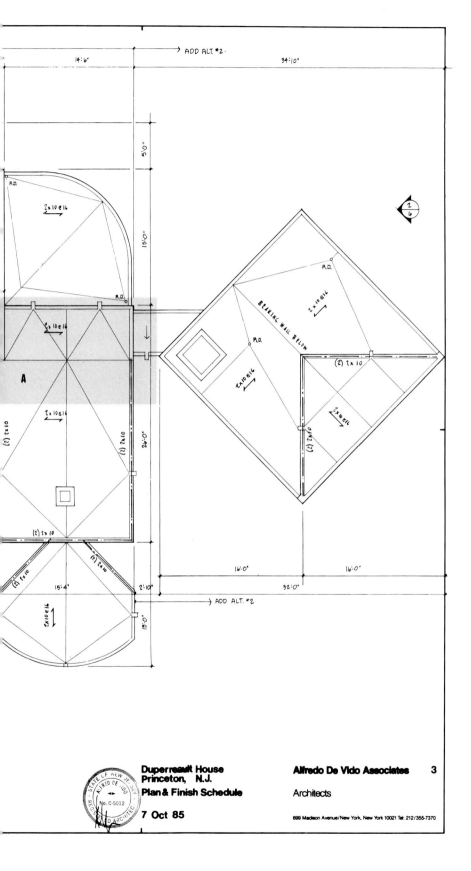

Duperreault House
Princeton, N.J.
Plan & Finish Schedule
7 Oct 85

Alfredo De Vido Associates   3

Architects

699 Madison Avenue/New York, New York 10021 Tel: 212/355-7370

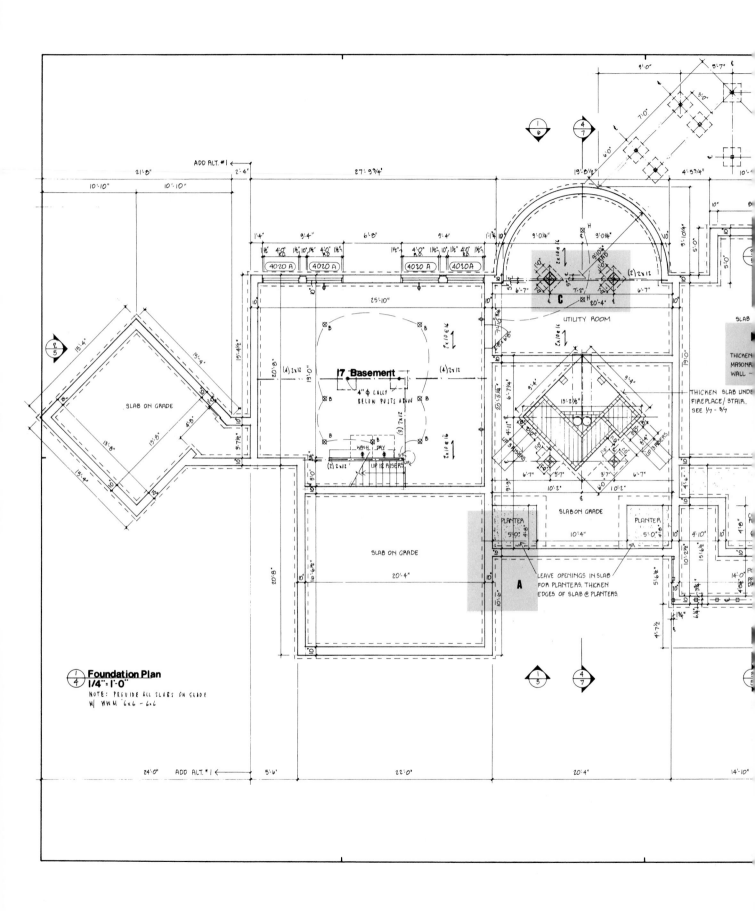

Foundation Plan
1/4" = 1'-0"

NOTE: PROVIDE ALL SLABS ON GRADE
W/ W.W.M. 6x6 - 6x6

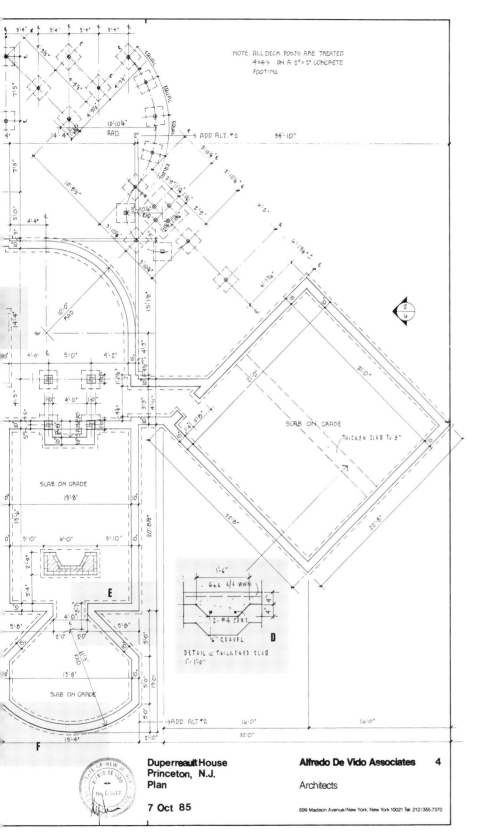

NOTE: ALL DECK POSTS ARE TREATED
4x4's ON A 2°x 2° CONCRETE
FOOTING

ADD ALT.#2   34'-10"

SLAB ON GRADE

THICKEN SLAB TO 9"

SLAB ON GRADE
13'-8"

SLAB ON GRADE
13'-8"

1'-6"
6x6 6/6 WWM
4"
2-#4 CONT.
6" GRAVEL   D

DETAIL @ THICKENED SLAB
1"=1'-0"

SLAB ON GRADE

ADD ALT.#2   16'-0"   16'-0"

2'-10"   32'-0"

E

F

Duperreault House
Princeton, N.J.
Plan

7 Oct 85

Alfredo De Vido Associates   **4**

Architects

699 Madison Avenue/New York, New York 10021 Tel: 212/355-7370

4. Foundation Plan

A. *Thicknesses of the foundation wall are shown, with footings outlined below and sizes of footings called out.*

B. *Thicknesses and reinforcing patterns are shown on the plans.*

C. *Centerline dimensions are shown to foundation piers so they will line up with posts in the structure above.*

D. *Any special foundation details are shown on this sheet. Footing and foundation details are otherwise shown on Details/Specifications Sheet 8.*

E. *Time-consuming hatching of foundation walls is not done. The heavier outline is sufficient to indicate the location of the wall.*

F. *Dimensional coordination of the foundation walls with upper floors is important on this sheet, inasmuch as the mason is a separate subcontractor and will not check or coordinate upper floor dimensions.*

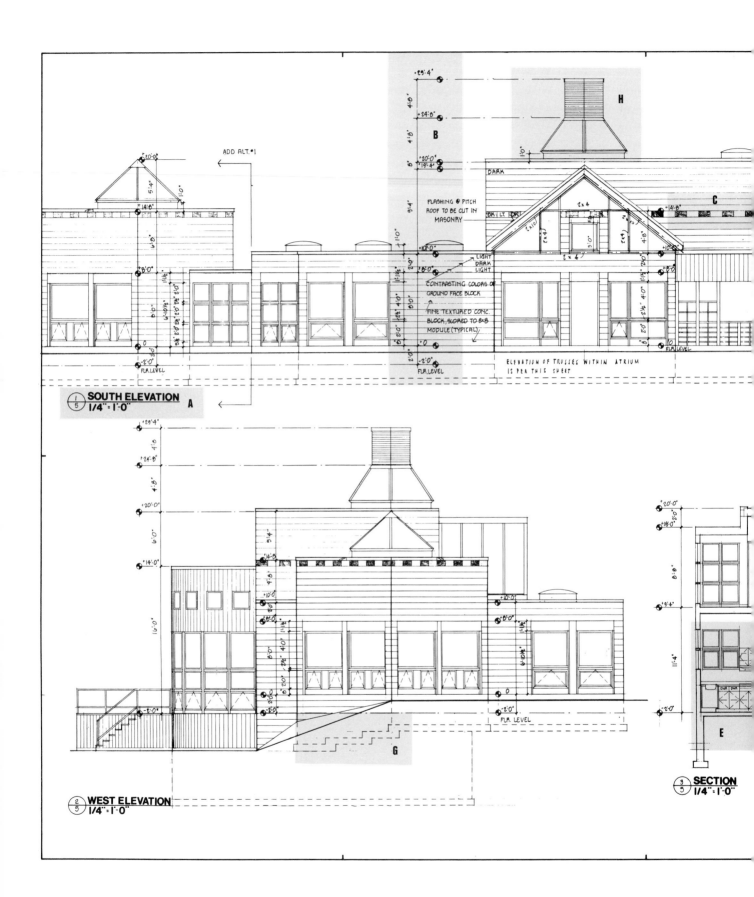

ADD ALT.#1

+29'-4"
+24'-0"
B
+20'-0" +19'-0"

DARK

FLASHING @ PITCH
ROOF TO BE CUT IN
MASONRY

DK | LT. | DK

2x4

H

C

LIGHT
DARK
LIGHT

CONTRASTING COLORS OF
GROUND FACE BLOCK

FINE TEXTURED CONC.
BLOCK, SCORED TO 8x8
MODULE (TYPICAL)

ELEVATION OF TRUSSES WITHIN ATRIUM
IS PER THIS SHEET

①/⑤ **SOUTH ELEVATION** A
1/4"= 1'-0"

②/⑤ **WEST ELEVATION**
1/4"= 1'-0"

G

③/⑤ **SECTION**
1/4"= 1'-0"

E

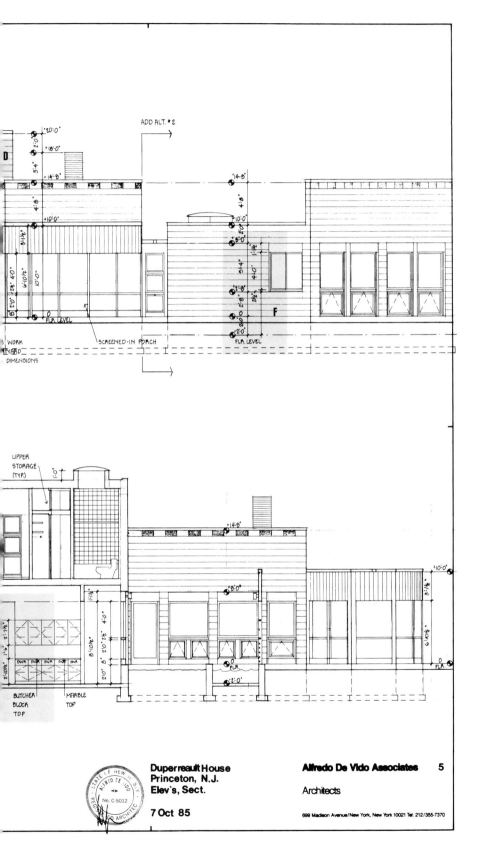

ADD ALT. #2

SCREENED-IN PORCH

FLR. LEVEL

WORK
YARD
DIMENSIONS

F

UPPER
STORAGE
(TYP.)

+14'-8"

BUTCHER
BLOCK
TOP

MARBLE
TOP

Duperreault House
Princeton, N.J.
Elev's, Sect.

7 Oct 85

Alfredo De Vido Associates   **5**

Architects

699 Madison Avenue/New York, New York 10021 Tel: 212/355-7370

5. Elevations/Sections

A. *The elevations and sections are done at the same scale as the plans ($\frac{1}{4}$" = 1'0").*

B. *Vertical dimensions are shown to critical points, such as lintel, floor, and roof heights. Because masonry is the predominating material used for this house, these dimensions are coordinated with stock masonry dimensions.*

C. *Special decorative features, such as the multicolored band of masonry on the facade, are shown in relation to the coursing of the masonry.*

D. *Horizontal masonry joints are shown clearly and accurately.*

E. *Because the section/elevation reveals the interior of the kitchen and the bath, the section portion is used to show the interior elevation of the rooms that are sectioned.*

F. *Window opening directions are shown on the elevations.*

G. *Depths and stepping of footings are shown.*

H. *Height and materials of chimney are indicated.*

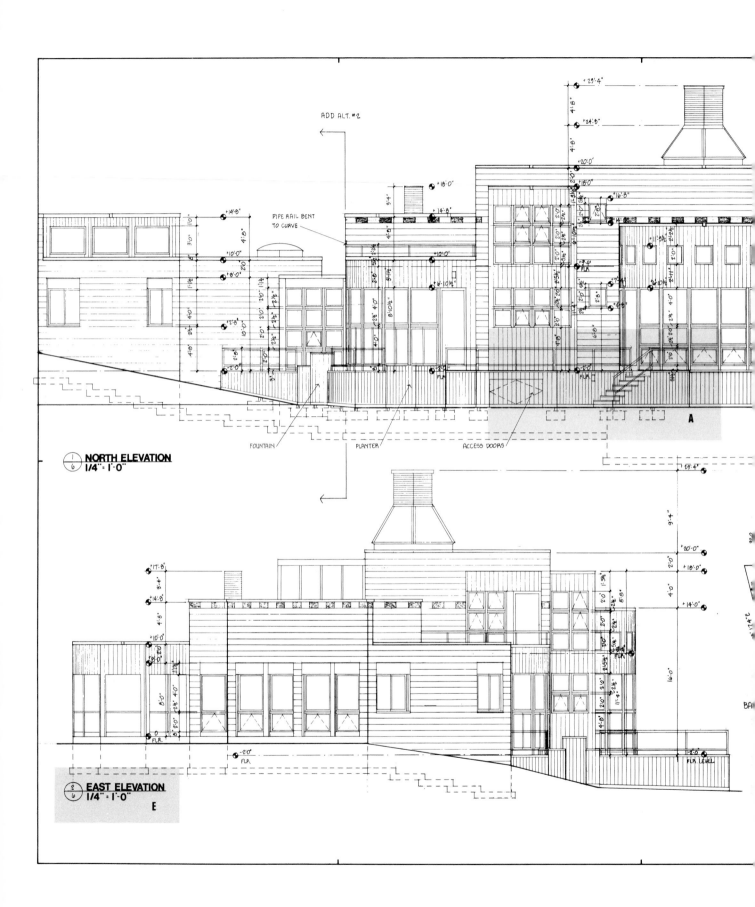

ADD ALT. #2

PIPE RAIL BENT
TO CURVE

NORTH ELEVATION
1/4" = 1'-0"

FOUNTAIN   PLANTER   ACCESS DOORS

EAST ELEVATION
1/4" = 1'-0"

E

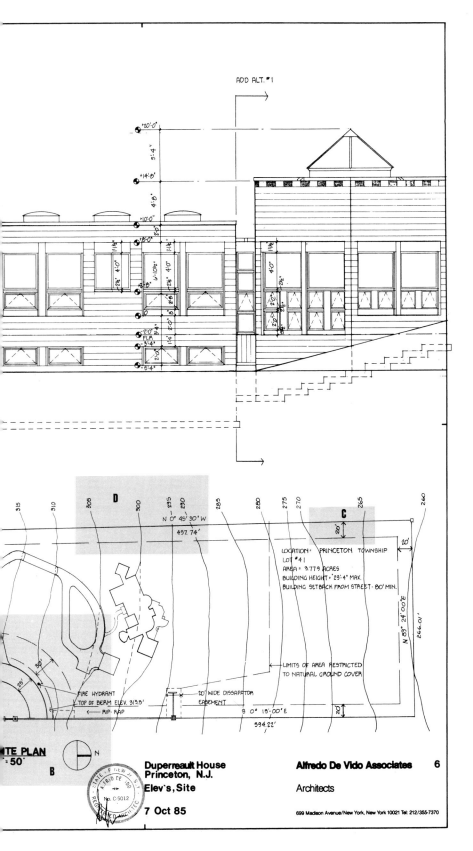

6. Elevations/Site Plan

A. *Elevations show decks in front of the house and the post footings of the decks.*

B. *The site plan is shown on this sheet because there is room available.*

C. *The site plan shows the required setbacks as called for by the local zoning ordinance and the environmental restrictions. This inclusion is for the benefit of the building inspector. The exact location of the house in this case is not shown, since it will be sited at the time of clearing in the general buildable area.*

D. *Contour lines are shown on the site plan, and finished contour lines are shown on the elevations.*

E. *The scale of the drawings is clearly shown, and all drawings are accurately and crisply drawn.*

ADD ALT. #1

LOCATION - PRINCETON TOWNSHIP
LOT #41
AREA = 3.779 ACRES
BUILDING HEIGHT = 29'-4" MAX.
BUILDING SETBACK FROM STREET - 80' MIN.

LIMITS OF AREA RESTRICTED TO NATURAL GROUND COVER

FIRE HYDRANT
TOP OF BERM ELEV. 313.5'
RIP-RAP

20' WIDE DISSAPATOR EASEMENT

N 0° 45' 30" W
457.74'

N 89° 24' 00" E
266.01'

S 0° 15'-00" E
594.22'

SITE PLAN
1" = 50'

Duperreault House
Princeton, N.J.

Elev's, Site

7 Oct 85

Alfredo De Vido Associates   6

Architects

699 Madison Avenue/New York, New York 10021 Tel: 212/355-7370

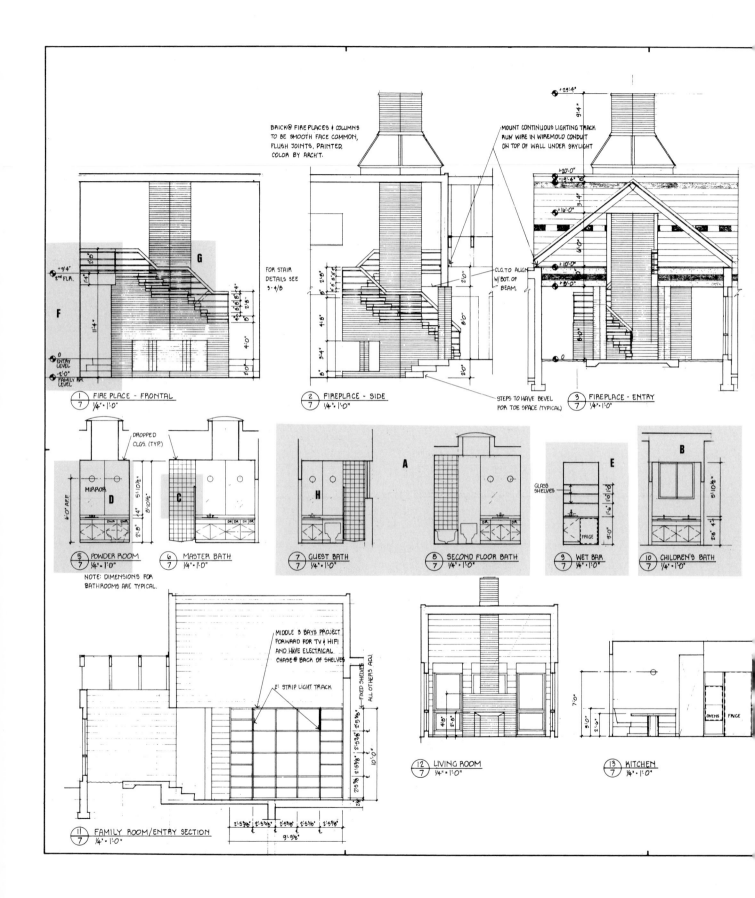

BRICK@ FIRE PLACES & COLUMNS
TO BE SMOOTH FACE COMMON,
FLUSH JOINTS, PAINTED,
COLOR BY ARCH'T.

MOUNT CONTINUOUS LIGHTING TRACK
RUN WIRE IN WIREMOLD CONDUIT
ON TOP OF WALL UNDER SKYLIGHT

FOR STAIR
DETAILS SEE
3-4/8

CLG. TO ALIGN
W/ BOT. OF
BEAM

STEPS TO HAVE BEVEL
FOR TOE SPACE (TYPICAL)

1/7 FIRE PLACE - FRONTAL
1/4" = 1'-0"

2/7 FIREPLACE - SIDE
1/4" = 1'-0"

3/7 FIREPLACE - ENTRY
1/4" = 1'-0"

DROPPED
CLGS. (TYP.)

MIRROR

D

C

A

H

GLASS
SHELVES

E

FRIGE

B

5/7 POWDER ROOM
1/4" = 1'-0"

6/7 MASTER BATH
1/4" = 1'-0"

7/7 GUEST BATH
1/4" = 1'-0"

8/7 SECOND FLOOR BATH
1/4" = 1'-0"

9/7 WET BAR
1/4" = 1'-0"

10/7 CHILDREN'S BATH
1/4" = 1'-0"

NOTE: DIMENSIONS FOR
BATHROOMS ARE TYPICAL.

MIDDLE 3 BAYS PROJECT
FORWARD FOR TV & HIFI
AND HAVE ELECTRICAL
CHASE@ BACK OF SHELVES

2' STRIP LIGHT TRACK

11/7 FAMILY ROOM/ENTRY SECTION
1/4" = 1'-0"

12/7 LIVING ROOM
1/4" = 1'-0"

OVENS   FRIGE

13/7 KITCHEN
1/4" = 1'-0"

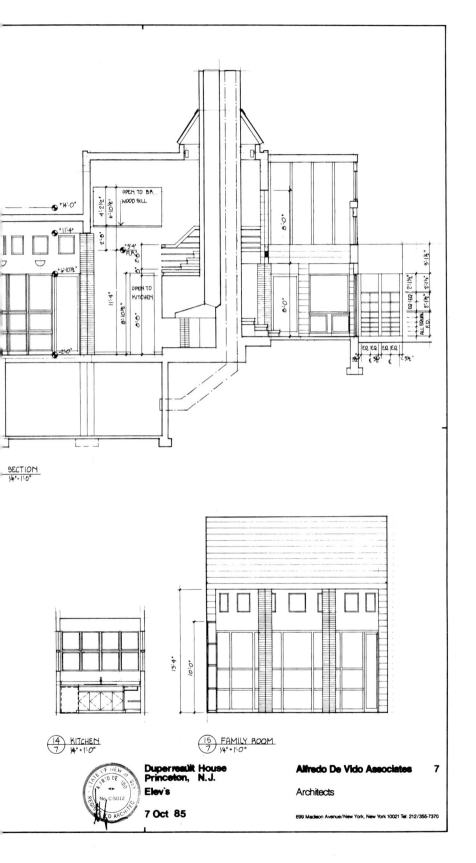

SECTION
1/4" = 1'-0"

OPEN TO BR.
WOOD SILL

OPEN TO
KITCHEN

(14/7) KITCHEN
1/4" = 1'-0"

(15/7) FAMILY ROOM
1/4" = 1'-0"

7. Interior Elevations/Sections

A. *Interior elevations not previously shown on other drawings are placed here.*

B. *Cabinetwork is shown, including door swings and numbers of shelves.*

C. *Tiled areas on walls are indicated.*

D. *Interior heights of special situations are shown.*

E. *Sections and interior elevations are restricted to special situations. Walls within the house are not shown unless they have special features.*

F. *The elevations and vertical heights are again indicated. These coordinate with the datums and vertical dimensions on other drawings.*

G. *Materials, such as brick and masonry, are delineated. Windows are shown from the interiors.*

H. *Lighting fixtures on walls, such as sconces and mirror lights over vanities, are shown and dimensioned.*

Duperreault House
Princeton, N.J.

Elev's

7 Oct 85

Alfredo De Vido Associates   7

Architects

699 Madison Avenue/New York, New York 10021 Tel: 212/355-7370

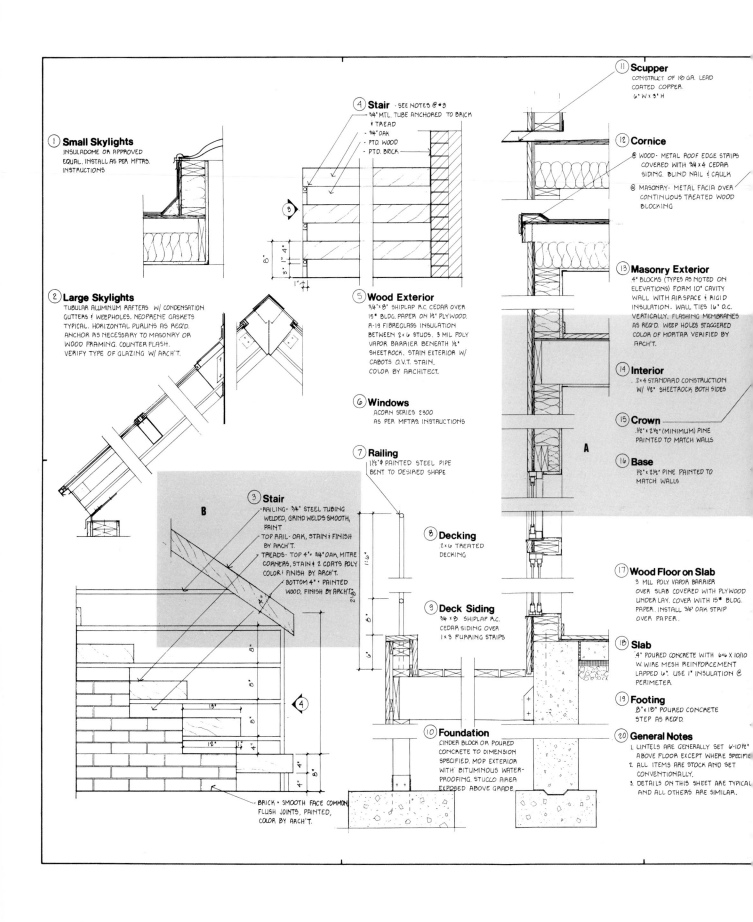

① **Small Skylights**
INSULADOME OR APPROVED
EQUAL, INSTALL AS PER MFTRS.
INSTRUCTIONS

② **Large Skylights**
TUBULAR ALUMINUM RAFTERS W/ CONDENSATION
GUTTERS & WEEPHOLES. NEOPRENE GASKETS
TYPICAL. HORIZONTAL PURLINS AS REQ'D.
ANCHOR AS NECESSARY TO MASONRY OR
WOOD FRAMING. COUNTER FLASH.
VERIFY TYPE OF GLAZING W/ ARCH'T.

④ **Stair** - SEE NOTES @ #3
- ¾" MTL. TUBE ANCHORED TO BRICK
  & TREAD
- ¾" OAK
- PTD. WOOD
- PTD. BRICK

⑤ **Wood Exterior**
¾"x 8" SHIPLAP A.C. CEDAR OVER
15# BLDG. PAPER ON ½" PLYWOOD.
R-18 FIBREGLASS INSULATION
BETWEEN 2x6 STUDS. 3 MIL POLY
VAPOR BARRIER BENEATH ½"
SHEETROCK. STAIN EXTERIOR W/
CABOTS O.V.T. STAIN.
COLOR BY ARCHITECT.

⑥ **Windows**
ACORN SERIES 2300
AS PER MFTRS INSTRUCTIONS

⑦ **Railing**
1½"Ø PAINTED STEEL PIPE
BENT TO DESIRED SHAPE

③ **Stair**
- RAILING- ¾" STEEL TUBING
  WELDED, GRIND WELDS SMOOTH,
  PAINT
- TOP RAIL- OAK, STAIN & FINISH
  BY ARCH'T.
- TREADS- TOP 4"= ¾" OAK, MITRE
  CORNERS, STAIN & 2 COATS POLY
  COLOR & FINISH BY ARCH'T.
- BOTTOM 4" = PAINTED
  WOOD, FINISH BY ARCH'T.

⑧ **Decking**
2x6 TREATED
DECKING

⑨ **Deck Siding**
¾"x 8 SHIPLAP A.C.
CEDAR SIDING OVER
1x3 FURRING STRIPS

⑩ **Foundation**
CINDER BLOCK OR POURED
CONCRETE TO DIMENSION
SPECIFIED. MOP EXTERIOR
WITH BITUMINOUS WATER-
PROOFING. STUCCO AREA
EXPOSED ABOVE GRADE.

- BRICK - SMOOTH FACE COMMON
  FLUSH JOINTS, PAINTED,
  COLOR BY ARCH'T.

⑪ **Scupper**
CONSTRUCT OF 18 GA. LEAD
COATED COPPER.
6" W x 3" H

⑫ **Cornice**
@ WOOD- METAL ROOF EDGE STRIPS
  COVERED WITH ¾ x 4 CEDAR
  SIDING. BLIND NAIL & CAULK
@ MASONRY- METAL FACIA OVER
  CONTINUOUS TREATED WOOD
  BLOCKING

⑬ **Masonry Exterior**
4" BLOCKS (TYPES AS NOTED ON
ELEVATIONS) FORM 10" CAVITY
WALL WITH AIR SPACE & RIGID
INSULATION. WALL TIES 16" O.C.
VERTICALLY. FLASHING MEMBRANES
AS REQ'D. WEEP HOLES STAGGERED
COLOR OF MORTAR VERIFIED BY
ARCH'T.

⑭ **Interior**
2x4 STANDARD CONSTRUCTION
W/ ½" SHEETROCK BOTH SIDES

⑮ **Crown**
½" x 2½" (MINIMUM) PINE
PAINTED TO MATCH WALLS

⑯ **Base**
½" x 2½" PINE PAINTED TO
MATCH WALLS

A

⑰ **Wood Floor on Slab**
3 MIL POLY VAPOR BARRIER
OVER SLAB COVERED WITH PLYWOOD
UNDERLAY. COVER WITH 15# BLDG.
PAPER. INSTALL ¾" OAK STRIP
OVER PAPER.

⑱ **Slab**
4" POURED CONCRETE WITH 6x6 X 10/10
W. WIRE MESH REINFORCEMENT
LAPPED 6". USE 1" INSULATION @
PERIMETER.

⑲ **Footing**
8"x 18" POURED CONCRETE
STEP AS REQ'D.

⑳ **General Notes**
1. LINTELS ARE GENERALLY SET 6'-10½"
   ABOVE FLOOR EXCEPT WHERE SPECIFIE
2. ALL ITEMS ARE STOCK AND SET
   CONVENTIONALLY.
3. DETAILS ON THIS SHEET ARE TYPICAL
   AND ALL OTHERS ARE SIMILAR.

RUBBER ROOFING AS PER MFTRS.
CTIONS. PROVIDE APPROVED FLAT
ENTS ± I2'-0" O.C.
ROOF TO DRAINS OR SCUPPERS.
5 REQ'D. USE R·3I FIBREGLASS INSUL.
OOFS. INSULATION MUST BE FACED
⎯ WITH CRAFT PAPER.

POCKET FLOOR JOISTS INTO
MASONRY WALL

E

= 1'-0"

SPECIFICATIONS:

1. GENERAL REQUIREMENTS: Plans and specifications are cooperative. All
labor and materials required to fully carry out the intentions of the
plans and specifications are part of this contract, whether or not
specifically documented. The contractor shall provide each item mentioned, indicated or implied to achieve the intended building according
to the methods of best construction practice. The contractor will comply with all State and local codes even in the event of conflicting
requirements in the plans and specifications at no additional cost to
the Owner. All equipment and materials to be installed according to
manufacturers' recommendations and are to be new. The architect shall
be the final judge of the quality of the workmanship, and reserves the
right to reject any work he considers inferior.
2. SITE WORK: Clear as required. Minimum damage to existing trees. Remove debris. Excavate as required for foundations, electrical and
mechanical work. Backfill well compacted. Comply with Town regulations.
3. CONCRETE: Minimum strength 2500 psi. Mesh reinforcing all footings
and slabs 6" x 6" x 10/10 wire mesh lapped 6". Approved hardener
(Sonneborn or equal). Steel trowel finish.
4. MASONRY & STUCCO: Concrete block per drawings as supplied by Consoli-
ated Brick Company or approved equal. Submit samples for architect's
approval prior to commencing work. Durowall reinforcing every third
course. Provide weeps 2' o.c. at base of cavity walls. Poured concrete foundation and basement walls, thickness shown.
5. METALS: Black anodized aluminum all flashing, all anchor bolts, framing
anchors and hangers galvanized.
6. CARPENTRY AND MILLWORK:
   A. FRAMING: Douglas fir, construction grade, 1500 psi. Bridging blocking maximum 8' o.c. all floors and roof. 2" x 6" studs all exterior
   wood walls, block horizontally 8' o.c., where otherwise unbraced.
   B. PLYWOOD: All exterior grade, ½" walls and flat roofs.
   C. ROOF AND DECKING: Dibitin installed in accordance per manufacturers'
   instructions for flat roofs.
   D. BUILDING PAPER: #15 asphalt-impregnated felt, horizontally applied
   in long lengths. Lapped 6" all directions, extra strip 6" wide
   all door and window jambs.
   E. SIDING: 8" tongue and groove rc cedar, vertically applied, #2. All
   exposed nails aluminum, 45 degree cut all horizontal joints. Provide sample.
   F. MILLWORK: Fabricate and install cabinets in kitchen and baths,
   formica, concealed hinges. Built-in shelving and closets per
   drawings.
   G. INTERIOR FINISH: ½" sheetrock on ceilings and walls. Coated nails.
7. MOISTURE PROTECTION:
   A. DAMPPROOFING: (One) 1 layer 4 mil polyethelene under all slabs on
   grade. All joints lapped 6", sealed and taped. Mopped waterproofing entire perimeter foundation.
   B. INSULATION: Fiberglass, R-19 unfaced all exterior walls, R-30
   in roof, Kraft faced, 6 mil vapor barrier all exterior walls.
   2" rigid insulation in cavities exterior masonry walls.
   C. SEALANTS: Silicone type, clear. Where opening more than 3/8"
   deep, pack with Neoprene joint filler to 3/8" of surface.
8. DOORS, WINDOWS AND GLASS:
   A. DOORS: Exterior doors: Acorn steel doors, sizes indicated.
   Interior doors and closet doors: 1 3/8" hollow core birch.
   B. WINDOWS AND GLASS: All Acorn sizes per drawings. Insulating
   glass. Provide w/screens. Safety glass where required.
   C. WEATHERSTRIPPING: All windows and doors not factory stripped,
   Accurate or approved equal, tops, sides and sills.
   D. HARDWARE: Furnish and install Schlage Plymouth hardware, brushed
   chrome, coated hinges.
   E. SCREENS: Provide for all operating sash.
   F. SKYLIGHTS: Insula Dome or Velux or equal installed per manufacturers'
   directions.
9. FINISHES:
   A. PAINTING: All Pratt & Lambert, Samuel Cabot, Minwax or approved
   equal. Interior doors: 1 coat stain, 1 coat polyurethane. Exterior doors: 2 coats oil base. Sheetrock: 1 primer, 1 coat
   latex flat. Exterior wood walls: one coat Olympic stain. Trim
   and base: stain plus 1 coat poly.
   B. CERAMIC TILE: Install tile per Handbook for Ceramic Tile Installation, latest edition.
10. EQUIPMENT: Install kitchen and laundry equip. furnished by Owner,
providing all necessary ducts, plumbing and wiring.
11. SPECIALTIES: Two (2) 24" towel bars, soap dishes, medicine cabinets,
shower rods, paper holders to be furnished and installed each bath.
12. HEATING, A.C. & PLUMBING:
    A. HEATING, A.C.: Forced hot air, two zones with humidifier and
    electrostatic precipitator. Bryant or equal.
    B. PLUMBING: Furnish and install (American Standard) all fixtures white:
    Two (2) Fiat cast stone shower receptors, sizes indicated on
    drawings with 1363.096 fitting.
    Two (2) Spectra tub 2605.103 with 1363.119 fitting.
    Four (4) 2065.018 toilets
    One (1) 7132.019 kitchen sink with 4160.17 fittings
    Six (6) 3301.025 lavatories with 2103.886 fittings
    Two (2) Bar sink 7055.025 with 1825.103 Duolux fitting and
    4320.024 strainer.
13. Electrical:
    A. SCOPE: 200 amp service for layout and complete wiring job. Con-
    form to local and state regulations and National Electric Code.
    Buried electric service.
    B. DISTRIBUTION: Circuit breaker type, Square D or approved equal.
    All labeled. 2 extra single-pole circuits, 6 extra double pole
    circuits. Meter concealed, location approved by architect. Hook
    up water system and electric.
    C. FIXTURES: Install fixtures furnished by Owner. Switch plates
    36" above floor.
    D. DEVICES: Pass & Seymour or equal. Murray panel. Leviton devices,
    silent. Smoke alarms per code.
SEPARATE PRICES:
    1. House without left and right diagonal element (Study 10 and guest
    rooms 19 and 20).
    2. Study 10.
    3. Guestrooms 19 and 20 and attached spaces.

A. *Details are typical and are used throughout the house. Special conditions are shown on the plans and elevations, and these are discussed with the contractor and clarified in the field as necessary. The aesthetic and general principle of the detailing intent is revealed in the typical section.*

B. *Some special details, such as the stairs, are shown.*

C. *Specifications are given in an outline format. Boilerplate jargon is avoided. Products and quality standards are selected and called for after coordination with the owner in the design phase.*

D. *Separate prices required by the bidding process are called out at the end of the specifications.*

E. *Structural beam sizes are not noted inasmuch as they are noted on the plans.*

Duperreault House
Princeton, N.J.
Details

7 October 85

Alfredo De Vido Associates   8

Architects

699 Madison Avenue/New York, New York 10021 Tel: 212/355-7370

SKETCH PLANS DURING THE DESIGN STAGE

PROJECT: GERSTENHABER HOUSE, *Eastern Long Island, New York*

Architect: Alfredo De Vido, FAIA

- These plans were drawn up during the design stage and were the subject of numerous revisions by the architect in collaboration with the client.

- The house was designed on graph paper at a scale of 1" = 10'0". The architect uses a minor module of 3'4" and a major module of 10'0".

- Levels, stairs, and exterior decked area with trellises are shown.

- Elevations and sections are worked out simultaneously with the plans, and the point of cut for the sections or the vantage point at the elevations is shown. Elevations of key heights are indicated.

- It is possible to give plans like these to an associate to complete the final working drawings, since they are modular and windows and doors are shown on the grid lines.

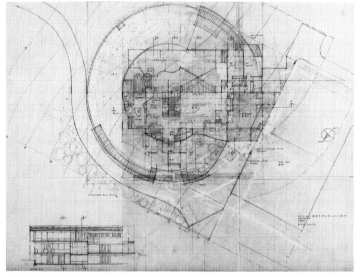

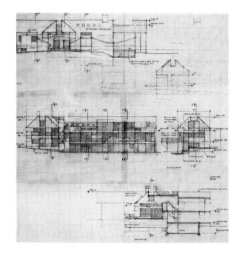

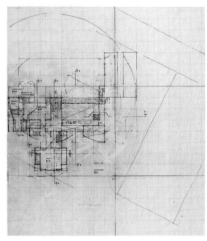

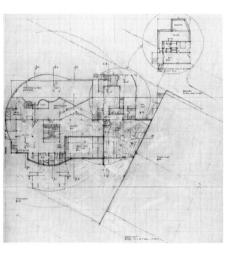

6 | CONSTRUCTION

THE BUSINESS OF CONSTRUCTION

There are many approaches to construction: competitive bids, construction management, and design/build. The main choice is whether a general contractor or outside construction manager will handle the job or whether the architect will do it. It's a good idea to explain the options to clients, discussing the pros and cons of each option and making your recommendation.

COMPETITIVE BIDS

The selection of a general contractor for an entire job used to be the conventional approach. Indeed, the American Institute of Architects formerly recommended this as the only acceptable, ethical way. The theory was that a conflict of interest between the designer of a structure and its builder should be avoided. It has now been generally recognized that this method can be time-consuming and expensive. It can also put the architect in an adversarial position in working with the general contractor. However, it is still a time-honored and good way of building homes.

If this traditional method is to be used, the architect should vet the contractors' qualifications and availability prior to soliciting competitive bids. The architect should also explain the job to the contractors, because it is difficult to comprehend a complex project, such as building a house, without some introduction. This early meeting will serve to introduce architect and contractor to each other, to see if they can work together.

Contract documents should then be distributed to the selected bidders. Do not solicit bids from more than three contractors. Even though construction is the nation's largest industry, the contracting world has a good networking system, particularly in low-density areas such as suburban or exurban areas. If you solicit too many bids, contractors will tend to be uncompetitive, not knowing what criteria you will use to select the successful bidder. Architects react in a similar way when they hear that a client is interviewing many of their colleagues. Allocating considerable time to getting the job becomes a gamble.

COMMUNICATING WITH BIDDERS

Once you've distributed the contract documents, it's a good idea to follow up with phone calls. Cover the following points:

- Does the bidder have enough information in the drawings to understand the job?

- Does the bidder have sufficient sets of drawings? General contractors usually need more than one set, since they commonly distribute a set to each subcontractor: plumber, electrician, heating/air-conditioning contractor, mason, and others. It is important to ask this question, because many contractors are reluctant to ask for more sets, thinking they are expensive and troublesome for you to make up. However, more sets mean faster bids.

- How long will it take the bidder to get the bid together? You may have set a bid date when you distributed the drawings, but, until the contractor has had a chance to review the drawings, he won't know the scope of the job and, therefore, what length of time is needed to estimate. Because it is common practice to have the local materials supplier do the quantity survey and pricing of materials, it's a good idea to ask whether the contractor will get it from a supplier. Many of the bidders may use the same supplier. The supplier will probably advise all bidders that he is doing the takeoff, thereby "networking" the job and eliminating some of the competitive edge.

- Once he's gotten into the job and talked to his subcontractors, ask the contractor again whether he has any questions. Be sure to ask this question in a friendly, solicitous way. Some contractors may feel that they are not sufficiently trained to understand drawings. Indeed, some of them are not. It is important to determine this qualification if you have not worked together before. If the bidder has questions, try to ferret them out carefully, because some of them may indicate gaps in your drawings or better ways to achieve the end result. You may discover that your design is too complicated or that it uses technology beyond the capability of the contractor. You'll get warnings of such a possibility if you are in touch during the bidding process. If the contractor is genuinely reluctant to take on the work, or if you think he simply cannot do it, it may be appropriate to ask whether he's comfortable about completing the bid. This can be tricky. Be a diplomat.

• Are there any details, material use, or structural aspect that the bidder thinks you should reconsider? This question will bring surprising answers if properly asked. Most contractors feel that an experienced architect knows about the practicalities of building. Architects know that this is not always the case, inasmuch as an architect's training concentrates on the design and coordination of a building project, rather than on detailed specifics. Posing this question to the contractor also signals that your working relationship will not be an adversarial one. This is an important point to communicate, because it may result in lower bids and an easier time during construction. However, you should stop short of giving the contractor license to do whatever he wants, which may signal an unknowledgeable architect who can be taken advantage of. In short, consulting the contractor helps establish a good working relationship between partners in the complicated process of construction.

CONSTRUCTION MANAGEMENT

Construction management is commonly used for larger projects, where time and money are of key importance. Although these factors are equally important in residential design, the process is rare in current residential practice in the United States. However, it is a management technique whose time has come, and the architect should consider it. Though it means more work, there is also additional compensation for the architect.

Construction management is not for novice architects. To successfully complete a project using this approach, the architect must know what trades are required, the sequence in which they must work, and whether it's necessary to get prices before the start of construction.

If the architect thinks this technique will result in lower costs for his or her client, better, faster construction, and additional compensation, and if the client is at ease with this method, the architect should draw up a list of qualified bidders for the various trades.

Within the broad field of construction management for residential building, there are several basic approaches. These are discussed in the following paragraphs.

Architect as Manager and Coordinator

One approach is for the architect to act as manager and coordinator and depends on the client's coming up with cash on demand. Many subcontractors are small operators who need to be paid as soon as they finish the work. If this is explained to the client, and if it is further explained that prompt payment of subcontractors and suppliers will save money, the client is usually agreeable to this approach.

If the payment for the job is tied to periodic payments from a lending institution, the approach cannot work unless all subcontractors and suppliers are willing to wait for receipt of funds from the lending institution. It is important to determine this situation first and to make sure that all parties understand and are willing to put up with a hiatus between completion of work and receipt of funds. If the client is able to pay the required amounts out-of-pocket as soon as the architect certifies that it's appropriate to do so, the job will proceed more smoothly and will probably be done faster. Because the architect is not a middleman in the payment process, this approach will not generate cash-flow problems for the architect.

Architect as Construction Manager

Another approach is for the architect to function as construction manager. In this case, greater capital must be at the architect/construction manager's disposal, because material suppliers offer discounts for payment within a set period of time after the bill is rendered, commonly 10 days, or by the tenth of any given month. Interest payments are also due if a bill is left unpaid longer than 30 days or by the end of the month. Before deciding to use this approach, the architect/construction manager should be sure that the client will pay the bills promptly. If there is any doubt, do not use this approach.

NEGOTIATED CONTRACTS

There are two types of negotiated contracts: lump sum and cost plus. Negotiated contracts are those whereby a contractor is selected at the outset of the job and the cost of the work is negotiated. It is sometimes appropriate to reveal the budget to the contractor at the schematic or preliminary stage in order to check costs at that stage.

Lump Sum

If there is a contractor in whom you or the client has confidence, you can negotiate a lump-sum contract with that contractor. This is an acceptable way to procure construction services if your contractor is trustworthy and does not require a large markup for coordinating services. Overhead and profit markups are normally 10 percent overhead and 10 percent profit. Overhead usually covers the contractor's costs of such things as equipment, clerical services, offices expenses, mandatory workers' benefit premiums, and other indirect costs. Some contractors work to a lower overhead and profit figure. Lower percentages can also be negotiated.

The advantage of a negotiated lump sum with a reliable contractor is the removal of any perceived need for him to cut corners in a competitive market to get the job. The disadvantage is the converse: an absence of other bidders tends to lessen the desire to be efficient. Do not use this approach with a contractor whom you or the client does not trust; there are many opportunities to pad costs along the way.

To negotiate a lump-sum contract, supply the contractor with the contract documents, as in a competitive bidding process, and ask for an estimate. The contractor will then solicit bids from subcontractors and material suppliers and furnish a list of expenses plus markups for overhead, general conditions, and profit. General conditions cover a variety of items, such as compliance with local wage rates, if appropriate, mandatory worker benefits, and payment of fees for building permits. There can also be a category in the contractor's estimate for contingencies. Contingencies include coping with unforeseeable site conditions, owner's field changes, or wrong estimates. Contingencies represent the contractor's "cushion."

Cost-Plus

A variation of the negotiated lump-sum approach is to ask the contractor to do the job and to submit itemized labor and material bills each month for payment by the owner. These submittals will generally include a previously negotiated percentage markup or a fixed management fee. The cost-plus arrangement is every contractor's dream, because there's no risk, other than to his reputation, if the bills total far in excess of the owner's resources.

This approach can also be coupled with an early estimate from the contractor. The architect can ask the contractor to give such an estimate, based on an experienced look at the documents.

Some builders will work only in this manner, particularly if they are working on an unusual or experimental design. (Conventionally built houses are within the experience of most contractors. They can therefore estimate these projects within 10 percent of the probable final figure with a reasonable expectation of meeting that figure.) Many architect-designed houses do not fall into the conventional category, and contractors cannot figure them based on previous experience. Indeed, for certain kinds of design, many contractors will not agree to lump sums. They base this policy on previous unprofitable experiences with unusual design.

HYBRID APPROACHES

There are other ways to get a house built. In fact, architects have their own ways of accomplishing a project, depending on their individual work approaches. A number of these methods are discussed in the following paragraphs.

Architect as Builder

Some architects like to work with their hands. To work in the open air and use the muscles as well as the brain is a rewarding experience. The architect as builder has a long history. Many architects in indigenous societies, ranging from those of ancient Egypt and the Middle Ages through Colonial times, were builders, rather than fitting the modern concept of an architect. The advantage of this approach is a reasonable certainty that the end result will equal the desired artistic one. The disadvantage is the limit on how much work the architect can do. Construction work is limited to good weather unless the job is closed in. It is also exhausting physical work. If the architect spends daylight hours working on the construction site, he or she will have little or no energy left over for design work at the drawing board at the end of the day.

Architect as Full-Time Supervisor

Engaging the architect, or deputy architect, as full-time construction supervisor was an approach commonly used by Frank Lloyd Wright. He routinely advised clients that they would have to pay the wages and maintenance for an on-site assistant who would supervise the builder and see to it that the work was executed in the intended manner. In Wright's day, this was an important requirement, because his designs were unusual and could not be built easily in many of the then-rural sites for which he got commissions. This is still a good way to do a job. However, the client may need to be convinced of the necessity for a full-time assistant as a job cost. Most clients regard the supervision of the work as a contingent part of the architect's services.

Owner-Built Houses

Sometimes an owner is interested in doing the actual construction of a house, either partially or in full. This approach can work, but it frequently requires a long construction time, assuming the owner is not also a full-time builder. The architect who becomes involved in this approach should count on having to spend a lot of time looking in on the job. This will be necessary not only because the construction time will be long, but also because the owner may want to make changes along the way. Owner changes without the architect's involvement can work, provided the owner has a good sense of design and construction. The latter is of great importance because of the physical danger involved with improperly placed foundations or badly fastened structural members.

There are situations in which the owner has a friend who can offer a deal or a special talent. For instance, many owners seem to know someone who can sell them lighting or plumbing fixtures at cost. Owners rightly perceive this as a significant cost saver. However, the architect should point out that the installer of the fixtures is not responsible if one of the fixtures is defective. The owner will then be required to take the unit back to the supplier. This can be time-consuming and sometimes beyond the owner's capability, for instance, if the item is a large tub.

Owners sometimes want to accomplish certain parts of the work themselves, such as painting and landscaping. This kind of work can be easily removed from the contractor's specifications, but it should be made clear just what the contractor will leave for the owner to do. For instance, a "rough grade" for "landscape work by owner" can mean that the owner will have to cope with construction debris scattered all over the site and hillocks of unspread excavation that require machinery to move and spread. The specifics should be precisely spelled out to both the contractor and the owner, so that there will be no arguments. It should also be pointed out how heavy construction work really is. Many clients who commission the design and building of a house lead sedentary lives in their daily occupations and do not understand that construction work can be quite physically demanding.

Still another cost-saving approach for an owner is to pick up certain expensive items from a discounter such as Home Depot or Wal-Mart. This is acceptable on its face, but the architect should discourage such an effort. For example, a trip to Home Depot sometimes involves long waiting periods and a search for the right article. Sales personnel are generally helpful, but they simply do not have the time to figure out how many nails, and of what sizes, it will take to put the house together. Moreover, the building business has a language of its own that is loaded with jargon. Try to make the owner aware of this in a politic way. People don't go to a materials discounter and order "nails." The needs are too technical for lay people to determine by themselves. It also takes a certain temperament to deal with the myriad complexities of the construction process. Most owners do not have the training needed to handle this task.

THE STRUCTURE OF A HOUSE

A common comment of builders speaking about architects is that "they don't even know how to frame a house." There is some truth in this, because architects learn difficult conceptual and visual skills in school. There's little time to learn many practicalities; in fact, students are expected to learn them later in apprenticeships with practicing architects.

LEARNING HOW TO DESIGN AND BUILD STRUCTURES

To design better houses, it is important for the architect to learn the techniques of house building. The following paragraphs suggest some ways to gain practical experience.

Work on a Construction Site

The value of working on a construction site or building a small shed or other structure can't be overestimated. By doing this sort of work, the architect gains experience that is useful in designing and in dealing with builders.

Build a Simple Framing Model

Building a simple framing model of your design is a valuable aid. If the model is of an entire house or a significant portion of it, it will be a useful tool for the contractor and enhance your own understanding of construction.

Study Materials Describing House Construction

In the course of studying various manuals describing the construction of houses, go over the diagrams until you understand them. Such diagrams are included in most manuals commonly found among an architect's reference materials. However, if something seems difficult, don't hesitate to ask a friendly builder how to do it. The chances are good that the builder will be delighted with the question and take as much time as necessary to explain the concepts. He will feel that the architect appreciates his knowledge and skills and will become a friend in the professional sense, rather than the more common adversary.

Work with a Structural Engineer

Many architects think that the structural design of a house is easy. It is true that loads and connections are not difficult to calculate if the design is simple.

However, most architect-designed houses are complex, and site conditions and wind loads must be taken into account. Unless the architect has had special training in structural design, it is advisable to find an engineer and work with him or her. Architects frequently counter this suggestion with the statement that it is not possible to pay engineering fees from the traditionally small architect's fee. But that depends on what you ask the engineer to do. If you ask for a full set of engineering drawings, the fee will be large. Still, it is possible to ask the engineer to red mark a set of prints with the necessary structural layout and sketch out the connections freehand. This approach has the additional merit of enabling the architect to check the beam sizes and layouts when they are being transferred to the architectural drawings.

Go to the Construction Site

Visiting the construction site is not only an excellent way to broaden your experience for future houses but also will enable you to work better with the contractor.

USING THE STRUCTURE AS A DESIGN TOOL

It is important for the architect to appreciate that houses have structural dimensions, because beams and their cladding or finish have thickness, and to express that knowledge in drawing a house. That will enable the architect to do a more accurate job of seeing the design on paper, and the house will also look more realistic on paper. Because a knowledgeable-looking set of drawings shows that the architect understands structure, the contractors will be convinced of that as well.

LEARNING A VARIETY OF STRUCTURAL TECHNIQUES

There are many ways to frame houses, depending on their size, number of rooms or units put together, and local codes and usage. Climate and geography will necessitate different techniques, as well as the location of a house in an earthquake or hurricane zone. Through framing methods that feature the structure and proclaim the skill of the builders, structure can be an expressive and decorative element.

There are various ways of framing a house or low-rise multifamily building. Among the more common are the wood stud balloon frame: Wood studs are continuous for the full height of the building, floor joists rest on continuous sill plates let into the exterior frame, and wood studs are arranged to form platforms at each floor. Other, less common, ways that also merit attention are discussed in the following paragraphs.

Post and Beam or Post and Girt

Post and beam techniques generally use a system of beams placed on top of evenly spaced posts. These structural members are usually heavier than conventional wood studs and are frequently left exposed as decorative elements. Post and girt systems, which date from Colonial times in this country, feature widely spaced posts braced with horizontal members that serve as nailing surfaces for the exterior skin. Both of these systems have the advantage of using less structural lumber, and they can be quite decorative. They have the disadvantage of a thin exterior that is not up to current insulation standards in temperate or cold climates. Colonial houses, owing to the lack of insulation, were notoriously cold, despite the fact that the window areas were small.

Masonry

The type of construction that uses through-the-wall masonry or load-bearing masonry can be fireproof, a big advantage, particularly in areas in prone to brush or forest fires. This kind of structure is also good in hot climates, because it keeps out heat during the day and radiates heat at night when the sun goes down. It has the disadvantage of lengthy construction time unless it is combined with a backup frame of lighter, more easily handled construction members such as wood or metal. Masonry must also have properly braced reinforcement in regions prone to earthquakes or high winds.

Masonry walls can be built with cut or irregular pieces of stone, brick, concrete block, or adobe. The walls can also be pierced in a variety of decorative ways, ranging from straight rectangular openings, in which the masonry above is supported by steel or reinforced concrete, to various types of arches—flat, rounded, or pointed. The history of architecture is amply illuminated with examples of different kinds of openings in masonry construction. The type of masonry and the opening selected can convey a strong sense of history and establish a link with older architecture.

Steel Frames, Exposed and Otherwise

Lightweight steel members, evenly and closely spaced, are commonly used in urban areas where people live in close proximity and fire is an important consideration. Spaces between the structural members are filled with insulation, in much the same way as between wood members, and exterior and interior finishes are then applied to the surfaces of the structural frame. It is also possible to use steel frames expressively, just as wood is used, by exposing the posts and beams. A steel frame has advantages, such as additional fire resistance and greater strength, which permit longer distances to be spanned. Steel is not fireproof, however, and will require covering with fireproof materials to comply with code requirements in multistory construction and in other instances where fire resistance is mandatory.

Elaborate Joinery Techniques

Little used today are the techniques of careful wood and metal joinery commonly found in important buildings of older cultures such as China, Japan, and northern Europe. These techniques are ancient and were developed to provide longer spans for larger spaces, as well as deep roof overhangs to shelter exterior walls. They consist of smaller dimension wood members overlapped and sometimes crisscrossed to build up a stepped appearance. Metal fasteners were frequently ornamental, shaped and engraved. These structural systems have proven their worth by lasting for many centuries. However, they are expensive to duplicate, because the joinery process is laborious.

In more modern times, however, such structural systems were used to handsome effect by the Greene brothers and others in a handsome series of California houses. They were also used by Frank Lloyd Wright to achieve deep overhangs. Wright built up layers of small-dimension wood members to achieve daring cantilevers. These layers were frequently clad on the underside of the overhangs to good decorative effect. Deep overhangs look better from below when they are shaped and modeled, as the Asians and Mr. Wright knew so well.

Steel Joinery

It is possible to build up layers of lightweight steel in a decorative manner, although the joinery can become expensive. Using metal as a decorative element doesn't make much sense structurally, because metal is strong and capable of longer spans than wood. It can, however, be used to create unusual and distinctive effects.

TECHNIQUES OF DETAILING

Construction materials and the ways of joining them are richly diverse. Materials must be combined to keep the elements out and to provide structural strength. There are myriad connecting devices for fastening materials: nails, plates, and brackets in wood construction; plates, bolts, rivets, and welds in steel construction; and mortar and reinforcing for masonry and concrete construction. Fasteners can be concealed or exposed decoratively. The architect should consider the various methods and select those most economical and efficient for the particular job. The expressive aspects of joinery and the connectors are also to be considered.

SELECTION OF DETAILING

The architect should decide what sort of detailing the house should have, or must have, from an economic point of view. It should be remembered that contractors are traditional in their techniques. They firmly believe that exterior joints must be covered to keep out the elements and that the structure, wiring, ducts, and piping inside must be covered by finish materials, trimmed where the finish material abuts windows and doors and where joints occur, as with ceilings, floors, and cabinets.

In these areas it is best to stick to the tried and true. Not only may "original" details not work, but the contractor may place a premium on their fabrication and installation. Ask yourself if the detail you want is really essential to the design concept. If so, research it thoroughly in advance so you know what it will really cost and can be certain it will work. When budget considerations dictate, it is best to focus on a rich organization of space, light, texture, and color to make your design statement. Limit yourself to a few details and techniques and keep to "builder's standards" in executing them.

Many different skilled workers are involved in the construction of houses. Some are more skillful than others where careful joinery is concerned. In general, masons who pour concrete footings are not as tidy as those who do stonework and brickwork. Similarly, finish carpenters who do trimwork are more fastidious with joinery than are framing carpenters; however, some carpenters do both finish carpentry and framing. These workers can do framing with the precision of finish work, but you will need to explain why you want it that way. Otherwise, they will assume the framing will be covered and that it's all right to "dimple" the lumber with a hammer. Frank Gehry has done a series of houses with exposed framing that looks like rough framing to the initial glance. In reality, carpenters take care with his framing so that it looks like finish joinery.

EXTERIOR DETAILING

The outside of a building generally functions to control the weather—to let it in or to keep it out. The exterior is the skin of the space within. In addition to fulfilling its functional objectives, the exterior proclaims the aesthetic of the building.

Weatherproofing as a Protective Skin

The "normal" way of weatherproofing a house is to design walls that are either on top of the structure or cover it so that the structure becomes an integral part of the wall. It is also possible to prefabricate exterior walls with finishes that can be lifted into place and cover the joints afterward. Many prefabrication schemes have been developed over the years that are worth considering, especially in repetitive housing.

The exterior structure of a wood frame house is generally covered with sheathing, which is a thin layer of plywood, boards, or composite material. That layer, in turn, is covered with a layer of weatherproofing material such as building paper or another impervious material. This layer is finally covered with the material that will take the weather. The choice is wide. A word to the wise: window and door openings must be placed in their respective openings before the final finish material is applied. It is important for the architect to understand the correct sequence of placing materials to form the skin, in that it will make the architect a better designer. The architect should detail the sequential placement of materials on the job site, so as to cause less confusion and smoother work flow.

The principle in steel frame construction is basically the same as with wood. It should be noted that steel structural frames can be combined with masonry infills. But because the coefficient of expansion differs between these two materials, expansion joints must be provided. Masonry construction is different, however, in that the exterior skin is already doing the structural work by itself or in combination with other masonry.

Exposed Structure

If the architect wants to expose the structural rhythm on the outside of a house, it is possible to join the infill wall between structural members to the column or beam with a caulk joint or a cover trim piece that will cover the joint. It should be remembered, though, that structural members are made of tree species selected for their strength and economy. They are also large in cross section and are frequently not kiln-dried to any great degree, which means that over time they will develop shrinkage cracks and check and warp. Therefore, structural members are not generally designed for exposure to weather extremes and should be covered, except perhaps where the weather is dry, as in the desert. There, the architect can express structure by covering its location with a trim piece that matches the structure behind it.

It is much easier to express structure in steel construction. It was used, for example, in an interesting series of case study houses built in the fifties in Southern California, which enjoys little rain and an even temperature. In other parts of the country, exposed steel will rust and deteriorate, unless it's the type that forms a protective coating over itself as it rusts. That type of steel, commonly known as Cor-Ten, has the problem of staining adjacent materials, so it should be used carefully. Although he did not design many houses, Mies van der Rohe is widely recognized as a master of exposed steel construction. He usually covered the actual structure with other sections of steel. His exposed steel structures were, therefore, mainly expressions of actual structures protected from the weather.

Masonry structure can be readily exposed to the weather, because it is designed specifically for that function. The architect can expose different kinds of masonry expressively, for example, by butting infill brick or concrete block against concrete supporting columns and beams. Note that in this case the architect must remember to waterproof the joint.

Given that structure is not generally designed for exterior exposure in climates subject to weather extremes, the designer should make very sure from the earliest design phases that such a design will work appropriately in the desired site. Steel, for instance, has a high coefficient of heat transfer. If it is left exposed in extreme heat or cold, it will expand and contract dimensionally much more rapidly than abutting materials. Cracks will open in joints between materials, which will admit air and moisture. Moisture will also condense when warmer air comes in contact with steel that is exposed to colder air outside. A knowledge of the physical characteristics of materials is essential in the design of buildings.

Exterior Openings and Junctures

The most vulnerable joints in a house are the points where different parts come together: walls to foundations, windows and doors to the skin of the building, roofs to walls, and if the exterior finish changes on parts of the house, different skin materials to each other. There are several acceptable ways of waterproofing the junctures, the most common being the application of some sort of trim, which can be defined as a cover piece over a joint. By its very nature, trim is able to cover a joint against penetrations of weather. Sometimes this cover piece is caulked on its backside to secure the joint very tightly. Another acceptable way of waterproofing vulnerable joints is to overlap a horizontal or sloping joint with pieces of metal, such as aluminum, copper, or stainless steel.

Ventilation and Insulation

In latitudes with wide variations in temperature and humidity, it is necessary to stop the migration of water vapor through an exterior wall. Within a heated space, water vapor is present in the air. Because heat always travels to cold, according to laws of physics, the heated air in the house moves naturally toward the colder exterior wall and the cold air outside. At some point during its passage through the wall, the warm air reaches the "dew point," at which it turns into actual droplets of water. If allowed to remain inside the wall or roof, the accumulation of water will rot the structural members and wet any insulation, rendering it less effective. It is therefore necessary to place a vapor barrier, generally some thickness of plastic sheeting, on the warm, interior side of the wall. This material is similar to the plastic wrap used to keep food dry in a refrigerator.

The roof poses a slightly different problem, although the phenomenon is similar. Given that the roof is a horizontal or sloping plane, some of the moisture will even migrate through the sheet of plastic and collect on top of it, eventually working its way down and through the interior finish. The normal way of handling this situation is to provide a vent strip at the edge of the roof, which lets fresh air into the cavity and allows any moisture there to evaporate.

In hot, dry climates or consistently cold ones, the steps outlined in this section are not necessary. Instead, other precautions must be taken, such as adding insulation in a hot, dry climate to keep conditioned air in and hot air out; in cold weather areas, the reverse effect also requires insulation.

INTERIOR DETAILING

There are a number of ways to deal with interior detailing. Just be sure the one you choose is consistent with your overall vision of the house.

Structure Concealed with Finish Material

By far the most common way of detailing interiors is the traditional one of building the structure, setting windows and doors within prepared openings, installing the mechanical feeders and returns, and covering the whole with finish. This is the way the building trades have been trained to do it, and this is the way they like to do it. It's also reasonably fail-safe, in that any slight warpage or bad workmanship can be covered and fixed with trim. The traditional method also permits adjustments to be made when windows and doors are set.

Within this broad approach, there's lots of room for creativity. Deciding on the size of the trim to be used, where it will go, what colors to paint on it and between it, whether there should be a change in material on a wall or ceiling, perhaps a wood wainscot on the lower part of a wall, and where the various mechanical and electrical devices should go and how to treat them, requires imagination and ingenuity.

Note that trim is generally made of more expensive kinds of wood that have been subject to greater care during their preparation in the mill. If the designer selects large cross sections of trim or builds up an elaborate baseboard or chair rail, the cost will eventually mount up for both labor and material.

Reveals and Other Interior Treatments

A reveal is basically a groove between two pieces of finish material. It's an attractive way to detail a joint, but a good one can be achieved only with a perfectly straight and plumb wall behind the reveal. This is not always the case of the reveal backs up to the structure of the house, and the backup material may not be attractive to look at within the reveal. In such cases the backup material can be painted quickly with a spray can of dark paint to cover imperfections and render the joint less prominent.

Reveals eventually have to end somewhere, so the architect should be concerned about the overall pattern of a system of reveals before using them. The contractor should also be made aware of the widespread use of this detailing technique. It's not enough to put a small detail or two on the drawings and expect the contractor to pick them up and be aware that the architect is calling for an unusual detailing system throughout the job. Such detailing must be discussed and the price incorporated in the bid.

Easier for the contractor is a system of trim work that runs around the perimeter of a room without termination until it meets itself. This detail, which can be attractive in many ways, was commonly used by architects in the past. It serves to unify a space visually and can also be a useful place to stop all vertical pieces of trim at windows and doors. Explaining at an early stage that this trim work will be a consistent detail throughout the house can ease communication between architect and contractor.

The use of tile in interiors also requires attention. It is necessary to ascertain the backup material for the tile, whether on the floor, walls, or ceiling, and what the resulting thickness will be. It is necessary to think through these requirements early. In using a thick, handmade tile on a cement base, for instance, preparation may require setting the beams lower under that area than under an adjacent piece of floor that may be specified for a simple overlay of carpet on the wood sheathing.

Exposed Structure

Structure can be exposed inside a house with many fewer problems than encountered on the outside, because there is no need to protect an interior from rain, snow, and temperature swings. However, exposing the structure within requires care in locating the mechanical components of the house that are routinely placed within walls and roofs. These include heating/air-conditioning ducts and pipes and their accompanying registers and radiation elements, lighting fixtures and their wiring, and plumbing pipes and vents. Most of these systems are usually run between structures or through the structural members themselves early in the job, because exposed wires, pipes, and ducts require more careful joinery. Electricians, for instance, commonly run wiring through structural beams and studs. When drilling holes, they take the shortest possible route, knowing that the holes are generally small enough not to weaken the beam.

It is therefore necessary to think through carefully and work out the routes for these items before attempting an exposed structure. It is also a good idea to make the contractor aware of your intent. Mechanical subcontractors generally do not like to work on a building with an exposed structure, because it requires a tidier job than the normally concealed structure. There are also code requirements for exposed wiring. Not only will it have to be routed in a more orthogonal fashion, but it must be housed in some sort of conduit. An exposed structure also requires infill between the structural members. This job necessitates extra care by the workers who do it and greater supervision by the architect. An easy way to solve the problem is to have the infill material placed on the outside of the exposed structure. In that way, some insulation can be placed within the covering skin and joints, which is not so labor-intensive.

Though exposed structures do pose a variety of special problems, they can afford very rich decorative effects within the house. Many clients find some aspects of exposed structure very appealing, such as a beamed ceiling, which gives an impressive look to what otherwise might be a boring, flat ceiling.

Mechanical Considerations

In addition to addressing the concerns about exposing or concealing electrical wiring, pipes, and ducts, it is necessary to decide how the lighting fixtures, switch plates, thermostats, registers, radiators, heating baseboards, computer and telephone outlets, and many other modern conveniences will look. Their locations should be determined and explained to the contractor and the subcontractors doing the mechanical and electrical work. If the architect does not pay particular attention to the location of these items, they may be placed wherever the workpeople decide to put them. Because these people are generally respectful of each other's work, their tendency is to put the fixtures and devices in widely separated locations, giving the resultant wall a spotty appearance. The location of these seemingly minor items is important not only for the sake of appearances, but also for the client's convenience. The mislocation of a light switch or heating outlet can loom large in a client's opinion of the architect's performance.

COMMUNICATION

The importance of on-the-job explanations and conferences with the contractor and the subcontractors cannot be overemphasized if you are doing the design-building yourself. Failure to communicate often and well may lead the people doing the construction to conclude that you are not interested in the details of the work. The details will therefore be done the way the contractor normally accomplishes them. It is rare that anyone tries to subvert an architect's design intents, although this can happen if an adversarial relationship develops between the two parties. There are many ways to establish and maintain good communications with the contractor and subcontractors.

Personal Relationships

As in any other life situation, the architect should make every effort to establish a relationship, based on trust and respect, with the key people doing the construction. If you've researched the people to whom you've given the work on the client's behalf, they should be worthy of your trust. Be aware of the general maxim that architects and contractors don't get along, generally believed by clients and contractors. This is a primary cause of job problems and extra costs. The architect should explain to the client, to start with, that one of the intents of your work is to establish a good working relationship with the contractor. This should help to allay any fears that there may be some collusion between the contractor and the architect to do shoddy work at greater cost. The next step is to explain forthrightly to the contractor what your intentions are, that the contractor is part of your team, and that it is his or her responsibility to alert you to any job problems or possible bad details before they are built. It's amazing to see the results that a simple explanation like this, at the outset of the job, can produce.

From this good beginning, the relationship can develop. Talk to the contractor often; visit the job site as often. Meet the subcontractors and work with them as well. If the contractor is a reasonable person, he or she will not object to your doing this. By working directly with the subcontractors, you can be assured that nothing will get lost in your design intent. You may also find it good to know the key workmen; they're mostly capable and congenial people. See what you can learn from them. On the other hand, make sure you stick to business and keep your relationship professional. Remember that you are in charge of a major construction and the expenditure of a lot of money. To ensure that all goes well, you may have to make decisions that are not popular with the contractor or subcontractors, such as determining that poor work must be redone.

The Value of Good Drawings

The importance of good, clear drawings that explain the job carefully and in detail, yet minimally and succinctly, is discussed earlier in Chapter 5. If you have adopted a modular system, explain it carefully so that the workpeople will be able to understand how you have designed the job and, equally important, be able to pick up any errors that may have crept in as you worked through the job and made changes along the way.

Handling Explanatory Sketches Under Construction

You may discover that your drawings do not cover a particular area under construction, or you may see a space that does not satisfy your expectations or the client's requirements. When this happens, alert the contractor on the spot so that work will not continue in the area that you are thinking of changing. Tell the contractor what is troubling you, or that you will clarify what is troubling you about the job as soon as possible. If the change has been generated by the client, point out to the client that this will cost more money or possibly increase construction time, if that is the case. Then get to the change drawings or explanations rapidly. Note that communications of impending and actual changes do not always have to be in writing. It's true that written or graphic explanation will establish the change. It is also true that many contractors do not spend a lot of time doing paperwork. They are practical people used to working in the field, directing workpeople and moving materials. So don't flood the contractor and the client with a lot of paper, except to establish important points that are necessary to speed the work along.

Extras

Changes or requests for additional money to cover omissions in the drawings can sour relations among all parties on the job. It is best to explain to the contractor early in the job that you will not welcome many requests for extras. This will alert the contractor that you will not be openhanded with the client's money. You do not have to explain this in an adversarial way. Simply point out that it is not in the best interests of the job to have a number of requests for extra money. It means more paperwork and annoyance to all parties when they have to wrangle over how much a change is worth. It's always good for the architect to know how much the work is worth, because it is common practice to charge a high price for changes. In fact, changes can be a two-way street; as the job progresses, some things may become simpler and can lead to deductive change orders. A bit of horse trading in this respect is sometimes in the best interests of the job. It will also indicate to the client that you are running the job well, inasmuch as popular belief holds that extras are commonplace during construction. Anything that improves the reputation of architects is helpful.

Once the scope and the cost of an extra have been determined, it's a good idea to do the paperwork. Forms are available for this purpose, such as the excellent series developed by the American Institute of Architects. Keep the paperwork short and to the point; note the money involved and what is added or deducted. Obviously, all this must be discussed with the clients beforehand, because it's their money.

If the Relationship Sours

Despite your best efforts in selecting a contractor, it may become apparent that he or she is not competent or is dishonest. If you're on the job site and keep in close touch with the execution of the work, you can observe this complication. A more common difficulty is that the work may not be progressing rapidly enough. Slow-moving jobs are fairly common in the construction industry. Contractors may take on too much work, when it's available, because most of them have experienced slowdowns when they've had little or no work. If this is the case, discuss it first with the contractor. Ask why the work isn't progressing and when it will speed up. If you're not satisfied with the answers and excuses, put the contractor on notice without threats, advising him or her that you expect the work to move in accordance with the previously agreed-upon schedule.

Watch the distribution of your client's money as well. If the contractor is asking for a high percentage of the agreed-upon contract amount early in the job, but that amount does not correspond with the work in place or the materials delivered to the job, that's a reasonably good sign that the job is being used to make up losses on another project or that the contractor is having financial problems unrelated to your work. It is never beneficial to cut off funds completely, because that just exacerbates any financial problems already present. If you know the subcontractors, it may be useful to ask them whether they are being paid. If they are not, it's a fairly sure sign that the contractor does have financial problems that are not of your job's making.

You may discover that your work is beyond the capabilities of the contractor selected; some contemporary houses are quite unusual in their use of materials or in the jointing of materials. A contractor who can otherwise handle a stock tract house may not understand the complex relationships some designers are capable of producing. If this becomes apparent during construction, it's best to terminate with the contractor as soon as possible.

It may also be desirable to discharge a subcontractor for the same reasons: not doing the work rapidly enough or being incompetent. If the base agreement your client has is with a prime contractor, do not take this action without his or her approval. Begin by advising the contractor that you are not happy with the speed or quality of the subcontractor's work, and that it is the contractor's responsibility to complete the overall job satisfactorily. As always, be careful about how you do this. Pride is at stake here, and contractors do not like architects telling them they are not doing a job properly.

If a contractor has to be terminated, it is likely that the process will cost your client additional money, because contractors tend to bill generously in the early stages of a job to ensure a steady cash flow. It will also be difficult to find a new contractor or subcontractor who will be willing to understand the balance of the job for the amount of money left in the contract. Therefore, terminating a contractor for cause is a last resort. The architect should first exhaust all other possibilities.

Keeping the Client Fully Informed

The client will expect the architect to "supervise" the work and see to it that the design intent is carried out. Most clients, however, do not understand the complex relationships of a construction site, especially if this is the first house they've commissioned. It's best to explain to clients early in the game that you do not want them ever to give instructions to the contractor or subcontractors. Sometimes clients feel that such instructions are harmless or may simply want to save the architect's time. Yet client intervention in construction is almost always bad for the job; it confuses the contractor, undermines the architect's authority as coordinator of the work, and usually dilutes the clarity of a carefully worked-out design.

However, it is a good idea to keep in touch with the clients, advising them of your site visits and conversations with the contractor. It's best to stop short of long, detailed explanations of arcane technicalities. Most clients are not interested, which is why they came to you in the first place. They are interested in matters of function, design, and money. Be sure to keep them fully informed on all of these subjects, and on the schedule as work progresses.

If you have a client who visualizes poorly from drawings and models (if you've made models), the construction period can be traumatic, because he or she may not comprehend what the house looks like until it exists. There's no easy way to handle this problem, but it helps if you recognize the situation in the design stage. It is a good idea for you to walk the client through the site when it is framed out and explain where things go and what the sizes are. That's not a sure cure, but it helps to do this before the mechanical systems are in place and the finish goes on the walls.

ILLUSTRATION CREDITS

The numbers after the name of the person receiving credit refer to pages on which their illustrations appear. When more than one person is credited for illustrations on the same page, reference is made to a specific illustration on that page.

Antonakakis, Suzana and Dimitris: 22, 23

Bogert, Catherine: 16, 17, 138, 139

Borel, Frederic (drawings): 148, 149

Borel, Nicholas: 148, 149

Charles, Frederick: 70, 71, 144, 145

Chatham, Walter: 96, 97, 150, 151

De Vido, Alfredo (sketch): 102, 216

De Vido, Alfredo, Associates (drawings): 14, 15, 18, 19, 24, 25, 66, 67, 70, 71, 75, 95, 99, 103, 140, 141, 145, 152, 153, 192, 193, 194, 195, 196, 197, 198, 199, 200, 201, 202, 203, 204, 205, 206, 207, 208, 209, 210, 211, 212, 213, 214, 215

Dikeos, Meliti: 2, 3, 4, 5, 6, 7, 8, 9, 10, 36, 37, 38, 40, 43, 44, 46, 48, 50, 51, 53, 54, 55, 56, 57, 58, 59, 60, 61, 62, 83, 84, 85, 86, 87, 88, 89, 110, 111, 113, 114, 115, 116, 117, 118, 119, 120, 121, 122, 123, 124, 125, 126, 127, 128, 129, 130, 131, 132, 133, 134, 135, 136, 165, 167, 168, 169, 170, 171, 172, 173, 175, 176, 178, 179

Gullichsen Kairamo Vormala Architects (drawings): 12, 13, 65

Hursley, Timothy: 20, 21, 68, 69, 78, 79, 100, 101

Kokoris, Moki: 11, 26, 63, 80, 81, 82, 91, 106, 107, 108, 137, 154, 155, 156

Koning Eizenberg: 92, 93

La Cima Minowa: 146, 147

Lake/Flato: 72, 73, 142, 143

La Pena/Torres (drawings): 146, 147

Lautman, Robert: 14, 15

Levi, Jonathan: 76, 77, 104, 105

Maris, Bill: 102, 103, 140, 141

McGrath, Norman: 98, 99, 152, 153

Predock, Antoine (drawings): 69, 101

Reens, Louis: 94, 95

Rista, Simo: 12, 13, 64, 65

Stoller, Ezra: 24, 25

Warchol, Paul: 18, 19, 66, 67, 74, 75

Wei, Wesley (drawings): 16, 17, 138, 139

INDEX *

* Italicized pages refer to illustrations.

Livability (continued)
  and living patterns, 34
  and long vs. spread-out house, 35–36
  and materials, 35
  mechanical equipment, location of, 39
  and odors, 39
  and pets, 39
  and room size, 35, 36
  safety concerns, 43–45
  and "smart house" features, 51–52
  and sound insulation, 37
  thermal comfort, 39–42
  and traffic flow, 32–34
  and weather, 35, 49
  and windows, 37, 38, 57–58
Living patterns, see Activities of inhabitants
Living room, 160
Long house, 35–36
Low-rise units, 7, 8
Lump sum contracts, 220–221
Lutyens, Edwin, 11

Machinery, 39, 116
Macroclimate, 167–170
Marvin house, 91
Masonry, 129, 189, 226
Materials:
  and client's program, 163
  privacy and interior, 35
  in rooms, 128–132
McCombe house, 59
McConomy house, 56
Melone house, 110
Mercer house, 62
Merz house, 154–155
Metric modules, 190
Michelangelo, 124
Microclimate, 170–173
Minton house, 120, 179
Mockbee, Samuel, 20–21
Mockbee-Coker, 78–79
Modernism, 121
Modifications of existing designs, 31
Modules, 185–190
Moellentine house, 127
Monticello, 6, 112
Moore, Charles, 89, 135–136
Moore house, 98–99
Morton house, 37, 123
Movable items, see Furniture and furnishings
Multiple access, 7, 9
Murcutt, Glenn, 156

National styles, 28
Natural disasters, potential, 170
Natural lighting, 127–128
Natural materials, synthetic vs., 131–132
Natural vegetation, 169–170
New Farm, 137
Nooks and crannies, 87
Nornay, 26

Odors, from kitchens and bathrooms, 39
Oil prices, 40
On-site parking, 172
Open planning, 111, 111–112
Organization, sense of, 89
Ornamentation, 121–122
Overhangs, 2, 22, 49, 122–123, 123, 124
Overhead materials, heavy, 44–45
Owner-built houses, 222–223

Palladio, 89, 109
Palmer house, 136
Parking, on-site, 172
Pastiche, 85
Paths, 61
Pedestrian approaches, 171
Perret, Auguste, 82
Pest control, 42
Pets, 39
Pierrakos house, 22–23
Pipes, 117
Place, sense of, 86
Placement on site, 109–110
Planned units, 8
Planning, site, see Site planning
Platforms, raised, 2
Plumbing walls, 115
Plywood sheathing, 131
Point blocks, 9–10
Pollutants, airborne, 42
Porches, 2, 15, 18, 123
Precipitation, see Rain; Snow, effects of
Precipitators, 42
Predock, Antoine, 68–69, 100–101
Privacy:
  activities requiring, 34–35
  changing norms of, 34, 89
  and interior materials, 35
  and microclimate, 170
  and rooms, 35
  and social needs, 3
  and windows, 38
Process, design, 157–190

and environment, 166–178
  modules, use of, 185–190
  phases in, 178–185
  program, 157–166
Procession, 88
Program, client, 157–166
  and budget, 164–166
  data collection for, 157–162
  stylistic/aesthetic considerations, 162–164
Protrusions, awkward, 45
Pugin house, 150–151

Quinones-Bieganek house, 66–67

Rafferty house, 110
Rain, 49
Raised levels, 61
Regional styles, 28
Regulations, city/town, 171
Reveals, 232
Richardson, H. H., 110
Rietveld, Gerrit, 133
Rittenhouse Square apartments, 16–17
Rohe, Mies van der, 86, 111, 133, 230
Roof, 176–177, 231
Rooms, 125–136. See also specific rooms
  arrangements of, 112–114, 125–126
  focus of, 128
  and limits of spans, 126
  materials for, 128–132
  natural lighting of, 127–128
  and privacy, 35
  size of, 35
  spatial variety among, 126–127
Rothschild house, 43
Row houses, 8
Rugs, 58

Safety concerns, 43–45
  awkward protrusions, 45
  and code regulations, 43
  disabled people, designing for, 45
  door swings, 43–44, 44
  handrails/grab bars, 45
  level changes, 43, 43
  lighting, 45, 47
  overhead materials, 44–45
  slippery floors, 43
Sametz house, 18–19
Sara house, 57
Scale, 86
Schematics, 180

DATE DUE

MAY 14 2008		
MAY 17 2010		
GAYLORD		PRINTED IN U.S.A.

JUN '03